Not Your Average Travelers

Forty Years of Adventures in
All of the U.S. National Parks

Not Your Average
Travelers

Forty Years of Adventures in
All of the U.S. National Parks

Nancy-Ann Feren

ISBN 978-1-7337876-0-4

Library of Congress Control Number: 2019903338

Cover design by Sarah Beaudin
Photography by Richard and Nancy-Ann Feren

Printed in United States of America

Published by Feren Travels

Visit www.ferentravels.com

To our grandchildren: Sebastien, Alexandre,
Hannah, Sam, and Lily—
may you all enjoy our national parks
for many years to come.

Contents

Preface

Over the years, friends and acquaintances have urged us to write a book about our adventures in the national parks. I initially intended this book to be an informational resource for elementary school children, since I spent many years having my students do research on national parks, a multifaceted project that incorporated reading, writing, social studies, science, math, and art. A former student recently contacted me on Facebook and commented, "I will never forget the national park project you had us do in 5th grade. I truly found a love for geography and a respect for the environment from that project."

However, as I began writing, I realized my book was becoming more of a memoir. I have used my journals as a starting point for describing more than 40 years of travel in our national parks, and I have quoted parts of journals written by my husband, Dick; our children, Andrew, Tara, and David; as well as those of our two oldest grandchildren, Sebastien and Alexandre. This book includes only our visits to national parks and preserves. Since we visited some national monuments, national memorials, national seashores, and so forth on each trip, as well as spending time with friends and visiting other places, such as Disney World, you will sometimes notice a gap between dates.

Our travels go back to 1977 when our sons, Andrew and David, were just little boys and we spent a week at Acadia National Park in Maine, only a six-hour drive from our home in New Hampshire. In the summer of 1980 on a trip to California, we visited a few national parks, but it wasn't until 1992 that I suggested that we visit all the national park sites. Dick thought this was a good idea, and each summer we would visit a few more. In 2007, after we both retired, visiting these sites became a major focus of our travels.

There are now 418 national park sites. This list includes sites with many different designations—national park, national monument, national preserve, national historical parks, etc.—and attempting to visit them all has been a bit of a moving target as new park sites have been added almost every year. In September 2017, we visited our 416th national park site. Number 417, Honouliuli National Monument, was established in 2015 but is not yet open to the public; Camp Nelson National Monument, Kentucky, was established by Presidential proclamation on October 26, 2018, after I started writing this book. We plan to visit Camp Nelson in spring 2019.

In retrospect, it almost seems that visiting all these sites had been our subconscious goal from the beginning. In 1980 I wrote, "I do like National Parks. I wish we had planned to stay in more of them," and in 1986 I wrote, "For being such a homebody and not wanting to live anywhere but New Hampshire, I hate staying in one place on vacation and would rather be enjoying nature than paying for big-ticket attractions."

Each place is unique, which is not surprising, since that is why each one was designated as a national park site. **National parks** are usually large natural areas with varied characteristics. Sometimes they include historic places. Hunting, trapping, mining, and oil or gas exploration and extraction are not allowed, although sometimes there is a **national preserve** within a national park where those activities are permitted, such as Glacier Bay National Park and Preserve in Alaska, which permits subsistence and sport hunting as well as commercial fishing in the preserve but not in the park. The Antiquities Act of 1906 allows the President of the United States to authorize a **national monument** as long as it is on land that already belongs to the federal government, but only Congress can authorize a national park. A **national historic site** usually contains a single historical feature. These parks are generally authorized by Congress, but a few have been established by the Secretaries of the Interior. A **national historical park** extends beyond a single property or building, such as Manhattan Project National Historical Park in Tennessee, New Mexico, and Washington. A **national memorial** commemorates a historic person or event but does not necessarily occupy a site connected with its subject. An example is Mount Rushmore in South Dakota. A **national battlefield** includes battlefields, battlefield parks, battlefield sites, and national military parks. Some **national recreation areas** are centered on large reservoirs and feature water-based recreation. Lake Chelan in Washington is one such area, while others are urban parks near major population centers, such as Golden Gate National Recreation Area in California. **National seashores** have been established on both the Atlantic and Pacific Oceans as well as the Gulf of Mexico. **National lakeshores** are all on the Great Lakes. **National rivers** include national river and recreation areas, national scenic rivers, and national wild and scenic rivers. **National parkways** refer to a roadway and the parkland paralleling the roadway, such as Blue Ridge Parkway in North Carolina and Natchez Trace Parkway in Mississippi. They often connect cultural sites and allow for scenic drives. **National trails** include national scenic trails and national historic trails. One such trail is the Appalachian Trail, which stretches from Maine to Georgia. **Other designations** include units with unique titles such as the White House.

As I mentioned previously, in this book I have included only national parks and national preserves. The book is organized chronologically beginning with our first trip in 1977. We have visited a few parks more than once, so you will find entries for those (Acadia, Badlands, Big Bend, Gateway Arch, Glacier, Theodore Roosevelt, Mesa Verde, and Indiana Dunes) in more than one chapter.

Acknowledgments

Thank you to Gayle Paige and many other friends who have kept encouraging me to follow through with this project.

Several people deserve special thanks: Renee Nicholls, my writing coach and a student in my very first class, made excellent suggestions and guided me through the publishing process. Sarah Beaudin designed the cover, did the formatting, and also was a huge help in publishing. Nicole Grinnell, a friend and extraordinary proofreader, corrected my typos and asked good questions. Our sons, Andrew and David, both contributed memories of our travels; David read most of the first draft and did some editing as well. Most of all, thanks to my husband, Dick, who accompanied me on every step of our travels, took lots of pictures, and did a critical reading of all the drafts. I couldn't have done the traveling or the writing without him.

Introduction

Simplicity, frugality, and a love of both nature and history have led us to national park sites and to campgrounds across the United States. With almost no camping experience, we bought a used tent, new sleeping bags, pots and pans (which we are still using after more than 40 years) and started what has been a lifetime of travel and camping.

Our first, used tent was a large, canvas monstrosity, but it fit our family and sometimes even our dog. We have never had (or wanted) a motor home or even a pop-up trailer. Now that our children are adults, we have downsized to a two-person tent.

Recently, we had to replace our tent. The helpful clerk said we probably should get one of the larger, family-sized tents. The conversation went something like this:

> CLERK: There isn't room in a two-man tent for cots.
>
> US: We don't use cots. [Yes, we sleep on the ground on thin foam pads, and we love it!]
>
> CLERK: You need more room for your gear.
>
> US: We leave our gear in the car and just bring in two small cloth bags with clothes for the next day.
>
> CLERK: You won't be able to stand up.
>
> US: We don't stand up in our tent. We crawl in and go to sleep.
>
> CLERK: Oh, then maybe you do want a two-man tent!

Right—and that's what we bought.

We like to cook our meals whenever possible over an open fire, using a Coleman stove only when campground rules prohibit fires or when we need to cook quickly. Building and using the fire is fun, and pancakes, potato bake, grilled chicken, hamburgers, and, of course, s'mores prepared over the fire always taste so good![1]

I love the challenge of fitting all the food we need into our little ice chest, the challenge of preparing meals in the rain and rolling up a tent in the wind. I love hearing the sounds of nature and picking berries right at our campsite. And I love traveling inexpensively. In 2014, 41 days of camping (from New Hampshire to California and back) cost us just under $5,000 for everything—campsites, food, gas, admissions.[2]

On one recent trip, two different men at two different campgrounds came over to our site and commented, "I hope I can still be doing this when I'm your age." What? Do we look old? I'm planning on doing this for many more years—sleeping in a sleeping bag with only a thin foam pad underneath, in a two-person tent.

When we started, like many young families, we didn't have a lot of money for vacations, and camping seemed like a viable alternative. We were also both teachers with the luxury of having summers off. At that time, we didn't even dream that our camping vacations would take us to all 50 states or begin a lifetime of travel. However, we did know that we wanted more than just the outdoors experience. We wanted to see historic sites and spots noted for their natural beauty.

Camping itself offered new opportunities for learning by doing. We all got a real appreciation for the life of the early pioneers. Our van was the wagon train, our tent the primitive cabin.

When our children were young, we found jobs they could do to help: pick up small sticks for kindling, rub a bar of soap over the bottom of a pan so it will wash easily after getting blackened over a fire, sweep inside the tent with a small broom. They had important roles to play in this camping/travel experience. A spirit of cooperation grew. If no one helped Mom

---

[1] The recipe for the potato bake and other great camping meals and snacks appear in the appendix.

[2] This worked out to about $122 a day for the two of us or $61 per person.

and Dad set up the tent, hang a clothesline, gather and chop wood, build the fire, buy ice, prepare the vegetables, soap the pans, do the cooking, and clean up afterwards, then there was no time for swimming or other activities. With everyone's help, we could arrive at a site and be totally set up with dinner cooking (and sometimes done) within 40 minutes, leaving plenty of time for a game of Frisbee or a swim.

Besides helping with the fire, our son Andrew remembers placing water in one of our medium-sized pots and swinging the pot over his head in such a way that the water didn't spill out: a physics experiment. In our travels, Dick introduced many such experiments into our daily life, although I don't think he was responsible for that one.

Most national parks have a Junior Ranger activity-based program.[3] Examples of activities include attending an evening program, going on a ranger-led walk, interviewing a ranger, and scavenger hunts for park-related items. When the children have completed a certain number of these activities, they share what they have done with a park ranger. Then they receive a Junior Ranger patch and Junior Ranger certificate for that park. They recite the Junior Ranger motto—"Explore, Learn, and Protect"—and are sworn in as Junior Rangers. At some parks, the rangers announce this on the loudspeaker and invite visitors to observe the ceremony. Children can also earn some Junior Ranger badges at home.

Starting with our second trip, we all kept journals. My instructions to the kids before we left went something like this: "You have to keep a journal of the trip. You can tell about what we're seeing or doing, draw pictures if you want, anything that will help you remember this summer. Yes, Daddy and I will do it too."

Although I thought we might refer back to our journals in the future for use with schoolwork, I never viewed it as an opportunity for growing in the writing process. However, that is

---

[3] Information can be found by searching for Junior Ranger programs at www.nps.gov.

exactly what it became. We planted the seed, it took root, and it flourished. David actually used his journal from our second trip to make a book, and he won a prize in the New Hampshire Young Authors Contest!

Dick and I both enjoy taking photographs. On our first trips, we had film cameras. We mailed the film in to be processed as slides, so when we got home, we had hundreds of slides to sort and organize. A few years ago, I spent months digitizing all those slides and putting them in folders by points of interest within each state. Now we have digital cameras, but we still do most of the organizing on the computer after we get home. Our friends enjoy seeing the captioned pictures on Facebook. I have done slide shows for elementary school classrooms, and we have also done a slide show at our church.

In terms of transportation, we've taken most of our road trips in a station wagon with a rooftop carrier or in a minivan. The station wagon had a bench seat in the front, and when the kids were young, Dick made a denim carrier with large pockets for their books and projects, which hung over the back of the front seat. He also created a similar carrier that hung over the front of the front seat. We used this for maps, journals, and tour books; it really helped us stay organized.

Sometimes people ask how we chose our destinations. Since Maine borders our home state of New Hampshire, Acadia was the first national park we visited as a family. During that trip, Andrew was seven and David was five. We loved Blackwoods Campground, the ranger-led talks and walks, and the opportunity to experience the variety of natural features. After being there for a week, I made the comment that this was the sort of place we would like to visit again. How prophetic my words were. We have been back to Acadia many times, with our children, our grandchildren, and on our own, and now we have been to all the national parks in the United States. I would be happy to go back to any of them at any time.

Originally, we thought we'd branch out a little farther from New Hampshire each year until we'd seen the entire country. Initially, our children were anxious to see Disney World, but then everyone told us how hot it would be in Florida in the summer. Dick's sister lived near Disneyland and we had other friends in California, so we suddenly started talking California. I think I would have talked myself out of this trip, but it was too late—everyone was excited for us and kept inspiring me.

As we have traveled, we have come to know America and her people, both past and present. We read aloud Doris Gates' book *Blue Willow*,[4] about migrant workers in the southwest, as we traveled through that area and *Gone with the Wind*[5] as we drove through Georgia.

Wherever we have gone, we have enjoyed watching the animals, sometimes from a distance and sometimes up close as they tried to get our food. We watched a family of skunks walk up the road in Shenandoah National Park, and we reported the whereabouts of a tagged deer to a park ranger. At Great Sand Dunes National Monument (now a national park), a deer tried to take our breakfast doughnuts from the picnic table, and a ground squirrel tried valiantly to get into a box of cheese crackers I had set on the ground. In the Grand Tetons, another ground squirrel hungrily eyed our pancakes.

We have hiked through fields of wildflowers and snow in July, alternately, on the same hike, close to a glacier on Mount Rainier, and we have watched buffaloes wallowing in the dirt in South Dakota. We have traveled through record-breaking heat in the Midwest, where the butter melted into a yellow puddle as soon as it was removed from the cooler. We have enjoyed the dark night sky at Big Bend National Park in Texas, read by the Midnight Sun in Alaska, climbed the Great Sand Dunes in Colorado by moonlight, walked for an hour with a butterfly

---

[4] Gates, Doris. *Blue Willow*. Viking Press, 1940.

[5] Mitchell, Margaret. *Gone with the Wind*. Macmillan Publishing Co., 1936.

on my wristband at Arches National Park in Utah, and enjoyed s'mores by evening campfires in many parks. We've sampled Maine lobster, Louisiana crawfish, South Dakota buffalo, Arizona prickly pear jam, southern grits, Florida oranges, and Key Lime pie.

Travel has given each of us something that is uniquely ours, from an education in geology to thoughts of a career with the National Park Service to the joy of seeing textbooks come alive. It has challenged us to look beyond our everyday lives. These shared adventures have given us an appreciation for the immensity of our nation and its great diversity, and they have helped us develop a special family bond. We hope our story will inspire you to enjoy many outdoor adventures of your own.

1977

Acadia National Park, Maine

Acadia National Park[6], Maine

Saturday, August 6, 1977

Acadia National Park on Mount Desert Island in Maine preserves the beauty of Maine's rocky coast and its coastal mountains. In addition to this natural beauty, there are 45 miles of gravel carriage roads, which are reserved for hikers, bikers, horseback riders, horse-drawn carriages, and in the winter, cross-country skiers. The park also has 16 stone bridges, each one different from every other one, designed to blend in with the environment. As we planned this trip, we hoped to fit in as much hiking and sightseeing as time (and young boys!) would allow.

After the long car ride, Andrew, age seven, and David, age five, were happy to run around our campsite while Dick and I set up our tent. After we cooked and ate dinner, we drove to a ranger-led astronomy watch on the top of Cadillac Mountain.[7] We spread blankets on the ground and lay on our backs, looking up at the dark sky. We observed shooting stars and many constellations, such as Orion and the Big Dipper, and, for the first time ever, we clearly saw the Milky Way. It was a good introduction to astronomy as well as to Acadia National Park.

Sunday, August 7, 1977

We spent that day at Sand Beach, where the "sand" was actually finely crushed shells. It was the first time Andrew and David had been in 55-degree Fahrenheit (COLD!) ocean water.

---

[6] Additional entries on Acadia National Park appear in 2000, 2002, and 2010.

[7] Visitor Centers, ranger talks, ranger walks, and evening programs are always free. Some hikes or canoe trips have a limited number of participants and require reservations. Some parks have parts that are reached by commercial cruises, which involve a cost.

After playing in the surf for a while, David asked Dick why he did not go in the water. The conversation went something like this:

"Daddy, why don't you want to come in the water?"

"Because I'm cold, that's why."

"Well, if you went in the water, you'd get even colder!"

Oh, the logic of a five-year-old!

Monday, August 8, 1977

We drove in to Bar Harbor to take a two-hour ranger-guided boat trip on Frenchman Bay. The water was calm, and we were able to see bald eagles, osprey, porpoises, and seals in their natural habitat.

Later in the day, we hiked part of the way on the Jordan Pond Path. This trail has very little elevation gain. It is a good option for young hikers and offers beautiful views of The Bubbles, a pair of mountains in the Mt. Desert Range.

Tuesday, August 9, 1977

We tried horseback riding for the first time. At Wildwood Stables, a guide matched each of us to a horse, gave us some instructions, and led us along carriage roads and trails in the park. The boys were excited to be on horseback. After this adventure, we enjoyed popovers at the Jordan Pond House and then picked blueberries on our way back to camp. Blueberry pancakes for breakfast!

Wednesday, August 10, 1977

Perhaps more fun than swimming in the notoriously cold ocean water of Maine was exploring the tidepools, where we found mussels, sea urchins, sea cucumbers, hermit crabs, and other small sea creatures that live in the intertidal zone, that area between high and low tide where pockets of seawater get trapped in rock basins. We also went to Thunder Hole, a naturally formed inlet. When the right-size wave rolls in, it causes a deep thunderous sound and water splashes high in the air.

After dinner we went back to Cadillac Mountain to see the sunset. Before the sun actually set, we happened upon a wedding in progress. It was very windy and cold, and the couple looked absolutely frozen!

Thursday, August 11, 1977

Dick wrote these details about fire-building:

I really enjoy making a fire. It is more than just creating a structure that will produce heat to cook our food. For me, each fire I set up becomes a creation. The careful stacking of the sticks and kindling becomes a work of art—almost an end in itself. However, the goal of this care is to produce a stack of wood that will ignite and burn cleanly with just one match. When I achieve the one-match fire I am pleased; when I don't, I am frustrated. The boys are learning a bit about fire building. Andrew built a beautiful one-match fire (with my supervision) yesterday. David helped provide kindling chips and splinters by shaving pieces off a small log with the hatchet. Eventually, I want them to be able to take charge of a fire from start to finish. I want them to be able to select their own wood and kindling, stack it properly, and light it all without guidance. Then I want them to maintain the fire at the proper heat and extinguish it when we are all through using it. Not only do I want them to be capable of doing these things, but I also want them to assume full responsibility for the fire, to the extent that the meal doesn't get cooked until their fire gets going.

Building fires, eating special "camp foods," exploring ocean and mountain habitats, and learning new things all contributed to making this a special week. We particularly loved the huge, delicious popovers at the Jordan Pond House, and the wild blueberries, which visitors can pick to their heart's content.[8] We all agreed that we should plan to come back again

---

[8] Berries are one thing that people can take out of a national park, and blueberries are abundant in Maine.

1980

Jefferson National Expansion Memorial
(now Gateway Arch National Park),
Missouri

Great Sand Dunes National Monument
and Preserve (now Great Sand Dunes
National Park and Preserve), Missouri

Mesa Verde National Park, Colorado

Grand Canyon National Park, Arizona

Rocky Mountain National Park, Colorado

Saturday, July 12, 1980

Our five-week cross-country camping trip started at 4:30 AM. Despite the prospect of long car rides, Andrew (10), David (8), and our foster daughter, Tara (8), who had been with us since April, were all very cooperative. I started reading *Blue Willow* by Doris Gates[9] to them, they read their own books, we all played auto bingo, sang, and we all looked for license plates from different states. Even though this was only our first day of travel we found license plates from 24 states! Andrew recorded in his journal the states we drove through each day. We had a picnic lunch at a scenic overlook in Fishkill, New York, a Revolutionary War landmark.

I suggested that we make special note of the changing scenery and everyone was very observant. New Hampshire, Massachusetts, Connecticut, and New York were all hilly, mostly forest land—pines, maples, and oaks. When we got into Pennsylvania, it became rolling farmland with cattle grazing in the fields. As we drove, it was interesting to watch not only the countryside change, but also the changes in rock formations and types. New Hampshire, Massachusetts, and Connecticut are mostly igneous in nature, but through Pennsylvania the rocks are mostly sedimentary and in flat layers, at least in each of the road cuts.

When we reached our first campground, I heard a cheeping in the grass. It almost sounded like a cricket, but crickets usually stop when footsteps come near, and this didn't. When I investigated, I discovered a tiny baby bird. It was gray, about 1½ inches in diameter (it looked like a little fluff ball), so it really blended in with the rocks. Eventually the mother came—she was small too. David got out the bird book, but we weren't able to identify her. She went down to the baby several times and we could hear them talking to each other, but when

---

[9] Gates, Doris. *Blue Willow.* Viking Press, 1940.

we returned from a walk, the baby was dead. Dick dug a grave, and Tara wrapped the bird in a big leaf. Each of the kids made a gravestone from a rock and wrote on it.

The campground had a nature trail that we walked on after dinner. We saw wild grapevines, woodpecker holes, and sassafras. (David knew it was sassafras thanks to a *Ranger Rick* magazine.)

Jefferson National Expansion Memorial (now Gateway Arch National Park), Missouri[10]

Wednesday, July 16, 1980

We had about 300 miles to go, so we left at 5:15 AM to avoid driving in the hottest part of the day. We had never experienced such hot weather before. As we approached St. Louis, we could see the huge arch that represents the Gateway to the West. On the spur of the moment we decided to stop, especially since an exit led directly to the arch. I'm glad we were flexible enough to allow for an unplanned stop because it was really worthwhile. We bought tickets for a scheduled trip to the top of the arch and then had time to look around the underground museum, which commemorates westward expansion. There were a lot of displays there, including many on Lewis and Clark, a covered wagon, and many other things related to the westward migration. Imagine what it must have been like to walk beside a covered wagon 10 to 20 miles a day in all kinds of weather.[11]

Dick wrote,

The ride to the top of the arch was in a train of barrel-shaped cars, each one with five seats. Riding in the car was like riding in a giant tumble-type clothes dryer. It ascended in a curved path, so each of the cars had to be rotated a fraction of a turn every so often to keep it level. Tara did not want to go at first, claiming she was afraid of heights, but once we were at the top, she was really excited about the view. The placement of the windows was such that we

---

[10] Another entry on Gateway Arch National Park appears in 2016.

[11] Over the next few years, we visited many more parks that helped us learn more about the westward expansion of the United States and appreciate how difficult it must have been for those early settlers.

could look down and see the bottom of the arch. When we came down from the top and went outside, the heat was oppressive. There were groups of people clustered under the shade of trees along the walkway.

Thursday, July 17, 1980

After several long days of driving during the day without air conditioning during an extreme heat wave, we decided to try driving at night. Dick and I took turns driving, stopping at rest areas for short naps when we were both too tired to drive. The kids did really well sleeping in the back seat, sitting up and sort of leaning on each other. It was certainly more comfortable than driving in the heat of the day. After arriving at a campground and setting up the tent in the morning, Dick and I slept for a couple of hours while the kids played around the campsite. Then we all went for a swim. We continued this pattern for two more days and nights. After the second long night's drive, we were all happy to end up in the mountains of Colorado.

Great Sand Dunes National Monument (now National Park) and Preserve, Colorado

Tuesday, July 22, 1980

We were now ready to visit parks, so we went back to daytime driving. The countryside changed to rolling plains soon after we left Colorado Springs. Our elevation was still high—more like a plateau. As we drove, Dick commented on the small, sandy mountains in front of the higher mountains. I said they were probably the dunes, and I was right!

Great Sand Dunes National Monument became a national park in 2000. The dunes are located in the northeast end of the San Luis Valley in Colorado at the base of the Sangre del Cristo mountains. The prevailing winds blow from the southwest, so the sands begin to pile up in front of the mountains where the winds slow down. The creek carries away the sand from the area between the dunes and the mountains, and it brings the sand around south of the dunes. From there it gets blown back onto the dunes again, and the process keeps repeating itself.

Fortunately, we went to the Visitor Center as soon as we arrived that afternoon, because a barefoot walk up the creek was scheduled for 3:30. The walk was really interesting. There are warnings not to climb on the dunes without shoes because the sand gets very hot during the day. Yet right in front of the dunes is a temporary creek, which comes from melted snow in the mountains. The ranger said it would probably dry up in a couple of weeks. In early spring it is knee deep, but by late July the deepest area is one or two inches deep, and then only in spots.

GREAT SAND DUNES NATIONAL PARK AND PRESERVE

11

The air and water were both warm from the sun, but when I dug my toes a couple of inches into the sand, it got cool, almost cold. The flowing water forms ripples in the sand, and the ripples grow larger until they collapse flat and then form again. There was not much wildlife on the walk except for some insects, including a rubber rabbitbrush beetle, a June beetle, and a camel cricket.

On the sandy banks of the stream, the guide showed us two examples of sand movement on a slope. One type was "slump," which was where a large amount of sand came loose and fell, usually from an upper edge or ridge. The second type was "flow," where the sand acts like a liquid and actually flows down the slope. At the conclusion of the walk, David and Tara made sandcastles in the creek bed.

The campground here was really different. It was almost like an oasis in the desert with a lot of trees, the tallest of which was only about 20 feet. Trees grow slowly in the arid soil, but they do provide shade. The surrounding area was mostly cactus, sage, and other small scrub. There seemed to be more trees at the campground than we had seen during the entire drive that morning. The sand dunes were in plain sight, and we could see mountains in the distance.

The animals in the campground were very friendly and tame. We saw deer, rabbits, ground squirrels, and chipmunks browsing and begging for food in or near campsites. There were frequent warnings by rangers and by printed signs not to feed the animals, but no doubt there had been some feedings by well-meaning people. David wrote,

Everybody including me liked this campground best because deer and rabbits could run loose.

The evening program at the amphitheater was on birds of the area—very few that we have in New Hampshire. The only familiar ones were robins, hawks, sparrows, and flickers. At the conclusion of this presentation, we went on what was supposed to be a moonlight walk on the dunes. It turned out to be a flashlight walk much of the time, since the sky was very overcast. Toward the end of the tour, the moon finally came out from behind the clouds. Parts of the walk were really quite strenuous—climbing a mountain of sand is not easy. Where the slope was steep, my feet sank quite deep, and the sand made a groaning or grunting noise when I stepped on it. I don't know how high we went, but some of the dunes are 700 feet high. Andrew commented,

On the way up, we had to climb a slip face (if you step on it you fall on your face).

As an adult, he still remembers being shown how to slide on the dunes by crouching down for a controlled slide.

Dick was fascinated by how the sand appeared to change texture. Wherever the sand was undisturbed, it was well packed and fairly easy to walk on because it did not give much when we stepped on it. Once someone had walked along the sand, however, the footprints disturbed it and it became very difficult to walk on. We would sink in and slide from side to side. The kids held up well—I was exhausted. We hiked from 10:00 PM until 12:15 AM! It was definitely a unique experience.

Wednesday, July 23, 1980

It was a pleasant morning when we woke up, and we decided to have eggheads—doughnuts dipped in an egg-and-milk mixture and toasted over an open fire—for breakfast. The deer at the campground were quite tame and came right up to our site begging, but as I mentioned, park rules forbid feeding them so they don't become dependent on humans. That morning one came right up to the table while Dick was preparing breakfast and tried to take a doughnut. Just as I started to take a picture, Dick shoved him away. But when I was washing dishes, another deer came up, and Dick got a picture. While I was doing some packing, I moved a box of food onto the ground and briefly left it unattended. I looked up and on two separate occasions, a ground squirrel was trying to get into our cheese breadsticks.

Great Sand Dunes National Park provided unique experiences: huge sand dunes, hiking by moonlight, and having wild animals very close to us. Our kids were really impressed with the animals and how much life there was at a desert park.

Mesa Verde National Park, Colorado[12]

Thursday, July 24, 1980

Mesa Verde National Park has cliff dwellings of ancient Native Americans. This park was created in 1906 to preserve the archeological heritage of the Ancestral Pueblo people.[13] The dwellings on the cliffs themselves were from the period 1100 AD to 1300 AD; they were made by the Ancestral Pueblo people, ancestors of the Hopi and other tribes. The views here were spectacular—I could easily identify a butte,[14] a mesa, and a canyon.

We took a ranger-guided tour through the dwelling called Balcony House where 40 people once lived. The walls are still intact in many places. The buildings were made of adobe brick and had no doors as we know them, but rather windows for entry and exit. Travel on the rock face was accomplished by notches cut in the rock; travel between buildings was likely accomplished by a series of balconies (basically narrow platforms) protruding from the face of the dwellings between each floor or level. To get into this dwelling, we had to climb a 32-foot ladder. To get out, we held only a railing and put our feet in cut-out places in the rocks.

The most interesting structure in this dwelling was the kiva, which was designed to serve both religion and ventilation. The kiva was basically a six-foot-deep cylindrical pit with a place for a fire in the middle and seats all around inside the perimeter. An air shaft went from the outside of the cylinder and down to the floor of the pit to bring oxygen to the fire to keep it

---

[12] An additional entry on Mesa Verde National Park appears in 2014.

[13] These people were called the Anasazi by early archeologists, but since *Anasazi* is from a Navajo word that is sometimes translated as "ancient enemies," the word is no longer used.

[14] An isolated hill with steep sides and a flat top; it is narrower than a mesa.

burning. Once the air was inside the kiva, it hit a deflector and went around it to the fire. The smoke went out a hole in the roof or cover of the kiva. Today, the Hopi and Zuni, the descendants of the Ancient Pueblo people, don't want the rangers to explain much to visitors about the religion, so we did not learn a lot about that.

We went to a couple of roof-top dwellings where we could look down at the houses. The kids loved the one where the tops of all the walls had been paved. It was like a maze; they ran off some excess energy.

Seeing these ruins made me feel as if I'd gone back in time. It was a shock afterward to be heading for a modern grocery store.

Grand Canyon National Park, Arizona

Friday, July 25, 1980

Grand Canyon National Park is one of the best-known national parks in the United States. It is about one mile deep and ranges from 600 feet to 18 miles in width. The Colorado River flows through the park.

Generally, the roads through this part of the country are very straight, flat, and without much variation in scenery. One exception is the road through Grand Canyon National Park. On the way into the park, we stopped at an overlook where we all got our first look at the Grand Canyon. WOW! Its size and grandeur almost defy description. Even with the books I had read about the Grand Canyon and the many pictures I had seen of it, I was not really prepared for its true magnificence.

Saturday, July 26, 1980

The park is so large and has so many things to do, we found it difficult to choose which to try first. We signed the kids up for a Junior Ranger program for the next morning and decided to hike into the canyon that afternoon. We were advised to carry at least one quart of water per person, so we had to go buy another canteen.

We chose the Bright Angel Trail because it had a rest stop with water at 1½ miles. That was far enough for Tara's first major hike and probably enough for the rest of us also because it was so hot. We took it very slowly going down, stopping frequently for water, rest, and views of the scenery. We had been told to allow twice as long for the return trip, but we went down so slowly it took about the same length of time coming back as it did going down. The trail was wide and easy to follow, but very dusty. There was even a fair amount of shade. At one point on the trail, we met up with a begging squirrel. He ventured within a couple feet of some hikers, stood up on his hind legs, and reached out toward the visitors with his forepaws. What a performance!

We watched two mule trains pass us on their upward trek. Tara was thrilled.[15] The first part of the upward trail wasn't too bad. Then the wind started to blow. It was really like a sandstorm. It kept blowing and the sun was behind the clouds, so we moved very quickly. The sand blowing on our skin hurt! When I got back, I was covered with a sandy film.

Sunday, July 27, 1980

Andrew, Tara, and David all went to a Junior Ranger program of outdoor activities from 9:15 to 10:45. They were divided into groups by age. Andrew commented that his group

played the web of life followed by the park game. You have an area of land no larger than the length of your arms and you make your own park on it.

---

[15] We would have liked to try a mule trip into the canyon, but our children were not old enough. The minimum age was nine.

David wrote that his group learned

what all the rangers and animals did at the Grand Canyon. Everybody got second names. My second name was Deer, Tara's was Toadflax which is a blue flower. We got certificates that said we were junior rangers.

The kids all enjoyed these activities.

At that point, we had already checked out of our campground, so we went to a picnic area to cook our noon meal before another night of driving. There was no water supply and we didn't want to waste our drinking water, but we managed to wash the dishes in a really small amount of our water. We stopped at Baskin-Robbins for ice cream and started to drive toward California.

It was off and on cloudy, so the heat wasn't too bad for a while. Then it became oppressive. Even though the sun was setting, it felt just like fire. We ate a fast supper at a closed truck-weighing station. It was in the shade but that really didn't help.

Just as the moon was rising—a beautiful full moon—we stopped at a rest area for a bathroom break. It was still unbearably hot. I had a brainstorm. We bought a bag of ice cubes. We put some in the cooler, some in the water jug, and gave ourselves two glasses of ice water each. This was very refreshing.

Rocky Mountain National Park, Colorado

Sunday, August 10, 1980

As we started getting into the foothills of the Rockies, we were happy to see real trees and lakes! Rocky Mountain National Park was spectacular—there's no way to describe the snow-covered peaks, alpine tundra, and meandering streams. Not only were there terrific vistas but also there was variety: dense pine woods to high alpine tundra, whitewater streams to slowly meandering streams, straight and level roads to winding and precipitous roads. Some of the peaks are more than 12,000 feet high. At one stop, birds and a chipmunk ate out of the kids' hands—until we noticed the sign saying not to feed them.

Some barn swallows gave us a couple of starts during lunch. They had a nest under the corner of the shelter roof, about 10 feet from the table. They were pretty birds: black with orange breasts. They did quite a bit of darting around for insects.

This was the last park on our trip, and we were all feeling anxious to get home. I decided that I'd like to come back on some future trip and spend more time here hiking and attending ranger programs.

Thursday, August 14, 1980

Once again, we were driving past fields of corn. It was still flat and boring to us, who are accustomed to hills and lots of trees; after five weeks we were all ready to get home. Andrew made up a song:

Hi ho, hi ho, it's off to home we go
We'll keep on driving all day long
Hi ho, hi ho.

No matter how wonderful the trip has been, it's always good to get home.

1982

Shenandoah National Park, Virginia

Everglades National Park, Florida

Shenandoah National Park, Virginia[16]

Friday, June 25, 1982

Because we were building an addition to our house, we didn't travel in 1981, so we were all anxious to begin our travels in 1982 to the southeastern part of the United States. During this trip, Andrew was 12, and Tara and David were 10. Our day began with a trip to the county courthouse for Tara's adoption, followed by cleaning the house and packing the car. After our success in 1980 with driving at night, we left home at 6:00 PM, which we expected would get us to Virginia, just outside Washington, DC, at around 6:15 AM. I was amazed at how heavy the traffic was all night long. Dick and I alternated driving and sleeping. The first hour I laughed to myself. There wasn't a sound from our children—the boys were reading, and Tara was writing in her journal. Seasoned travelers!

Tara noted one quasi-problem en route:

Mommy heard a clinking noise which turned out to be the ice cubes in the water jug.

We decided if that remained our worst challenge, we'd be in very good shape.

Monday, June 28, 1982

We made black raspberry pancakes for breakfast and took our time leaving the campground, so we didn't get to the Skyline Drive until almost lunchtime. We ate at the first picnic area we came to and watched a doe and her two fawns cross the road. Then Andrew found a bird's nest on the wall outside the men's room with some tiny birds in it. Skyline Drive, the only public

---

[16] Additional entries on Shenandoah National Park appear in 1986, 2007, and 2012.

road through the park, is 105 miles long with a speed limit of 35 miles per hour. It is curvy with many overlooks for scenic views and pictures, so it was a slow drive.

On the spur of the moment, we decided to stop at Loft Mountain Campground, which is part of Shenandoah National Park. David's journal reflects that he must have been studying prepositions that year. He wrote,

We drove along Skyline Drive in Shenandoah National Park to Loft Mountain Campground.

There were a variety of organized events and self-service nature activities. We went for an evening hike on the Deadening Nature Trail, a 1.3-mile loop up and down the mountain. Tara rushed ahead and became our official animal spotter. She saw deer, a rabbit, and then a bird. We couldn't decide whether the bird was a quail or a bobwhite (or as David called him "Robert 'Bob' White"). A few minutes later, Tara was startled when another large bird flew out of the bushes right next to her.

The boys spent some time with Dick looking at rocks, and we all looked at some interesting wildflowers. When we got to the parking lot, there were eight deer grazing. Some of the deer had yellow tags with numbers on them. The kids got some of the numbers and were able to report them to the ranger. There were 25 yellow-tagged deer and 25 blue-tagged deer being tracked. We watched them for quite a few minutes.

As Tara and Andrew continued to watch the deer, Dick, David, and I went off to the side to investigate what appeared to be two white-tailed rabbits hopping around and grazing in the grass by the side of the road. It turned out to be a skunk with a white patch on the end of its tail, and another white patch on its head. It was busily digging for something in the ground and let us approach to within 20 feet so I could take its picture. Back at camp there was another huge skunk in a vacant campsite where people had left some garbage. We were fortunate they didn't acknowledge us with their spray.

Watching the animals here was the highlight of our stop at Shenandoah.

Everglades National Park, Florida

Saturday, July 10, 1982

We really wanted to see Everglades National Park because we'd heard so much about it, but the stories of the mosquitoes in the Everglades were making us all a bit wary. When we got to the Everglades Visitor Center, the ranger told us that camping in the park was free, but the mosquitoes were so bad we might want to camp elsewhere. As we drove through the gate of the next campground, we read this sign:

Mosquitoes are abundant. Sorry, no refunds.

David worked hard to help us set up. Andrew and Tara stayed in the car because of the bugs. We even ate in the tent, since the bugs were awful.[17] Andrew wrote,

We had at least two million problems if you count each mosquito in the campsite as a problem.

We could have had the mosquitoes for free at the campground in Everglades National Park; here we had to pay for them!

Sunday, July 11, 1982

There was a huge snake at another campsite, but fortunately no snakes at our site. Andrew spotted (and we all saw) a heron in the sawgrass. It was really graceful as it flew.

The only things consistent about the everglades were the water (which varied from a few inches to a few feet in depth), the mosquitoes (which were everywhere), and the flatness (the highest point was 20 feet above sea level, and that was a

---

[17] We have since learned that eating in the tent is not a good idea and we do not recommend it; the residual smell can attract animals.

man-made Native American mound). An elevation change of just a couple of feet changed the vegetation from the sawgrass of the swamps to willows or pine or hardwood trees, which grew on mounds ("hummocks") of dry land.

The everglades were really quite varied, with a section of pine forest, another of mahogany forest, sawgrass prairies, mangrove forests, willow groves, ponds, marshes, and hummocks of dry land where hardwood trees grew. There were trails to all of these different types of features. We drove the whole route from Royal Palm to Flamingo. At the first stop there were two trails. We went on the first without much difficulty and saw a coral snake on a tree, several lizards, a locust, and fish. The second trail was awful. We were attacked by mosquitoes before we went 10 feet, so we turned back. When I say attacked, I mean being able to kill 10 mosquitoes with one swat. Even after we left the trail, there were still mosquitoes on us. On most of the other trails, we were able to go somewhat farther. We did see the largest mahogany tree in the United States.

There was an alligator crossing the road and an owl on telephone wires. The road was only built in 1959, and a lot of the area is still uncharted. I could not even imagine wanting to explore with all those bugs, but we were told it's not bad in the winter. We decided to keep that in mind for future trips.

1983

Badlands National Park, South Dakota

Wind Cave National Park, South Dakota

Yellowstone National Park, Idaho,
Montana, Wyoming

Grand Teton National Park, Wyoming

Theodore Roosevelt National Park,
North Dakota

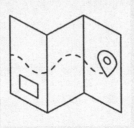

Tuesday, June 21, 1983

At this time, Andrew was 13; Tara and David were 11. We started our trip with a route through Canada so we could see Niagara Falls. Going through customs was strange. The agent asked whether we were all born in the United States. Dick said yes; I said no. (Andrew was born in Germany while Dick was stationed there with the U.S. Army.) She asked if we were all one family and if Tara was adopted. We all said yes, and I wondered how she could possibly know. Next, she asked to see citizenship papers. Thank heavens I had all the birth certificates. Then she looked really confused. She explained that she had thought Tara was the one born in Germany and hence adopted!

Andrew's journal entry for that day was,

Today is the longest day of the year scientifically as well as psychologically. Twelve hours makes for a long day.

Tara, however, had a more upbeat attitude as she wrote,

This is neat! I like this. We're going up a mountain and my ears are popping. I can smell the fresh air. It tingles in my nose. This is the life.

This is the life I'd love to have.

Trees, birds, flowers, mountains, and streams,

All these are all going by me

Like the going of memories.

Badlands National Park, South Dakota[18]

July 10, 1983

My very first experience with a national park was at the Badlands. My parents, grandfather, and I were driving most of the way across the country in the summer of 1959 when I was 12. We stayed at a motel very close to Badlands National Park and went to an evening campfire program. Although I don't remember the content of the program, I remember being fascinated with the whole idea of campgrounds, national parks, and informative ranger programs. When we started planning our trip for the summer of 1983, I knew I wanted to return to Badlands National Park. Half of the park is mixed-grass prairie where bison, bighorn sheep, prairie dogs and black-footed ferrets live; the other half is geologic deposits with rich fossil beds. The sedimentary layers were cemented together millions of years ago and eroded to form rugged spires and deep canyons.

Although I remembered that park from my childhood trip, it was Dick's first time in the area, and he was really impressed. His journal reflects his excitement. He wrote,

The scenery was so different from anything I had ever seen before, and so varied that I was bouncing up and down in the seat as I drove along. I was like a little kid with a new toy.

After an early dinner, we went to the Visitor Center and checked out the offerings. We decided to drive about 25 miles toward the Sage Creek Wilderness Area, where there is often a herd of bison, but we didn't see them. There was an evening campfire program at 9:00 and a walk (Night Prowl) at 10:00.

To bide our time until the evening programs started, we took a ride along the main route through the park. On the way

---

[18] An additional entry on Badlands National Park appears in 2011.

back from our drive, we rounded a curve and almost ran into a deer, which was standing partway into the road. We got back just in time to see the slide presentation: "Why People Came to the Badlands." Tara and David were really tired, so they went to the car and slept after this, but Dick, Andrew, and I went on the Night Prowl. We spotted a rabbit, and a "paleontologist from the past" spoke to us. He gave a good talk on fossils.

Monday, July 11, 1983

We got up very early so Dick and the boys could go on a canyon climb at 6:30. This was a bit more strenuous than the usual nature walk to which we had been accustomed, but they all enjoyed it. Andrew wrote,

Today David, Dad, and I went on a hike in one of the canyons in the Badlands. On the hike we found some fossils and saw some interesting rocks and saw some formations called "armored mud balls" because they are little balls of mud rolled in the pebbles in the bottom of a gully. When the gully dries up you are left with little balls of mud armored with pebbles.

Tara and I walked the mile to the amphitheater for an 8:00 AM nature walk. The guide pointed out flowers, rock formations, and a meadowlark; we had bluebirds at our campsite.

After lunch we attended a program on fossil preparation and went on a fossil walk. On our way driving back to the campground, it seemed that we stopped at every overlook. Dick (who was teaching earth science and geology) just couldn't drive by them. We went to the Star Trek program which started at 10:00 PM. I didn't see a shooting star, but I did find the Big Dipper, North Star, Arcturus, Jupiter, and Saturn, and we watched a satellite moving across the sky. Then we used telescopes to see Saturn and Jupiter—they looked like marbles but were really clear, especially Jupiter. We could see Saturn's rings and Jupiter's moons very clearly. It was a beautiful night.

Our family left the Badlands with the same feelings I had experienced many years earlier: it is a special place and one where we knew we would like to return.

Wind Cave National Park, South Dakota

Tuesday, July 12, 1983

We decided to take a scenic road at the last minute—and were glad we did. Just after Tara commented that we hadn't seen any wildlife, she spotted a buffalo with twins. They were a short way from the road, but with binoculars and telescope we watched them for a while. About a mile farther on was a herd of buffalo—more than 50. We stopped to watch them too and drove by another huge herd later. We stopped to take pictures of one solitary bull that was close to the road.

Wind Cave National Park is comprised of limestone caves in the southwest corner of South Dakota. It is called Wind Cave because of the wind that blows either in or out of the cave depending on the air pressure. (Lower atmospheric pressure causes the caves to have relatively higher pressure and the winds blow out, while higher atmospheric pressure causes the winds to blow in.) We took a tour, which involved a one-mile walk that took 1¾ hours. The wind was blowing out of the cave that day. As we stood at the entrance, we could feel the cool air—53 degrees Fahrenheit. There were lots of steps down and some up, but we also took an elevator up. The most interesting feature of this cave was "boxwork" formed when calcite got into cracks in the limestone and the limestone dissolved. The thin blades of calcite project from cave walls and ceilings to form a beautiful honeycomb pattern. The caverns also had features called cave popcorn, which are round formations that look a bit like popcorn.

Yellowstone National Park, Idaho, Montana, Wyoming

Sunday, July 17, 1983

Yellowstone was the world's first national park, established in 1872. With its geysers, mudpots, mountains, hot springs, and wildlife it is one park very familiar to most Americans and one that we were all looking forward to visiting.

Tara was very excited when we finally reached Yellowstone National Park. She wrote,

Feelings of Yellowstone. We're at Yellowstone!

Today it is a very cold morning. It was cold last night too. When I woke up I had expected to be in my nice soft warm bed but no. I shook my head. Now I remembered. On the way here, it was so beautiful. You could see the Rocky Mountains in the distance. Occasionally I would see a mountain bluebird flying from branch to branch or a robin looking for worms or making a nest. I could feel my ears popping as my family and I went up the mountains. Sometimes it hurt, but most of the time I wouldn't mind.

As soon as we saw the sign that said "Welcome to Yellowstone National Park" coming into view I remembered the anxious feeling in my stomach through our whole trip from New Hampshire to Wyoming chanting, "Let's get to Yellowstone! Let's get to Yellowstone." The suspense had been killing me. Now we were there, free from suspense at long last.

On our first day of sightseeing, we spotted an osprey (sea hawk), a pelican, some bison, a chipmunk, and many other animals. Dick's observations centered on the campground and the temperature.

We entered Yellowstone and got a site at Bridge Bay. The ground squirrels had been there first, however, and the ground was quite lumpy. If we moved our bodies around so we fitted in between the lumps, it didn't seem too bad. The only thing that really bothered us was the prospect of cold nights and our lack of warm sleepwear. When we woke up this morning it was about freezing out. I couldn't tell you for sure whether it was above or below freezing, but it was cold!

The temperature warmed up quickly, however, so we figured we would make it. We also heard there had been snow on Friday, which probably meant a cold front had passed and that probably it would gradually get warmer over the next few days. Tara wasn't so sure about her ability to survive the cold and began to hint that maybe we should cut our trip a little shorter than planned and head home . . . NOW! She finally decided that if she slept in all her clothes including a sweatshirt and jeans, she might pull through. Sleeping in her clothes also meant that she didn't have to put on cold clothes in the cold morning air but could get out of her cocoon and start moving around to get warm.

Nanc also slept in all of her clothes plus two pairs of socks (mine). It didn't help, because her feet were still cold! The boys put their pajamas on over their underwear sometimes, but sometimes slept in their clothes also. I had enough with a t-shirt and shorts, and on the coldest night a second t-shirt and a pair of socks.

We stopped at one of the Visitor Centers to pick up a wildlife checksheet. Visitors scored 10 points for each animal sighted. A score of 70 was considered excellent; by the end of the day we had a score of 90, plus some animals not on the list. We checked off buffalo, several herds of mule deer, moose, pelicans, osprey, ground squirrels, red squirrels, chipmunks, and Canada geese. I think everyone enjoyed this even more than the scenery.

On the way to our first official stop, Tower Falls, we stopped at some patches of snow. The boys got out and made snowballs. At Tower Falls, we hiked down to the base of the falls (about ½ mile), where we could enjoy the cooling mist. We saw a petrified redwood tree and a whole colony of ground squirrels. Then we went to Calcite Springs, which was in a canyon carved by the Yellowstone River. In the canyon there were some interesting volcanic and glacial formations on the walls.

Mammoth Hot Springs was next, where we walked on a trail to see the different springs. These springs deposit minerals in various formations, mainly tiered terraces. The area has a very interesting collection of hot pools, fumaroles,[19] and travertine mounds[20] along with the terraces. Since this is an active geologic area it is constantly changing.

Monday, July 18, 1983

When Dick got up that morning, he was surprised to find a thick layer of frost on the top of our picnic table! Within an hour it had warmed up considerably, and the frost was gone. The rest of us stayed in bed until after 7:30, and it really wasn't too cold. I slept with all my clothes on—sweatshirt and jeans too! Soon after we left our campsite, we saw an elk. He was really beautiful, and we were able to get fairly close.

We walked around the Mud Volcanoes area, where there were lots of bubbling mud pots and a strong smell of sulphur. Yuck! We then headed back to Norris, the geologically hottest spot in the park, to view the geyser basins. We watched one good-sized geyser erupt by chance—it only erupts four to six times a day. There were many steam vents, whirlpools, and multicolored pools due to different bacteria that inhabit areas of

---

[19] Fumaroles are openings in or near a volcano, through which hot sulfurous gases emerge.

[20] Travertine mounds are limestone formed by mineral springs.

different temperatures. While viewing Bear's Den Geyser, Tara noticed that a little stream started because of the water spurting out. She and David ran down the hill so she could get a close look at the water as it ran under the little footbridge. All of a sudden David, who had been moving in slow motion all day, came running back at full speed, saying Tara had fallen flat on her stomach. At first, I thought he meant into a thermal area, but fortunately it was on the path. She scraped both knees—one fairly badly—but she was brave. She washed it off the best she could with water from our canteen and rather gamely limped back to the Visitor Center.

Fortunately, we had no more long walks planned for the day. Our next destination was a scenic drive along the Grand Canyon of the Yellowstone. The only walking was out to overlooks and back. The canyon is a deep gorge and very pretty. Dick said it was gorge-ous.

Tuesday, July 19, 1983

It wasn't quite so cold that morning. We especially enjoyed the multi-colored water at the Grand Prismatic Spring located in the Midway Geyser Basin. The colors are produced by a variety of heat-loving bacteria which live at the spring. The center of the spring reaches 189 degrees Fahrenheit which is too hot for microbial growth, so the water remains clear and appears blue. The water cools as it spreads out from the source and different bacteria live at the decreasing temperatures, yellow at about 169 degrees Fahrenheit, orange at 149 degrees Fahrenheit, and red at 131 degrees Fahrenheit. It was like a thermal rainbow.

The ranger-led hike through the area near Fountain Paint Pots was fascinating. The ranger explained the difference between geysers and hot springs and how to tell them apart. A geyser has to be 204 degrees Fahrenheit. Algae can't live above 167 degrees Fahrenheit, so if there's algae there, it can't be a geyser. Also, a geyser has a beach where the water washes over. Some geysers are very small but very regular; others erupt only every few years. There were also huge mud pots and fumaroles. The other thermal area is a cauldron like we saw yesterday. The ranger kept stressing the dangers involved—like stepping backward into a mud hole.

Dick wrote,

One of the things that intrigued me was the frequent evidence of changes brought about by the 1959 earthquake. It opened up new cracks and closed others. Sometimes when it opened up new fissures, the heat got very close to the surface. On this walk there were a great many trees that had had their roots cooked by the heat and had then died and been blown over. Because of the prevailing winds, they were all lying pointing in the same direction.

After a picnic lunch, we went to a map and compass program given by the same ranger who had given the morning program. This time he presented a short course on orienteering skills and then offered participants the chance to test their skill by trying to find a small pond from a given starting point. The boys picked up the techniques quite readily and were anxious to try it on their own in the future.

The ranger told us where to find a family of trumpeter swans. They are a fairly rare bird but apparently not too difficult to see if you know the right places to look. We found two adults and three cygnets swimming around. The side trip to see them was worth it, especially to Tara. Ever since she had seen that trumpeter swans were listed on that wildlife checklist, she had been hoping to see one, I think because she remembered reading E.B. White's book *The Trumpet of the Swan*.[21]

Then we went to Old Faithful—almost an anticlimax after all we'd seen, but something we certainly couldn't miss. It was spectacular. We decided against any more hikes there and went

---

[21] White, E.B. *The Trumpet of the Swan*. Harper Collins, 1970.

back toward camp, stopping at Fishing Bridge so Tara could see the pelicans at her leisure. We got a good look at some pelicans, and we also enjoyed the California gulls and their antics. We even saw some fish as they were grabbing insects that landed on the surface of the water.

As our visit to Yellowstone ended, Dick wrote,

As I looked at the Yellowstone canyon, I was reminded of both the Badlands and the Grand Canyon of the Colorado. When we went to the Grand Canyon in Arizona, I was struck by the immensity of it all. It was almost too big for me to fully comprehend. Everywhere I looked it was just enormously huge and seemed to look the same from every angle. We ceased stopping at overlooks because they all seemed so much the same.

When we hiked down inside it, we hiked for almost four hours, and were only able to get less than halfway down and come back up again. In the Badlands when we went on the canyon climb, the walk lasted for less than four hours but in that time, we were able to go all the way to the bottom, walk around, climb up some smaller hills inside, and come back to the top.

I felt as if I could get it inside my head and comprehend the extent of the Badlands better than I could comprehend the Grand Canyon. Maybe I just had a better understanding of nature's force or maybe I had a better understanding of my place in the world, or some combination of things, but I thoroughly enjoyed the Badlands in a way that I have enjoyed few other things.

Grand Teton National Park, Wyoming

Wednesday, July 20, 1983

The mountains of the Grand Teton Range provide extraordinary scenery. There are clear alpine lakes, more than 200 miles of trails, and a huge variety of wild animals including moose, bears, pikas, and yellow-bellied marmots.

There was a line when we got to the campground in Grand Teton National Park. They assigned sites and gave us a beauty! The view was magnificent. The site was also huge, and there was nothing behind us but woods. Dick said he felt like a pioneer in a lean-to. The site was rustic and bumpy but very scenic and quiet. Earlier in the week, we had bought a camper's solar shower, a heavy, two-gallon plastic bag that was clear on one side and black on the other and included a hose and a nozzle. This would be our first chance to try it out. Tara filled it with water, and we set it out in the sun to make it hot. Later we

discovered that as long as it remained in a sunny spot all day, it worked fairly well. We decided to cook our dinner at noon so we could go for the trail ride that Tara wanted from 3:00 to 5:00 PM, and a ranger-led hike at 6:30. Tara enjoyed the trail ride, so it was worth the money. We saw a beaver dam and a moose, but that was about it.

The walk at 6:30 was terrific. We covered 2½ miles in a little less than 3 hours, and we stopped frequently to look at wildlife and signs of wildlife. The ranger was the park's resident naturalist, and he was very good. He pointed out porcupine scars on trees, where the porcupine had stripped the bark to get the cambium for food. The ranger explained how the teeth marks showed that it was fresh. According to him, bears do a similar thing but rip the bark off.

He had just finished telling us about a time he had watched an osprey circle, dive straight down to catch a fish, and take off again when we saw one do the very same thing. We also watched a beaver carry pond lilies all the way back across the lake to his lodge. When we got to Swan Lake, the trumpeter swans, which are usually there, were nowhere to be found. However, we saw a cow moose and her baby drinking from the water and a mother duck with her ducklings.

Thursday, July 21, 1983

Our morning began with a ground squirrel attempting to share our breakfast.

We watched a Native American woman who did demonstrations at the park erect a tipi this morning. As she worked, she explained the procedures and symbolism of building a tipi.

Then we went to a dance demonstration. The guide, a full-blooded Navajo, had the audience demonstrating three different Native American dances: the owl dance, the two-step (which was a modified owl dance), and the circle dance (which was similar in many ways to American square dances). We didn't dance the first, but Dick and I did the next two. We couldn't convince the kids to try it. The dances were very simple ones that visitors could do at a Native American celebration. We also learned that Native American babies learn rhythm at birth from their presence at dances. The baby rests on a cradleboard on the mother's back, and the mother taps the board rhythmically.

I did some shopping while Tara went on a tour of the Native American museum and participated in a craft activity. She got to make a necklace, and the instructor gave her enough beads to make another. She was thrilled.

In the evening, we went on a 90-minute float trip down the Snake River. The boys would have really liked a whitewater trip, but this was rough enough for me. We all had to wear lifejackets, and some people got wet. We spotted an eagle family (two parents and one baby), a cow moose and her baby, a pronghorn antelope up on the bluff, beavers, and some osprey. We got a good view of the Gros Ventre slide[22] and beautiful views of the mountains.

There was a strange rainbow today that Dick said foretold rain within 15 to 24 hours. He gave us a mini-science lesson to explain what we were seeing. The sun was high and in front of us. As the sunlight passed through the water droplets in the clouds, it produced a first-order rainbow, which arced upward (encircling the sun). The usual rainbow we see is a second-order rainbow, when the sun is behind us. We'd have to wait and see if his weather forecast was correct.[23]

There were so many things to do in this park. Again, we enjoyed learning more about the flora and fauna from a park

---

[22] This mile-wide landslide occurred on June 23, 1925. It blocked the Gros Ventre River and formed Lower Slide Lake.

[23] His forecast was correct!

naturalist, getting more information about Native American customs, and floating down the Snake River. We had been looking forward to a long hike on our last day, but we abandoned those plans due to the heavy rain.

Theodore Roosevelt National Park, North Dakota[24]

Saturday, July 23, 1983

The ride to Theodore Roosevelt National Park was monotonous. However, with nothing but rangeland on both sides and all interstate with little traffic, we made good time. I tried to imagine what it must have been like when Theodore Roosevelt came to this area to hunt bison in 1883. Although he was hunting big game, he was also very aware of the gradual eradication of many of these animals. He became very concerned with conservation of wildlife and public lands. As president, he created the United States Forest Service and protected about 230 million acres of public land.

As we walked in the door of the Visitor Center, a ranger announced a tour of Roosevelt's cabin—the Maltese Cross cabin—which had been part of his ranch out here. Roosevelt had this cabin built to use as a temporary home when he was there hunting. The cabin's original ponderosa pine logs (which were not native to the area) survived; the native wood doesn't last. There are two original items in the cabin, a small brown writing desk and a large light-weight trunk. As we walked back into the Visitor Center, we heard an announcement about a movie on the history of the park, so we went to that. We always find these movies very informative.

---

[24] An additional entry on Theodore Roosevelt National Park appears in 2018.

Then they announced a snake demonstration. The kids really enjoyed that. Andrew wrote,

My favorite part was getting to hold a live bullsnake.

We found out that there were sites available at Cottonwood Campground in the park, so we left the kids at the Visitor Center for a talk on skulls and went to set up.

The camp is in a beautiful grove of cottonwood trees. Right behind it are badlands, extensive tracts of heavily eroded land with little vegetation. Quite a contrast! After dinner we toasted marshmallows before we went to see the evening campfire program about prairie dogs. We could see bats and hear June bugs flying around over our heads. Dick commented,

One of my most vivid memories as a kid was when I went for an evening walk with Grandpa Jennings and he pointed out flying bats to me.

We hoped that our children would vividly remember some of the experiences from our trips.

1984

Big Bend National Park, Texas

Carlsbad Caverns National Park,
New Mexico

Hot Springs National Park, Arkansas

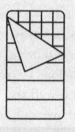

Big Bend National Park, Texas

Saturday, July 14, 1984

During this trip, Andrew was 14; Tara and David were 12. The temperature was exceptionally hot. The scenery became more desert-like as we went along. Sometimes it appeared very much like grassland with rolling hills and sometimes more like desert with rocky soil and scrubby growth. The desert is much greener than most people imagine. The soil in the desert is also less sandy and more rocky than most would think.

Just getting to Big Bend made an impression on Andrew. Thirty-five years later he remembered the town of Marathon, Texas which to him was an intersection with a gas station on each corner and nothing else. In reality it is a tiny town with hotels and restaurants that provides a pleasant break before continuing the long drive to get to the southwestern part of Texas where Big Bend is located. The miles we traveled gave him (and all of us) a real appreciation of just how big the United States is.

Andrew wrote that when we got to Big Bend National Park, we asked a ranger which of the park's several campgrounds we should stay at. According to Andrew's notes, she said, "Well, the Chisos Basin is usually 20 degrees Fahrenheit cooler than the other campgrounds." Based on that news, we all agreed that Chisos Basin was the place to camp. We looked forward to a more comfortable night for sleeping. The view alone in the national park makes it worth camping there. It's really beautiful.

Dick and I went for a short walk after dinner and finally spotted the insect that was responsible for much of the chirping noise that is heard for a while after sunset, but we weren't able to identify it. We met the kids at the amphitheater for a program called "Travel Through Time." The geologist made us all 46 years old and related the history of this area to that time period, with man appearing in the last four minutes. It was very well done.

The best thing was the terrific breeze that developed. Some people left the program because it was cold, but we thoroughly enjoyed being chilly. It meant a good night's sleep ahead.

Sunday, July 15, 1984

We all continued to write about the heat. Dick wrote,

Last night was the first time since Delaware that it was cool enough to use a sleeping bag. Sleeping was a real pleasure, especially after the night before, which was uncomfortably hot. When the sun set last night, I watched as the sun-lit portions of the mountains gradually got smaller and finally disappeared off the peaks. This morning I watched as the sunlight gradually lit the mountains from the peaks down. I took a picture showing our tent, a sunlit mountain behind it, and the two-days-past-full moon just above it.

After a stop at the Visitor Center and a walk on the Panther Trail, a short self-guided trail that pointed out different plants (mostly cacti), we drove to Santa Elena Canyon, the farthest point we wanted to see. We stood at the headwaters of the Rio Grande. Half the cliffs were in Mexico and half in the United States. We were only one mile from a border crossing. We really would have liked to cross, but it was hot, and we didn't know what we might be getting into. Dick and I decided that maybe someday we would do it by ourselves—when we had no one else to worry about. As it was, we made lots of stops for short trails and exhibits. It was hot. Fortunately, we had filled the canteens and had juice too. We bought a huge head of lettuce and ate almost the whole thing.

Among the things we saw on the way back were the ruins of three ranches and a small town. No settlement lasted very long out in the Big Bend area. Perhaps the only reason there is anything remaining now is that Big Bend National Park brings in tourists, many of whom are looking for motels, gas stations, and restaurants or grocery stores. I liked the stop at Sam Nail's ranch the best. It was built in 1919 of adobe. Parts of it are still standing. We sat on a bench where he and his wife sat. My parents were 10 years old in 1919 and were living in the city where we live today, but out here it was still wilderness. I couldn't imagine surviving here without ice or cold water or ice cream. Guess what I was craving!

One interesting local plant is the century plant. The base is a very thick-leaved cactus. Once in 15 to 40 years, a giant stalk grows from the center with big yellow flowers (sort of like sunflowers), and after it blooms the whole plant dies. There were several varieties of prickly pear cacti. A lot of them were blooming with a purplish flower.

There were many hawks and turkey vultures. Javelinas (pronounced havelinas), which are similar in appearance to small pigs, were supposed to be there, but we didn't see any.

After dinner Dick, Andrew, and I went on a trail to the Window Viewing Area to see the sunset. There were three small deer—one was just getting antlers—eating the cactus. I was surprised to learn that white-tailed deer do eat cactus, although it is not their main food source. When we stopped to talk with some other people on the trail, we noticed a large skunk ambling across the road. Dick pointed out a hummingbird, but all I saw was a whir as it flew away. The sunset wasn't particularly colorful, but it was pretty anyway between the two cliffs.

Big Bend was Dick's favorite park on this trip. He wrote,

It is one of the most beautiful areas I have ever been in, more because of its uniqueness and diversity than for any amenities it may have to offer. It is very quiet and peaceful yet teeming with life if you know where to look.

At that point in our trip, Dick and I decided that after the kids were no longer traveling with us, we would come back to visit all the National Parks and spend more time in each one.

Carlsbad Caverns National Park, New Mexico

Monday, July 16, 1984

We got a campsite right across the street from Carlsbad Caverns National Park and went to the Caverns to check "bat time." Although the caverns, which are limestone caves, are interesting, the real attraction here is the bats, which fly out of the caves at dusk and return in the pre-dawn hours.[25] After dinner we went to see the bats. The ranger talked for about half an hour before they came out. The caves were discovered because of the bats' evening flight. It is really an interesting phenomenon. It was fairly dark, so it was a challenge to see them, and it was hard to distinguish bats from birds. At one time, more than a million bats came out each evening to catch insects. Now it's about 100,000, due partly to the use of pesticides. DDT is still used in Mexico, where the bats spend the winter. They leave Mexico in April and return there in October.

Tuesday, July 17, 1984

We took the self-guided walking tour so we could see more of the caves and proceed at our own pace. They offered us radios to carry that described what we were seeing. The reception wasn't the greatest, but the things we saw were spectacular. Most of the stalactites[26] and stalagmites[27] are not growing. Dick liked the nodular and branch-like growths on the walls. The nodules

---

[25] Since 2007, a fungal disease called White-nose Syndrome has been killing bats in North America. If you visit these caves, do not bring in any gear or wear shoes or clothing that has been worn in another cave.

[26] Stala**c**tite—c for ceiling; stala**c**tites attach to the ceiling.

[27] Stala**g**mite—g for ground; stala**g**mites form from the ground up.

are called cave popcorn, and the branching growths are called helictites. They form when absorbed water seeps out from the pores in the walls or other surfaces. One section of the cave was called "Fairyland," and that's really what the whole thing looked like. The Big Room had the same volume as four Astrodomes. We could appreciate the analogy because we had visited the Houston Astrodome earlier on this trip.

The cave was used first by the bats and then by the Native Americans as shelter. The Native Americans never went beyond the mouth of the cave because of a steep drop-off. Now there is a winding path that goes into the cave. It is three miles long and goes about 860 feet underground. The hike took about 3½ hours. At one part of the cave there was a narrow passageway, and Andrew's voice was just the right frequency to make it echo. Dick, David, and Tara all tried but couldn't make it echo. At the end was an underground gift shop and lunch room. It was sort of strange, with the walls and ceiling being natural cave formations and the rest of it being man made.

I couldn't imagine how the first explorers ever dared venture into the caves. We walked on trails that have been paved and lit, but the original explorers had only a kerosene lantern. If it had been left to me, they'd still be unexplored!

Hot Springs National Park, Arkansas

Friday, July 20, 1984

Most of our driving at that point was in wooded hilly country, and it got woodier and hillier as we went along. When we entered Arkansas, Andrew noted,

This is the 45th state I've been to and the last new one for this trip.

We stopped at the Hot Springs National Park Visitor Center to get a brochure and headed for the campfire program at a National Park campground area called Gulpha Gorge. We attended two programs. One of them was on the history of the city of Hot Springs, which became a city almost overnight because so many people came for the baths. The area was part of the land acquired by the United States in 1803 in the Louisiana Purchase. The first permanent settlers came to the area in 1807 and realized that the hot springs had healing qualities. By 1830, there were log cabins and a store for the visitors who were coming to the springs. Between 1880 and 1888, wooden Victorian-style bathhouses were built, although most of these were later replaced by fire-resistant brick and stucco bathhouses. In the 1960s and 1970s, the use of the bathhouses declined, and they gradually closed.

The second program was about the hot springs themselves. Minerals dissolve out of the rocks 8000 feet below the earth's surface into the water, which comes from natural thermal springs and flows out of the ground at an average temperature of 143 degrees Fahrenheit.

Saturday, July 21, 1984

We started our day's activities with a ranger-led hike up to an old Native American quarry where novaculite was mined before this area became a National Park. Novaculite is a type of rock formed by hot springs; the Native Americans used it to make arrowheads and spearheads because when it is chipped, it is razor sharp. It has also been used as flints for rifles, and fire starters. Today it is used for sharpening knives. It is said to be the best sharpening stone in the world.

The most eventful part of the walk occurred when someone disturbed a bee or hornet nest on the ground. Several people got stung, including Dick, who used to be allergic to bee stings but has been desensitized by a series of shots with gradually increasing amounts of bee venom. I guess the desensitization has worked because he didn't get a reaction, although when swatting at the bees, he also swatted off his glasses. I went back for them because he didn't want to go near the nest again.

After the hike, we went into the city portion of the park. We went on the bathhouse tour first. The first bathhouses were crude structures built over the thermal springs, but they soon became much more elaborate. They must have really been something in their heyday. Today eight bathhouses can be seen on Bathhouse Row. The Fordyce Bathhouse, which we went in, reminded me a lot of Ellis Island. Both places had a lot of the original furniture and had not yet been restored, so they had an "old" feel to them. The bathhouse has three floors and two courtyards, plus a basement, which once had a bowling alley. There are marble benches and stairs, terracotta fountains, and stained-glass skylights. Many services used to be offered, such as hydrotherapy, electrotherapy, and massage. There were also many other amenities, such as a beauty parlor, a fancy room with a grand piano, and a men's parlor with a pool table. The Fordyce went out of business in 1962.

When we were there, the Fordyce was in the process of being repaired,[28] but we were able to see how the bathing was done. Andrew noted that the bathhouses were also used to

---

[28] Today it is a historically furnished museum and the national park's Visitor Center.

exercise, sunbathe, and discuss business. There are still some places where visitors can go for baths, but that didn't interest any of us. We ate lunch in a park; for a drink we had hot chocolate made with the hot springs water that we got from a "hot water jug fountain" nearby. The water does not have much iron or sulphur, and it is odorless, colorless, and tasteless.

Our final tour was on thermal features. We saw some of the springs, including one that is under a bathhouse. We all enjoyed Hot Springs National Park. It was so different from most of the other parks we had visited, since it was located right in a city with a focus on nature (hot springs) as used by people.

1985

Glacier National Park, Montana

Mount Rainier National Park, Washington

Olympic National Park, Washington

Crater Lake National Park, Oregon

Craters of the Moon National Monument
and Preserve, Idaho

Glacier National Park, Montana[29]

Friday, June 28, 1985

During this trip, Andrew was 15; Tara and David were 13. As we approached Glacier National Park, we could see the mountains of the park looming above the prairie. Dick guessed it was formed similarly to the Grand Tetons, and he was partly right. The Tetons were formed from a fault block, and Glacier was from an overthrust fault. Dick commented that these two formations both start in the same way but develop differently depending on pressures and position. In both cases, the uplifted portion is what wears away to form the mountains. The fault block formation happens when the uplifted portion stays at the fault. The overthrust formation occurs when the uplifted portion slides past the fault and over the land next to it.

In the evening we went to a campfire program on geology. The park is not named for the glaciers here now but for the ones that formed it. At one time—1.8 billion years ago—there was an inland sea here. Then there were four periods of glaciers—the remains of the fourth being what visitors see now.

Our campsite had some very friendly ground squirrels and chipmunks who came right up near us as we got food ready. As we were eating supper, we heard a whistling or chirping sound, which Andrew correctly identified as coming from a squirrel.

Saturday, June 29, 1985

That morning we started out on the "Going to the Sun" road, which is the major (only) east-west road through the park. Andrew wrote,

---

[29] Another entry on Glacier National Park appears in 2018.

Along the way there were little turnouts that told about different geological features and historical events. With Dad's explanations and the little turnouts, I learned a lot about geology.

The snow in Logan Pass on the side of the road in places was 10 feet deep! The kids wrote their names and drew little pictures in the snow, using rocks as markers.

Andrew, Tara, and David were particularly anxious to go white-water rafting. They knew that I was scared and that I almost didn't go. David wrote,

Believe it or not, Mom went, and she actually enjoyed it.

Andrew described the trip well:

The rafting company put our family and all the other groups on three buses and took us several miles up the river. When we got off the buses, we all put on life jackets and walked about 3/4 of a mile until we got to a place where we could board the rafts. Before our raft got near white water, another raft came up behind us and started a water fight. We all got wet, but it was nothing compared to when we hit white water. Our end of the raft got flooded. At first, we tried to bail the water out during calm stretches, but we soon gave it up. By the end of the trip, we had four-plus inches of water in the bottom of our side of the raft; the other end barely had an inch. All in all, it was a great ride.

On the way back to camp, we looked at the place where the kids had written their names in the snow, and they had melted almost completely away.

We could see rain off in the distance, so we made and ate supper quickly. Just as we finished, it started to rain, so we never got the dishes washed. We just put them in plastic bags in the car to wash the next day. It stays light incredibly long here. I read by daylight until 10 PM!

Sunday, June 30, 1985

We had a hard time deciding exactly what hikes to take. We would decide on one, then discover it didn't start until July or until the trails were clear of snow.

That morning we went to the Many Glacier region. On the way, we stopped to get a picture of some mountains reflected in Lake Sherburne. It was just like a mirror. We hiked the trail to Iceberg Lake, although we knew we couldn't go all the way and still get back for the 2:15 flower walk. The scenery on the hike was lovely, but there were also plenty of black flies and a few mosquitoes. Along the trail we crossed several small streams. It seemed that around each one there was a cloud of little blue butterflies. I think they were pretty, but I'm not sure because they never seemed to sit still long enough for me to truly find out.

We all enjoyed the hike. The very first part was steep, but then it leveled off. It alternated between sun and shade. There were some streams and mini-waterfalls to cool us off. Someone coming down the trail said a bear had been spotted at the falls, but we didn't see it.

After lunch we went on the "flower walk," which was a naturalist-led walk through plains and woods. We learned that back in the early 1900s, there were Native Americans camped a few hundred yards away near the river. We stopped at the park ranger's original cabin, which was built in 1913. The ranger at that time had a wife and two children; it must have been quite an adventure for them. The ranger's wife was still living when the house was restored about 10 years ago. She contributed the furnishings and a lot of information, including an anecdote about skunks in her root cellar and another about a mountain lion in her attic. According to her story, the mountain lion came in from a tree through an open attic window. She was home alone and could hear the footsteps and scratching above her on the attic door, so she left. The next day the mountain lion was gone, but she was able to identify it by its footprints!

Most of the trail wound alternately through pine woods and forest meadows, providing interesting contrasts. I loved the yellow-bellied sapsucker we saw. We could see the hole in the tree where it lived and could hear its family inside. The last stop on our walk was at Red Eagle Lookout, which provided a fine view of St. Mary's Lake and the surrounding area.

We also climbed a fire lookout tower, which had a gorgeous view. As David said in his journal,

The __highlight__ of the hike was Red Eagle Point Lookout Tower.

Monday, July 1, 1985

In the morning, we took a naturalist-led boat trip and hiked to two falls: Baring Falls and St. Mary Falls. First, the boat took us partway up the lake and docked. After seeing the multi-tiered St. Mary Falls, we went a little way up a very pleasant trail to Baring Falls. Then we walked back to the boat, and anyone who didn't want to go on the next hike—which was 1½ miles each way—

boarded the boat again and got taken back. We, along with a ranger-naturalist, went on the hike to Virginia Falls, which was another spectacular multi-tiered waterfall. We saw a bird called a water ouzel, which had a nest in the rocks behind the falls.

The evening nature stroll at 6:00 PM was interesting. We went to an active beaver lodge but didn't see the beaver. Andrew, Tara, Dick, and I went to the campfire program about the history of the Blackfeet tribe, who controlled this area when the first white settlers arrived. Even today, the Blackfeet Nation is the largest Native American tribe in Montana. Their reservation is on the eastern border of the park.

Tuesday, July 2, 1985

On our way out of Glacier, we stopped briefly in Logan Pass to see if there were any mountain goats or bighorn sheep around. We didn't see any, but our walk behind the St. Mary's Visitor Center was really lovely. We started on the prairie near the Visitor Center and went to the woods right next to the stream. On the way, we noticed some barn swallows that had built their nest under a bridge. There were some beautiful alpine meadows. Along the road we saw some marmots and a couple of large birds, which looked somewhat like female pheasants, but we saw no sheep, goats, or bears.

Going from the east to the west side of Logan Pass produced a substantial change in scenery and vegetation. The topography was still basically features formed by glaciers, but some of the contours were more rounded because of increased rainfall and vegetation on the western slopes. We also noticed that the trees on the western side were more numerous, taller, and straighter than those on the eastern side, which tended to be sparser, shorter, and frequently bent and twisted.

Dick explained the formation of glacial terrain in his journal:

When enough ice collects in a valley, it can form a glacier, which can then start to move down the valley. This motion can cause two types of glacial terrain: one from erosion and one from deposition. As the glacier moves, it scrapes away rocks and dirt and causes the valley to become U-shaped with a smooth round bottom and steep sides. The top edges of the valley's steep sides are square and sharp.

The eroded material that was carried away by the glacier gets deposited at the front and side edges as the glacier moves and melts. These deposits are called moraines and tend to result in rounded or curved ridges or hills. Cape Cod, Massachusetts is an example of something that was formed by a moraine. Logan Pass was formed as a U-shaped valley. The glacier that formed it is gone, so some of the sharp edges are gradually becoming more rounded from weathering.

Mount Rainier National Park, Washington

Wednesday, July 3, 1985

As we drove along, the topography and vegetation began to change even more. At first, it was a plateau with an occasional river-cut canyon. The terrain became hillier and the vegetation thicker, larger, and greener as we got closer to Mount Rainier (pronounced Rah-neer) in Mount Rainier National Park. The mountain is almost totally snow/glacier covered.

After dinner we went to the campfire program. The ranger talked about how Mount St. Helens affected Mount Rainier. Our campground, Ohanapecosh, had been covered with an inch of ash. I couldn't imagine what that must have been like. Unlike snow, which eventually melts, the ash had to be carted away. For one year, almost no one camped here. Workers had to rake all the camp sites, clean out the fire pits, and sweep the picnic tables.

Thursday, July 4, 1985

We started hiking the Skyline Trail at Paradise. We got a close look at some glaciers and could see features such as moraines, crevasses, and pressure ridges. The glacier we saw was the Nisqually Glacier, which is one of the largest in the park. On the way there, the scenery was very pretty, and in some cases even spectacular. We stopped at the overlook by the Cowlitz River. The canyon was about 300 to 400 feet deep. The walls of the canyon are about the straightest and steepest we had ever seen. It was about 200 feet wide at the top and 20 to 50 feet wide at the bottom. We ate our lunch at Panoramic Point at 6800 feet. While we were there, a Steller's jay kept eyeing our food.

It didn't take any of ours, but it did take a plum pit from one of the other people there.

On the way up, we could see people who were hiking all the way to the top of Mount Rainier. They planned to get to Camp Muir at 10,188 feet that day. Then they would rise at 1:00 AM (when the snow was firmer) to go to the summit; they would come all the way down that same day. Later we heard a ranger say that a seven-year-old girl was the youngest and an 80-year-old man the oldest ever to get to the summit.[30] We also met a ranger who had been part of a rescue team for a man who was trapped in an avalanche the previous day. That's scary!

The trail was partly snow covered, partly wet, partly mud. Going up through the snow wasn't too hard. We could see the footsteps of other people. Coming down, I slipped on the mud once, but it wasn't as bad as I had expected. The views were fantastic. There were also beautiful alpine wildflowers. It seemed so strange to be walking through snow in light-weight slacks and t-shirts and seeing people skiing in similar attire.

---

[30] These records were surpassed in 2005 when an 82-year-old man, William Painter, broke his own record of climbing the 14,411-foot mountain. When he reached the summit, 7-year-old Aidan Gold was on his way back down.

Olympic National Park, Washington

Sunday, July 7, 1985

Taking a ferry rather than driving down and around the tip of the bay to Olympic National Park worked out well. We learned that the Olympic Peninsula has both the wettest spot in the continental United States (near the Hoh Rain Forest, which is a temperate rain forest in Olympic National Park) and the driest spot on the West Coast outside of southern California (Sequim—pronounced Skwim—on the northeast corner of the peninsula). Truly a land of contrasts.

Our campsite was on the west end of Lake Crescent, known as the jewel of the Olympics. It used to be a resort area in the early 1900s. We started out to go swimming but went canoeing on Lake Crescent instead. Tara and I went together in one canoe; Dick and the boys went in another. The lake is 600 feet deep in parts and is very blue, partly because of its depth. It was a relaxing way to spend the afternoon.

After dinner, Dick, Andrew, and I went to the campfire talk on plants and animals. The tall purple flower on the roadside is foxglove, from which the drug digitalis is made. We all felt the leaf of the thimbleberry plant. It's very soft—and is nicknamed "the toilet paper of the woods." We saw some bats and heard a flying squirrel. I wished we had been able to see it.

Monday, July 8, 1985

Another beautiful day. Tara cooked breakfast and we started out for the Hoh Rain Forest. As we approached, the trees suddenly became very dense, a canopy of green hanging over the road. The forest was different from any we had ever seen before. The sun was shining through the branches, but it was a very different feeling from being in a forest in New England. The rain forest

65

was very green with moss and very dense leaves; in New England forests we can usually see more of the sky in between the leaves.

There were two hiking loops at the Hoh, and we went on both. We did the first one, the Hall of Mosses Trail, on our own. The mosses are called epiphytes. They don't take anything from the trees but hang from them. Because of all the rain, trees grow very large. Usually they get 144 inches of rain a year, but we were there on a sunny day.

That year's rainfall had been below average, an extremely rare situation in the Olympics. The weather had been dry for the past two weeks, so some of the mosses had shrunk a bit, and the forest was not as green and lush as normal. The forest was also less thick than it might have been because of the elk, which eat off much of the vegetation. The elk keep the lowest tree branches about seven or eight feet off the ground, and many of the bushes are cropped short. Otherwise, the first six feet of air space above the forest floor would be a tangled mass of vegetation. As it is, it is quite open.

We saw nurse logs, which are trees that have fallen down and have little saplings growing on them. When a tree falls over, seeds land on it and sprout. The log decays very slowly because there is so much water from the rain (air is required for it to decay). This gives the seedling a long time to grow. Eventually— sometimes as much as 50 years later—the roots reach the ground. Then the log rots and leaves a tunnel through the roots.

We did the second trail accompanied by a ranger. He pointed out colonnades, which are straight lines of trees that are left after nurse logs rot away. The only other major thing we saw were salmonberries, which look and taste like raspberries; most of the ones we saw, we ate.

After lunch, we went on another ranger-guided hike, this time on the Spruce Nature Trail. On this hike, the ranger pointed out similar things to those we had seen on the other hike, but now we were with someone who could explain them in more detail. From there we drove to see a big Sitka spruce tree. The tree was 12 feet 6 inches in diameter and 230 feet tall. What an awesome sight!

Andrew and I went to the campfire program that night. It was about plants and animals that are endemic to Olympic (found here and nowhere else in the world). There are a lot of endemic animals here, including the Olympic marmot, the Olympic yellow-pine chipmunk, and the Olympic snow mole.

Tuesday, July 9, 1985

We started out by driving to Hurricane Ridge, which gave us a totally different view of mountains. These really are a ridge— almost a wall of mountains. There were glaciers on most of them and some snow. The area we could see at a distance is unspoiled—not even any roads. Less than one percent of the surface area of the United States is the way it was when white men first came, and this area is part of it.

Wednesday, July 10, 1985

We headed west, then south, going down the coast and stopping briefly at the seacoast portion of Olympic National Park. The kids played in and near the surf, but Dick and I just enjoyed the scenery. A wilderness beach is such a beautiful place. I enjoyed walking past the huge tree trunks that had been washed up on shore. A sign on the trail to the shore described them as the "bones of the forest picked clean by the ocean." They reminded David about the Bible passage about the valley of the bones.

Andrew wrote,

After supper, Dad and Mom cleaned up the dishes and David, Tara, and I went to a campfire program on Lewis and Clark. The whole program was interesting, but my favorite part was when they showed how to light a fire with flint and steel. I had done it before, but the way they showed was a lot easier than the way I learned.

Crater Lake National Park, Oregon

Sunday, July 14, 1985

Our destination for the day was Crater Lake National Park. Dick, Andrew, and I went to the campfire program on the history of Crater Lake. The lake was formed when the volcano Mount Mazama collapsed 7,700 years ago and formed a depression called a caldera. Wizard Island, in the center of the lake, is a volcanic cinder cone capped by a large volcanic crater. The lake was named because of this crater. There are no inlets or outlets, so all the water in the lake is from melting snow and rainwater. It is the deepest lake in the United States, 1,932 feet, and seventh deepest in the world. It is incredibly blue due to its depth and lack of dissolved particles. The lake was discovered independently several different times, and every time nobody paid any attention to the finding. Eventually one man, William Gladstone Steel, took an interest in the lake and spent his life first working to make it a park and then working to allow more people into the park.

Monday, July 15, 1985

We went to the 9:00 AM ranger-led hike to Discovery Point, where white men first saw the lake. The hike took 2 hours: 90 minutes to get there, and 30 minutes back because we returned on our own. There were some lovely views of the lake and of Wizard Island. When we started out, the lake was so calm the mountains were reflected perfectly in it. At the end of the walk, the ranger asked us for possible ideas of other names for the lake. Some suggestions included Azure Lake, God's Looking Glass, and Mirror Lake. Dick suggested (with apologies to Shakespeare) that one possible name might be Azure Like It. I liked Blue Mirror best.

Later we went to a brief geology talk. There was a neat model there showing Mount Mazama before it erupted. When we lifted the top off, there was Crater Lake.

After cleaning up from dinner, Dick, Andrew, David, and I hiked the Annie Creek Canyon Trail. We went backward by mistake, so we had to read the nature guide in reverse order, but it didn't make much difference. The hike covered virtually the whole gamut of geologic processes, from the effects of volcanic activities to the effects of ground water. It was a lovely walk, and we saw animal tracks and the American Dipper at a distance. This bird is common along rushing streams in the West and is noted for its bobbing or dipping movements. We hadn't really hiked right along a creek before. The only bad part was the steep climb up at the end.

Dick wanted to be on Rim Drive at sunset. The drive took us about three quarters of the way around the lake, so we could watch the sun set over Wizard Island directly across from us. We stopped at every turnout along the way—some spectacular views—and were at Kerr Notch at sunset. It was very pretty, although not particularly colorful.

We got back to camp just in time to hustle over to the amphitheater for the evening program. We attended most of the evening programs on our trips because they were always so interesting and informative. Andrew and I particularly enjoyed them.

Craters of the Moon National Monument and Preserve, Idaho

Thursday, July 18, 1985

As we approached Craters of the Moon National Monument and Preserve, we were driving through fields of lava—all black. We stopped outside the park to do some rock collecting. It was difficult walking over the jagged rocks.

We set up camp in what was described as "a novel campground." It certainly was. The ground was all cinders, and there were lava rocks everywhere. We could see cinder cones in the background. Our site was in the middle of an old lava flow with no plants around the site, just rocks.

After lunch we drove on the seven-mile-long one-way loop road. We timed it so that we could stop at pull-outs along the road and still get to the last stop by 2:00 PM for the ranger-led cave walk. I was hesitant about going on the hike after my last cave experience, where I felt very claustrophobic, but this one was fine. The cave had some places that let light in, and the rooms were quite large. I actually enjoyed it. Andrew explained,

The ranger took us to and through Indian Cave explaining the geology of the area on the way. One of the things he told us was that Indian Cave wasn't a cave but a lava tube. Lava tubes form during a lava flow when the lava on top hardens and turns to rock and the lava underneath flows out.

We were free to explore the other caves on our own; however, they are pitch black. Tara and I went back to the car, but Dick and the boys explored the caves with flashlights. Everyone agreed I had made the right decision, but they really enjoyed themselves. Andrew commented,

It was really neat to go into a cave that you had to crawl into and had no light other than your flashlight. My favorite feature of the caves was that they were such good insulators. They have ice year-round.

We stopped at the Visitor Center and then drove the loop again, this time stopping at all the trails. The most spectacular view was from the top of a cinder cone. A whole line of these cones formed because of the Great Rift, along which volcanoes shot up. When the lava was shot into the air, it cooled and returned to earth as cinders. A whole line of these cinder cones was formed. We also climbed up to look at some spatter cones, which were formed by the same process, but the lava returned to earth in larger chunks.

At the campfire program, we watched an excellent movie on volcanoes called "Heartbeat of a Volcano." It showed the Hawaiian volcano Kilauea, which had erupted a couple of years before. It's the same type of volcano as the one that formed Craters of the Moon. In the movie, we saw the molten lava and scientists measuring all sorts of things.

We were told that Craters of the Moon was overdue for an eruption. History shows it has erupted approximately every 2,000 years, but when we were there it had been 2,100 years since an eruption.

Tuesday, July 23, 1985

When we got to Illinois on our trip home, I felt like we were really getting east toward New Hampshire. Then we stopped for gas and a woman said, "My, you're a long way from home."

1986

Shenandoah National Park, Virginia

Great Smoky Mountains National Park,
North Carolina, Tennessee

Shenandoah National Park, Virginia

Sunday, June 22, 1986

In addition to Andrew, 16, and Tara and David, both 14, we had added one more traveler to our family: Jorg Gabelmann, an exchange student from Neustadt an der Weinstrasse, Germany, who had been with us since the previous August.[31]

Our children became much more creative with their journal entries. Andrew wrote,

After packing up, we boarded the "Feren Mobile" and were served a breakfast of strawberry bread, orange juice, and bananas. As we proceeded down Skyline Drive at nowhere near warp speed, we were able to enjoy the clearest view we had ever had there. The panoramic view, however, was still far from pristine. Upon awakening I was granted permission to serve as temporary pilot along the drive. I served in this capacity until slightly before the noon hour, at which point I surrendered control of our vehicle to the veteran navigator Richard B. Feren. At 1700 hours we arrived at a campground. We set up camp and ate our supper at a rapid clip, for our parents desired to see a fiddle hoe-down.

They suffered one minor setback when two cup covers wandered off by themselves. After the safe return of the covers, my parents and I went to the hoe-down. We managed to arrive only a mere 10 minutes late.

David wrote,

Captain's Log Stardate 6-22-86
We beamed aboard the Enterprise at 700 hours to continue

---

[31] When we returned from this trip, Andrew went to Germany to live with Jorg's family for a year.

our trip to the depths of space to boldly go where no man has gone before. This is OUR TREK.

(music interlude)

(3 commercials)

We zoomed along at just under warp speed so as to keep our bodies as well as our ship intact. After approximately 60 minutes of pleasant zooming we came upon a navigator's nightmare, Skyline Drive! It was somewhat like a beautiful tractor beam. Its beauty pulled you in, luring you with sights and sounds but its treacherous array of twists and turns shock you back to reality. At 1700 hours we docked for the night at a local orbiting space station that went by the alias of Roanoke Mountain Campground although I secretly suspected it of being a front for a Klingon Space Junk fencing operation.

My comments were much more mundane. I mentioned that we saw deer three different times. The first one was right on the yellow line in the center of the road. When we came along, it dutifully went to the side and posed for pictures! The second one went bounding across the road, and the third was in the woods. We also saw live woodchucks on the side of the road on two different occasions. (We usually see only road-killed woodchucks.)

Dick mentioned that Andrew did his first driving on a trip. It was very nice to have a third person to share driving chores. This was the first time that Dick and I could both look at the scenery at length while the car was still moving.

Great Smoky Mountains National Park, North Carolina, Tennessee

Monday, June 23, 1986

We stopped briefly at the Visitor Center in Great Smoky Mountain National Park to see an orientation film and then on to Cades Cove. The cove is a shallow, bowl-shaped depression. Geologically it is a fenster, or "window," where overlying rock has been worn away and the underlayer shows through. It is a beautiful place. Walking through the woods is like walking through a fairyland forest because the floor is covered with a luxurious-looking, bright-green vegetation. The tendency of the deer to allow us to get very close to them only added to the fairyland illusion.

Historically, it is a preserved historic area—basically pre-Civil War. There is an 11-mile, one-way loop drive, which took us about three hours. I could understand why anyone would be struck with the beauty of the place and decide to live there.

We visited the various farms and cabins with a ranger as our guide. He gave insights into the lives of the people, so it was easy to identify with these pioneers and picture them living out their existence in synchrony with nature's clock of the days and seasons. One description stated that these folks were not all that different from the other animals who lived there: they collected honey and berries like the bears; gathered nuts like the squirrels; and captured small game like other predators.

We saw three churches, only one of which we were allowed to enter. It was a very basic structure with nothing in it but rough, unfinished wood and an altar that was barely more than a table.

David continued his experimentation with different styles of writing.[32] His journal entry summed up our trip well.

See Dick. See Nancy-Ann. See their family.
See them wake up and yawn.
Yawn. Yawn. Yawn.
See them pack the car.
Pack, Dick. Pack, Nancy-Ann.
See them go for a drive.
Vroom! Vroom!
See the road. It has many turns.
Turn, Dick. Turn, Nancy-Ann.
See the family eat lunch.
Munch! Munch! Munch!
Yum! Yum! Yum!
See them eat prunes.
Slurp! Slurp! Slurp!
See them driving again on the road with many twists and turns.
Nancy-Ann is reading things from a booklet.
The family sees the things Nancy-Ann is reading about.

---

[32] David is now a high school English teacher.

Read! Read! Read!

See! See! See!

See the family visiting old houses and churches in Cades Cove.

See the pretty girl.

Andrew and David see the pretty girl.

See them (Andrew and David) exchange looks and grin.

Grin! Grin! Grin!

See the family set up camp.

They are working hard.

Work! Work! Work!

After dinner David and Tara washed up.

They washed their arms, their backs, their legs, and their stomachs.

David combed his hair and the grease kept it there.

He also washed his hair.

Scrub! Scrub! Scrub!

See the family sleep.

Z-Z-Z-Z-Z-Z-ZZZZZZZ

Good Night Family.

1992

Indiana Dunes National Lakeshore
(now Indiana Dunes National Park), Indiana

Voyageurs National Park, Minnesota

Isle Royale National Park, Michigan

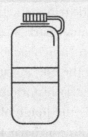

Indiana Dunes National Lakeshore (now National Park), Indiana[33]

Sunday, June 21, 1992

Six years had passed since our previous camping trip. In 1987, we traveled to Europe to meet Andrew, who had spent a year in Germany with Jorg, and we traveled with our family throughout much of Western Europe. After that, our children were in high school and college with summer jobs that kept them—and us— at home. In 1992, Dick gave a science workshop in Minnesota, and our children were old enough to stay home alone, so we finally had a chance to get back on the road.

Aside from occasional weekends we had spent at local campgrounds, this was our first camping trip in six years and our very first one without our children. Although I always loved having the kids with us, this was great too. Four hundred miles didn't seem as far as it did with a car full of children.

As I was driving, I saw signs for Indiana Dunes National Lakeshore. This was the year we had decided that we wanted to visit all the national park sites, so we made a serendipitous, spur-of-the-moment side trip to the lakeshore. Although Indiana Dunes is a relatively small park, it offers great diversity—from ponds, marshes, swamps, and beaches to dunes that were formed 4,700 years ago when the lake's water level was 25 feet higher than today. There are also historic buildings, such as the Bailly Homestead, which was the home of a fur trader who was one of the earliest settlers in northern Indiana, and the Chellberg Farmhouse, which was the home of a Swedish immigrant family.

The dunes are spread out for fifteen miles along the southern shore of Lake Michigan and because of the changing water level over the years, some of them are quite a distance

---

[33] Another entry on Indiana Dunes National Park appears in 2018

inland. Some dunes are forested hills and others are piles of shifting sand. We climbed the tallest dune, Mt. Baldy. There was an easy trail, but I didn't know that at first and tried to go up the side of the dune, which was almost impossible on the loose sand. In striking contrast to the lake scenery was the industry of Gary, Indiana, in particular Bethlehem Steel, which we could see in the distance.

Voyageurs National Park, Minnesota

Sunday, July 5, 1992

When I look back at our journals for 1992, it seems like I didn't do too much advance planning. On impulse, we took a different exit than we had originally planned for Voyageurs National Park and, by luck, ended up at the Kabetogama Visitor Center. We got there a little after 9:00 AM and discovered that there was an all-day boat trip leaving at 11:00 AM. We decided that would give us the best view of the park, which is 40 percent water. There are several hiking trails near each of the two Visitor Centers, but we didn't try any of those trails.

The boat trip was chilly but pleasant. Despite the cold, we got to see several bald eagles, including some young in a nest. The adults were sitting right nearby. A little further on was another eagle nest. This time I could see the two young eagles in the nest and then watched the adults fly, land, and sit nearby. We stopped by a rock covered with pelicans. I don't know where I thought pelicans lived, but it wasn't here! There were also cormorants there and a couple of loons, Minnesota's state bird, although they were not too close to us. One dove under the water almost as soon as we saw it and came up much farther away. Bears had been seen recently on one island. We stopped to look but didn't see them. I vowed that someday I would see a bear!

On the boat, we placed an order for lunch so it would be ready for us when we arrived at the Kettle Falls Hotel, an old resort hotel at the far point of our trip. At one point, it fell into disrepair and wasn't in use for several years, but it was eventually restored, and in 1976 it was added to the National Register of Historic Places. It had 12 hotel rooms for guests and a full-service restaurant. Dick had a walleye sandwich. Walleye is a popular fish there.

After lunch, we walked a few hundred yards down a small road and were able to straddle the border between the United States and Canada. It is one of the very few places in the United States where people can look south into Canada.

Isle Royale National Park, Michigan

Tuesday, July 7, 1992

Isle Royale National Park is an island in Lake Superior. It is far from civilization, which makes it a great place to enjoy solitude and scenic beauty. On a day trip such as we took, visitors can browse through the displays at the Visitor Centers at Rock Harbor and Windigo or take short hikes.

Because the park is so isolated, we left camp early in order to get to the dock for the boat tour to the island. It was a frigid day. That was the coldest I had been, and we were going on a three-hour boat trip: Brrr! It started to rain as soon as we got in the car, stopped, then started again very hard after we got on the boat.

Aside from the rain, the boat trip was uneventful. We moved from the first seats we chose to the cabin area, which was the only nonsmoking part. It also turned out to be the warmest! We ate most of our lunch on the boat. When we docked, we walked up to the store and met the ranger for a guided walk. She pointed out lots of different plants, moose tracks, and "moose berries," which are moose droppings. When she finished, we took the self-guided nature walk and saw both yellow and pink lady slippers. I thought we were getting back to the store just in time for another naturalist's talk, but we only got to hear the very end. We did see the lens that used to be in the lighthouse.

It was warm and sunny on Isle Royale, which I had expected to be the coldest part of our trip. I was almost sorry we had decided not to backpack and camp on the island. The trails are easy and the shelters accessible. Next time …

During the 1800s and early 1900s, many people built vacation cabins on Isle Royale. When the island became a national park in 1931, these people were given the choice of selling their land to the National Park Service or naming someone in their family who could possess the land until they died. In the harbor, we saw homes of some of the descendants of people who were living there when the National Park Service took over. Much as I enjoy wilderness, I would not want to live there.

1994

Haleakala National Park, Hawaii

Hawaii Volcanoes National Park, Hawaii

Tuesday, July 19, 1994

Dick and I were excited to fly to our 49th state: Hawaii. I was really looking forward to relaxing. It had been a very hectic spring, with the last day of school for the kids June 24 and Andrew's wedding June 25. Then I had to go back for two more teacher workdays.

I loved the flight from Boston across the mainland. I slept off and on but woke up in time for some fantastic views of what may have been Colorado. We could see mesas, then some very dry land, then what I think were the Rockies with patches of snow, and then irrigated circles of farmland. They were different shades of green, perhaps depending on the crop. I found it fascinating to realize that we flew over in minutes what usually took us days to drive across. The one picture I remembered from elementary school geography books was an aerial photograph of farmland in the United States. I could now vouch for its authenticity.

Haleakala National Park, Hawaii

Tuesday, July 26, 1994

On this trip we stayed at bed and breakfasts instead of camping, so it was a different experience. Our room at the first B and B in Honolulu was very airy and spacious. We had indoor accommodations with an outdoorsy feeling. Our particular room was located in such a way as to be hidden from outside view, so we were able to keep both the shades and the windows open, and it was very much like camping. The wind at times made some sounds that were new to us as the stiff leaves of the native trees rattled together. It was very pleasant indeed.

For our drive in our rental car to Hana, we rented a cassette tour, which gave good information. The road is noted for more than 50 one-lane bridges and more than 600 turns, many of them hairpin turns. We were in and out of rain, but the scenery was lovely.

My favorite stop was Black Sand Beach, which was formed from lava that had eroded into tiny sand-like particles. We had our picnic lunch here and then walked down a trail to the beach. The "sand" was very different. It stuck to my skin in little globules. There was a cave here formed by waves crashing against a lava deposit. We crawled through the opening; then we could stand up. The surf was gorgeous!

We didn't really stop in Hana but went beyond to the "seven sacred pools." There are not seven pools and they're not really sacred—apparently tour bus people called them this to lure visitors there—but the area is now an extension of Haleakala National Park. A series of falls form pretty pools, and many people were swimming.

Wednesday, July 27, 1994

We got up at 2:40 AM and drove to Haleakala, a 10,023–foot-tall dormant volcano, to see the sunrise.[34] I was amazed at how many people were there, many of them a good hour before sunrise. We were early enough to be able to drive all the way to the summit parking lot. That day the rangers closed that lot before sunrise because it was full.

Sunrise was lovely: vivid colors with clouds in the "crater," which was actually created by headward erosion of two rivers. What we thought was the horizon was really the other side of the rim about seven miles away! As the sun came up, we also watched cyclists getting ready to coast down the mountain. Apparently, there is a great demand from people who want to be driven to the top of the mountain so they can just coast downhill. I think we saw about a hundred cyclists that morning, and more were being driven up as we drove down. We saw only one person attempting to bike up the mountain.

Once the sun was up, we walked on several trails: one to the top of a cinder cone, another to see some rare silversword plants, and one last one for a view. The land was amazing. We could see craters and cones for miles with just scattered plants. It reminded me of Craters of the Moon in Idaho, also a volcanic region.

---

[34] Now reservations must be made 60 days in advance to view the sunrise. Reservations can be obtained at recreation.gov or by calling 1-877-444-6777.

Hawaii Volcanoes National Park, Hawaii

Friday, July 29, 1994

That day we went to Hawaii Volcanoes National Park. We were on Kilauea; its crater is a caldera, several miles across. In it are several smaller craters. Of these, the largest and most recently active is the Halemaumau crater. We walked on lava fields that I remembered seeing flowing on television in 1974. The volcano is still active. There had been a small eruption two days before our visit. I wished we could have seen it, but we still saw lots of steam and a small area of red molten lava flowing into the sea. There were lots of steam vents and craters of different types. Walking near the Halemaumau crater, we could smell the sulphur, and in part of it near the floor, we could see a bright yellow river of sulphur.

The Kilauea River Road was blocked off here, so we had to head back. We stopped for a wonderful buffet lunch at Volcano

House, which also provided a great view of Kilauea Crater.[35] After lunch we took the other part of the rim drive, which took us to the road that ran down the volcano to the ocean. There were some interesting stops on the way. One was a 500-year-old lava tube that was about 200 to 300 feet long. Another site was Devastation Trail, where a bare lava landscape was situated next to a thriving forest.

The road down to the shore was a fairly typical winding mountain road. But at the coast, things got different. The view was obscured by a fog or mist, which we discovered was steam from seawater produced by hot lava from a recent eruption. We got to see some spots of red lava (from a distance) where the lava entered the ocean. The steam cloud was blowing across the road near where we parked. When we got back to the car, it was covered with salt and looked like a salt dome.

We spent another day on the island of Hawaii visiting a couple of National Historic Parks before returning to Oahu for two more days in Honolulu. We were glad we had taken the time to travel this far from home.

[35] Kilauea is one of the most active volcanoes in the world. Its most destructive eruption in recent history began on May 3, 2018. Most of Hawaii Volcanoes National Park was closed due to increased and damaging earthquakes, corrosive volcanic ash, and continuing explosions from Halemaumau, the summit crater of Kilauea Volcano.

1995

Gates of the Arctic National Park
and Preserve, Alaska

Denali National Park and Preserve, Alaska

Kenai Fjords National Park, Alaska

Tuesday, June 20, 1995

We set forth for Alaska—finally! We had talked of this trip for years. This was a long summer: no snow days to make up and no school until after Labor Day. David was at home to take care of our dog, Shadow, the bills, and the house. No weddings or other commitments.

I'd been planning this trip for more than nine months. We had driven cross country with three children twice and taken many other lengthy camping trips, but this was by far our most ambitious trip to date.

We estimated that we would drive 10,000 miles and that we would spend 50 nights on the road.[36] I used a AAA camp book to find possible campgrounds and their cost.[37] Then I made a rough estimate of the campground costs for 50 nights and an estimate of the cost of food. Dick estimated the cost of gas, a car tune-up, and possibly some car repairs. We budgeted the cost of admission to national parks and several tours. When we lived in Europe many years ago, we learned to buy our Christmas gifts when we see them, so we budgeted money for this as well. We then knew we could afford this trip.[38]

Next, I used AAA maps and mileage charts to map out a tentative route, anticipating that we would make more changes as we dug deeper into the literature and still more once we were on the road. We felt that with straight driving we could easily do 400 miles a day, but we also planned to stop more frequently in Alaska. I fine-tuned the itinerary so we would arrive at places with campgrounds at the end of each day. It appeared that sometimes this would necessitate two shorter days of driving,

---

[36] It turned out to be just over 12,000 miles, and 53 nights.

[37] The AAA camp book is no longer published. Today, campers need to use the Woodall Campground Guide (which does not always include national park campgrounds); *Milepost Magazine*, which I also used; and national park websites.

[38] $4,900 in 1995.

because there just aren't a lot of towns in northwestern Canada and Alaska. Whenever possible, I selected campgrounds near towns that probably had grocery stores, garages, and maybe even a laundromat. This part of the planning ensured that we really would have enough time to attempt the trip.

As I continued planning, I realized that there was not a lot of choice once we got past Alberta. Most of the campgrounds were designated as "pit toilets, no showers." These were the types of campgrounds we'd always passed by, at my request. Now I knew how much I really wanted to go to Alaska. If it meant pit toilets, pit toilets it would be. It appeared that our solar shower might finally get daily use. On the plus side, there would be enough hours of sunlight in Alaska to heat the water, even if we arrived late in the day.

Next, I figured out when and where we needed ferries: Skagway to Juneau, Juneau to Sitka, Sitka to Ketchikan, Ketchikan to Prince Rupert, British Columbia. I couldn't figure out the ferry schedule, so I called the 800 number for the Alaska Marine Highway System.[39] The staff members whom I spoke with were extremely helpful. All the trips were overnight; some took as many as 23 hours. Some ferries that I wanted didn't run on the days I wanted, so they helped me revamp our schedule. One ferry was small and didn't have berths, but we were able to get berths on all the others. Staff members reminded me that the berths get booked quickly, so it is important to make reservations early.

My most valuable resource was a 700-page annual magazine, *The Milepost* magazine,[40] which contains maps for all the major highways and a guide with milepost numbers telling exactly where to find lodging (both campgrounds and hotels), restaurants, restrooms, services, and sightseeing attractions along the Alaska Highway both to and within Alaska. There are also advertisements for tours and shops. I used *The Milepost*

---

[39] 1-800-642-0066.

[40] www.themilepost.com.

magazine to find addresses for tour companies and wrote letters for information.[41] The brochures came in throughout January and February. I immediately looked at the ones with information on flights to the Arctic Circle and cruises, because these types of transportation all required reservations.

I typed out a new itinerary with the growing details and made the reservations for the Skagway train trip, a cruise at the Kenai Peninsula,[42] and a trip to the Arctic Circle.[43] We knew we would change some of those plans, but they gave us a framework. Making plans helped the time pass quickly, and soon enough, we were on our way.

Saturday, June 24, 1995

Over the first few days of travel, we kept rearranging the boxes in the car until we got them exactly as we wanted them, and we stretched a clothesline across the back storage area. We had what we needed (including two tires with rims), and not much extra. We also stopped at a garage to get additional springs for the car to help support the amount of weight we were carrying.

We planned to drive west through Canada, with stops in all the provinces en route, so we expected that it would take us about three weeks to actually get to Alaska.

---

[41] Today this can all be done online.

[42] We used Mariah tours (millerslandingak.com).

[43] We used Northern Alaska Tour Company (www.northernalaska.com), although the itinerary has changed since we went in 1995.

Wednesday, July 12, 1995

On July 12, after a quick trip across the Yukon River, we were on the Top of the World Highway. About 2:00 PM we entered Alaska. I got very emotional. The tears wouldn't stop. I think it was a combination of having achieved our goal of seeing all 50 states and a memory of my mother wanting to do that. I felt as if I'd done it for her. I hoped she was looking down and seeing us achieve this goal.

Gates of the Arctic National Park, Alaska

Saturday, July 15, 1995

We did a wonderful tour, starting in Fairbanks, where we were picked up by our Northern Alaska Tour van at our campground at 5:00 AM. When we got to the Arctic Circle, our tour guide, Andrea, made a big deal out of it, even putting out a red carpet and shaking our hands as we crossed the line. Then we had tundra (chocolate) cake with perma frosting (Cool Whip). It was delicious!

From there we drove to Prospect Creek to get a plane to Anaktuvuk Pass. This remote village of 250 people was established in the 1950s by the last remaining semi-nomadic tribe of Nunamiut Eskimo. The village is part of Gates of the Arctic National Park and Preserve.

At first our plane wouldn't start, but workers fixed the problem. Riding in the plane was an adventure. We were close enough to the ground to see a lot of geologic detail, and to see some animals. We spotted bear, moose, and caribou. The plane was so small that it was at the mercy of any wind shifts. Sometimes we bounced like a speed boat hitting waves. Other times, we dropped like we were going down the slope on a roller coaster. Still other times, we side-slipped as the wind blew us from the side.

Once we landed, we drove up to the museum because the mosquitoes were *really* thick (worse than the Everglades). It was a very interesting, small museum with items relating to Nunamiut history and culture. One exhibit showed a primitive Eskimo pack dog. The village residents still rely on caribou for most of their meat although they hunt other animals as well. We felt like we didn't have enough time at the museum. In fact, the bus left without us, and we had to brave the mosquitoes and walk back to the Community Center. I bought an Eskimo mask, which had been made here. We later saw an identical mask for sale at a shop near a cruise ship landing. There, it was priced more than five times what we had paid.

At the Community Center, a teenager named Brian, who was an Eskimo, sang and played the drum (a very shallow instrument—a skin stretched over something). We tried to ask him questions, but he was very shy.

This town, which is two miles from end to end, is not accessible by road, but it has roads of its own. They have a bus that runs constantly through the village. The driver is paid almost $2000 a week! Sometimes the children will pay a quarter and ride around the village for entertainment. The residents are still dependent on the migration of the caribou for their winter meat. Many of the men are employed by the pipeline. The school (120 children out of a population of 300) has an indoor swimming pool and a big gym.

When we got back on the plane, it wouldn't start—again. This time they couldn't fix it. Fortunately, there was another Frontier plane there to carry cargo. They sent us to the café while they put seats into the cargo plane. We finally got back to camp about 9:30 PM —to find a couple from Newmarket, New Hampshire,[44] camped next to us.

---

[44] A small town 35 miles from our home.

Denali National Park and Preserve, Alaska

Sunday, July 16, 1995

Fortunately, it wasn't a long drive to Denali National Park and Preserve, our next stop. We drove to the National Park Visitor Center to pick up our tickets for the next day's bus ride into the park. What a madhouse! There were long lines of people hoping to get tickets. We only had to pick ours up, but we still had to wait. Only one third of the tickets are sold ahead of time.

Monday, July 17, 1995

We got the 7:30 AM bus to the Eielson Visitor Center, about 60 miles into the park. Private cars are only allowed on the first 14 miles, but there are lots of tours—buses all over the place. Whenever anyone on our bus spotted wildlife, they yelled "stop" and our bus driver pulled over. It was a beautiful day: bright and clear with a few scattered clouds. The colors and texture were magnificent: charcoal grey to the left (south); beige, brown, and orange to the right (north). In some places the colors mixed, especially in Polychrome Pass. There were as many shades of green as we had seen on a previous trip to Ireland. There were areas of smooth sand, rough gravel, jagged rocks, rounded peaks, pointed peaks, and U-valleys with taiga (coniferous forests found in subarctic areas) and tundra (vast, flat, treeless Arctic region where the subsoil is permanently frozen) alternating and mixing.

People on our bus saw Dall sheep, but they were *far* up on the hillside. Even with binoculars, they were only white dots. Then we spotted two mother grizzly bears with their cubs. One mama went after a squirrel and left the babies alone; the other mama was nursing. We saw one caribou running—possibly crazed by flies.

We stopped a couple of times for spectacular views of Mount McKinley.[15] It is the tallest mountain in North America at 20,320 feet and is totally snow-covered. As we approached the mountain, it grew large, but it wasn't a gradual growth. It grew larger in jumps because we could only see it on a few occasions as we rode, when it peeked out between other mountains. The bright sun over its white top made a spectacular sight. We were really lucky to get a clear view. Our bus driver said he had recently met a visitor who had come seven years in a row and still hadn't seen the mountain. It's so large it creates its own clouds and its own weather; it is often covered with clouds.

At Eielson Visitor Center, Dick and I hiked a little way up a hill to view the tundra and the surroundings. The tundra initially appeared to be a rolling green carpet that is more or less uniform, but when we looked closely, we saw many shades of green, and many different and very colorful flowers.

When we came down, caribou were all around the Visitor Center. We were told that they're becoming quite the pests. The

---

[15] In 2015, it was officially renamed Mount Denali to reflect one of the native names for the mountain.

rangers kept trying to shoo them away. The caribou frequently walked down the road. One time, three of them were walking equally spaced in front of a truck so that they looked like Santa's reindeer pulling a multi-ton yellow sleigh with 10 wheels.

Dick walked back to take a picture of a waterfall we had seen on the way in. He described it this way:

Water tumbled over rocks arranged with the spacing and steepness of steps, but not so regular. They were spaced randomly, yet perfectly to make just the right effect. Moss grew between rock and edges, softening the view. Monk's Hood, bluebells, bear flowers, dwarf fireweed, and more covered the banks—mostly on the right where the slope was most gradual and sunny.

At 1:30 we went on a guided tundra walk. There were only five people on the walk, so it was very personalized. The ranger gave out little magnifying glasses and a list of things to look for. We looked at flowers and their survival strategies on the ranger walk. Some had short fat leaves; others had flowers with the shape of a satellite dish; some had hairy or furry stems and leaves; some were miniaturized; some grew in sheltered areas. All had adaptations to the harsh tundra environment. There were about two dozen varieties of wildflowers.

Temperature on top of the tundra measured 90 degrees Fahrenheit; six inches down into the soil it measured 40 degrees Fahrenheit. We were all kneeling on the ground when one tourist noticed the caribou heading straight for us. We moved fast!

On the bus ride back, we stopped for a bear with cubs (this one was hard to see) and one much closer, eating berries or something. Then someone spotted a gray wolf. I didn't see it until it came out of the brush and led the bus down the road! It looked like a large dog. We were almost back when we saw a moose. I had seen what looked like a horse in the field and was trying to process this when Dick realized it was a moose. We also saw hairy marmots and golden eagles.

Tuesday, July 18, 1995

That morning we went hiking. We climbed to the Mount Healy overlook, the only hike billed as "strenuous"—and it was! The first part to the scenic view was fairly easy, but then it got very steep, with many switchbacks. Most of that was a real trail as opposed to rocks, but it was difficult. We ate our lunch at the top and picked blueberries on the way down. Blueberry pancakes for breakfast the next morning!

We wore loud "bear bells," which drove me crazy, but I'm sure they're a good safety precaution. When we got down, we had just enough time to get ready for the sled dog demonstration. Denali is the only national park that raises sled dogs and uses them to patrol the park in the winter. Before the demonstration, we got to pat the dogs. Most of them were very sleepy. There were also three five-week old puppies. The dogs don't work during the summer, so they get most of their exercise from doing the demonstrations and from being walked by volunteers.

We all stood in a circle as the ranger started explaining things. She told us that to do the demonstration, most of us would have to move, but she said not to move until she gave the word. The dogs know that movement means some of them are going to be picked to perform, and they all want to do it—they love to run and pull the sled. Sure enough, when the ranger signaled for the audience to move and make room for the dogs, the dogs started to howl, bark, and hop around, saying, "Take me! Take me!"

To hitch them up, the rangers lead the dogs by their collar with their two front feet off the ground (two-wheel as opposed to four-wheel drive), because otherwise they'd pull the rangers over. Five were harnessed up: one lead dog, two swing dogs (to help turn), and two dogs that pull more of the weight. When the driver said for the dogs to go, they took off like a shot around a prepared trail, starting at about 15 miles per hour, and slowing to about 6 to 7 miles per hour after a short time. They can keep up that pace for hours. In winter, they often go 35 to 40 miles a day.

They each eat a pound of dry dog food a day. In winter, they get a fat supplement, and hot water is poured over their food. They have to learn to eat quickly or their food will freeze. All of them had *heavy* coats and were shedding a lot. Rangers adopt them for the summer, take them for walks, and give them TLC.

Another one of our tour guides told us about his experience as a musher. His tutor told him to never let go of the sled, no matter what. When he told his dogs to "mush," they took off so fast that his head snapped back. Shortly after that, they hit a bump and flipped over the sled. He hung on, while his face plowed a 75-foot furrow in the snow. But it was soft, so he was okay. He enjoyed working with the dogs, and he didn't really mind the whitewash. He got up, righted the sled, and they were off again.

Kenai Fjords National Park, Alaska

Friday, July 21, 1995

At the Kenai Fjords National Park Visitor Center, we watched two videos: one on the Harding Ice Field and one on the Valdez oil spill. Seeing the birds and animals covered with oil in the video made me feel sick.

Then we headed for Exit Glacier, which was very accessible. We went on a ranger-led hike first. The ranger pointed out a magpie's nest, which has a roof, perhaps because the birds winter here and need protection from the snow. He also said to watch the birds in the parking lot. They jump up to eat the dead insects on bumpers and windshields.

Next, we hiked up close to the glacier. It is so blue, especially in some of the deep crevices. I decided it could be a new paint color: glacial blue. We saw terminal moraines (dirt that collects at the front edge of an ice sheet or glacier), and different amounts of vegetation that increased on them as moraines got older. The earliest plants included fireweed. We saw them in patches out on the outwash plain, as well as in the fringes of the forest. The first trees to develop were alder, cottonwood, and willow. Alder and cottonwood often grow together because they provide mutual shelter, and alder provide nitrogen for cottonwood. Leaves catch dust from the air, and rain washes dirt to the ground, all of which helps soil formation.

Saturday, July 22, 1995

We lucked out again with the weather. Today was our day for the glacier and wildlife tour at Resurrection Bay, and it was gorgeous. Well … the sky was blue and the sun was shining, but there was some fog, and it was cold. I should have dressed more warmly. I also should have put sunscreen on. It never occurred to me.

The boat was small. (It's called "the small ship alternative for seeing Kenai Fjords," so I guess that isn't surprising.) It was 45 feet long and held 22 passengers. There was very little inside room—it must be awful on a rainy day—and the only seats per se (except for a couple inside) are storage boxes. The captain really knew his stuff and explained things very well.

A short way out of Seward Harbor, we met a sea otter. Dick described him as:

a placid old gentleman who was apparently familiar with tour boats. His gray face gave him a distinguished look. He rolled over every so often, but always keeping his face and front paws out of the water. He watched the boat and nonchalantly scratched his chin. He propelled himself at a leisurely pace using only his right hind foot. He was obviously wrapped up in a deep philosophical thought (or maybe theological if you consider the prayerful position of his front paws) and he couldn't be bothered with anything so mundane as a tour boat.

We got really close (the advantage of a small boat), but the captain was careful not to get close enough to bother him.

There were a lot of dead trees on shore near the ruins of a World War II Army munitions dock. The dead trees reminded us that an earthquake in 1964 dropped parts of the land in this part of the country about six feet, drowning many trees at the coast. Near the dead trees was one of the very few beaches in Resurrection Bay.

Nearby, we could see some bald eagles. They are majestic when in flight. We also saw humpback whales and could see their waterspouts. As we approached, I saw one breach. I guess they had been doing a lot of that before we approached. They were as big as the 45-foot boat we were on. It's good that the peoples and countries of the world are beginning to recognize the necessity to allow whales to live without our interference, let alone having us try to kill them.

The next stop was for a group of about 30 harbor seals. They were playing and fishing and sunning. There were also birds called black oyster catchers. The Bear Glacier which was visible in the distance clearly showed the medial and lateral moraines.

For lunch we stopped right in front of Holgate Glacier. This was the most spectacular part of the tour. We watched it calve.[46] We witnessed quite a few calvings—a couple of big ones and a lot of smaller ones. The big ones made a huge noise as they landed in the water. Just as we arrived, one broke off with a loud crack and hit the water with a bang that sounded like the report of a small cannon. The sun was in just the right position to highlight the grooves the glacier had carved in the rock walls as it moved along the valley years ago.

After lunch we went to Chiswell Islands to see the bird rookeries and also to see a large colony of Stellar Sea Lions. They were all over the rocks—adults and babies (the babies are darker colored). The adult males can reach a size of 1800

---

[46] This occurs when pieces of ice break off the front edge of the glacier and fall into the water—sometimes pieces that extend from the top of the glacier to the bottom.

to 2200 pounds, with females 700 to 900 pounds. Some of the males bore scars from territorial battles and other injuries. Most of the big males at this time were sunning themselves. They are quite good climbers, and some venture up onto the rocks far above the beach. The pups were mostly frolicking around on the low rocks by the water. Females were either nursing or just watching the pups play.

The second most spectacular part of the tour came as we were about halfway up Resurrection Bay when we went through a pod of orcas. For several minutes, we watched as an occasional dorsal fin would show itself at some considerable distance from the boat, but not always in the same place. Our captain said that he thought the pod was spread out over about a mile rather than clustered. Just as we were getting ready to leave, a few surfaced closer to the boat, then a few came even closer, and one came 10 feet off the stern of the boat! Wow! Unlike the Pacific gray whales that we had previously seen in Scammon's Lagoon in Mexico, orcas are not noted for coming so close to boats, so this was indeed a rare treat.

As we headed back to Resurrection Bay, we had to stop to help our boat's sister ship, which had had engine trouble. They tied the boats together, and the captains went back and forth getting parts and tools. It appeared to be a loose electrical connection, which they fixed quickly.

Sunday, July 23, 1995

We woke up early to the sound of rain. We stopped at the Visitor Center again. This stop was especially worthwhile: they had two ice worms they had found Friday night. Ice worms are about an inch long and very tiny. They look like black thread and are found in glacial ice, where they feed on snow algae, pollen grains, ice, and snow.

Saturday August 12, 1995

This marked our 54th—and last—day of that trip. It was beautiful in the morning, although it had rained during the night. I felt very nostalgic. I wanted to go home, but I also felt that I'd like to keep enjoying the relaxing life of travel—camping—away from routine.

1998

Black Canyon of the Gunnison
National Park, Colorado

Canyonlands National Park, Utah

Arches National Park, Utah

Capitol Reef National Park, Utah

Bryce Canyon National Park, Utah

Cedar Breaks National Park, Utah

Zion National Park, Utah

Petrified Forest National Park, Arizona

Black Canyon of the Gunnison National Park, Colorado

Sunday, June 28, 1998

We changed our original plans and went a little farther south to see Curecanti National Recreation Area and Black Canyon of the Gunnison National Park, another good decision. After watching a brief film at the first Visitor Center in Curecanti, we drove on to the campground at Cimarron. It was very scenic. The ground was desert-like, and we were surrounded by pinkish hills without much vegetation. I could hear water, so I knew there must be a river nearby.

Monday, June 29, 1998

It was cool enough for sweatshirts when we got up (before the sun rose over the hill). It was only a short ride to the Black Canyon of the Gunnison National Park. The canyon is about 2000 feet deep, 1000 feet wide at the top, but 40 feet wide at the very bottom. The Gunnison River is very fast-moving to have carved a valley with such steep walls, but from the top of the canyon, the water at the bottom seems to be slow moving, and there is not much volume of water.

We got to the Visitor Center before it opened so did not go onto its porch. If we had, we would have seen the path to the viewpoint. Instead, we took a different path. It was very well maintained, and there were beautiful wildflowers.

On the way back, I was a little ahead of Dick. A little fawn came very close to me and then ran into the woods. I asked Dick whether he had seen it. He responded that it was very big. That's because he had thought it was a jack rabbit rather than a deer! I wish we could have gotten a picture. It was so cute: big white spots.

At one point, we viewed the Painted Wall. At 2,300 feet, it is the highest cliff in the park. A sign at the site said that if the Empire State Building were placed on the floor of the canyon, it would reach only a little more than halfway up the wall of the canyon. The views throughout the park were spectacular.

Canyonlands National Park, Utah

Tuesday, June 30, 1998

Again, we changed plans en route and decided to camp at Canyonlands National Park rather than at the state park we had planned. We got a site in Willow Flat Campground with a little shade, enough for eating our early lunch. Later, I discovered the National Park evening program is held at the state park—and our campground not only had no flush toilets, but also no water.

Canyonlands is divided into three parts, mostly on the basis of the rivers that cross it and intersect in it. We were in a part called Island in the Sky, which is a high desert, and from which parts of the other sections can be seen. Needles is named for the tall, slender rock formations that are very common in it. The Maze is a remote, rugged area, and it is one of the most inaccessible areas in the United States. It gets its name from the labyrinthine maze of canyons that crisscross it.

Our first hike was The Rim Trail from Grand View Point. It would have been an easy one except for the fact that the temperature was 105 degrees Fahrenheit and the elevation over 6,000 feet. The hike was about a mile. It took us 90 minutes, exactly what the guidebook said. There were some beautiful views of red sandstone canyons and spires.

Dick was really impressed with the cryptobiotic crust found on the desert floor. It is composed of lichen, algae, fungi, and cryano bacteria. It is a living surface that serves as a way to provide nitrogen to the soil, and to stabilize the surface of the desert soil. It provides a place to aid the germination of plants.

The second hike was shorter. It was a half-mile loop to a sandstone arch. What a view!

It was then after 3:00 so we decided to drive to town (45 minutes one way). I wanted to look for Native American crafts and buy ice. We found a great dairy bar with delicious ice cream. It was 105 degrees Fahrenheit, and there was no line. I know New Englanders eat more ice cream than anyone else, but seeing no waiting line on such a hot day really surprised me. I should have asked about all the flavors before ordering. Mine was good, but Dick's "Mother Lode" with butterscotch chips, chocolate chips, and Heath bar chips was superb!

Back at camp we commented on how quiet it was at the park—not just Canyonlands but almost all the parks we visited. We had commented on it when we were at Colorado National Monument and Black Canyon of the Gunnison too. There were also incredibly clear blue skies all day and stars at night. I didn't try to identify constellations, but even I could see the Milky Way.

It was a beautiful evening when we got back. It would have been nice to sit outside but it was almost dark, and we were exhausted.

Wednesday, July 1, 1998

We got up early to hike in relative coolness. It was darker at 5 AM than it had been at 11 PM when the moon was casting shadows.

We hiked to Upheaval Dome, which has an uncertain origin still being debated by geologists. Apparently, they are not sure whether it is an impact crater or the eroded layers above a salt dome. Dick's opinion was that it is more likely to be from a salt dome than from a meteor impact. A material such as salt is left behind when the water it was dissolved in evaporates. A salt dome is formed when this salt, called an evaporite, is forced up by the weight of denser materials surrounding it. Dick described the formation in this way:

To picture the process of salt-dome formation, imagine a layer of material (like salt) that is softer and less dense than rock, and imagine a layer of rocky/sandy sediment on top of it. If there is a place in the sedimentary deposit that has a weak spot (is cracked or thinner than other parts), the evaporite will gradually be forced vertically up into the weak spot, raising the sediment slightly higher than the surroundings. As more sediment is deposited, the evaporite continues to get pushed higher, and a vertical column of evaporite is formed under the ground. The result above ground is a slightly dome-shaped uplift of the sedimentary material.

Arches National Park, Utah

Wednesday, July 1, 1998

After leaving Canyonlands, we drove to Arches National Park, which has been described as the Crown Jewel of the National Parks. We weren't sure whether this referred to all national parks, or just those in Utah. It was certainly interesting, with more than 2,000 natural stone arches plus hundreds of other red-rock formations. In retrospect, we might have been better off staying two nights at the state park as we had originally planned. This campground was fine but much more crowded. I liked the quiet of Canyonlands.

We set up camp and then did a hike to Turret Arch and North and South Windows. We passed by a monolith that looked like a profile of a person. The rest of that trail went around behind North and South Windows and gave the only really good view of both. We came back by the "primitive" route, which had fewer people. It was longer and more pleasant. But it was HOT. There are signs everywhere reminding us to carry and drink lots of water —at least one gallon per person per day. We tried to make sure we did that.

We ate lunch in the car. With the sun directly overhead, it was the shadiest spot we could find. We had just heard it was 108 degrees Fahrenheit the previous day. Even the natives thought it was hot. We couldn't sit on a rock to rest because it burned our bottoms. It burned our fingers to open the cooler. Luckily, we had been finding block ice, which lasts much longer.

I met a woman from Boston at the Visitor Center. She hadn't traveled in 30 years but had promised her daughter (a Harvard grad) that she would come for her graduation from med school. The daughter, Maria, wanted to work on the Navajo Reservation. The mother could not understand this. When she discovered we had driven cross-country she was shocked—and more so when she discovered we were camping—and even more when I said we were camping in a tent. She said maybe I was Maria's mother. When Maria came over, her mother told her what we were doing, and Maria's response was, "Neat."

I tried cold wet wristbands to cool down. I liked to believe it was helping.

On our way back to camp, we decided to go to the Delicate Arch viewpoint. There were two paths, and neither of us bothered to read the sign. We chose the viewpoint that required a steep half-mile hike—which I did in sandals! It is a pretty arch: much less massive than most of the others.

We finally got back to camp and prepared dinner as quickly as possible, so we could do another hike. We selected a short evening hike we could do from our campground and be back before the 9 PM ranger talk. It was a delightful hike because it was getting cooler as the sun dropped lower, and we saw lots of life: bugs, beetles, lizards, and tracks of various creatures. It was a different trail than we had expected: two different arches. The first arch was Broken Arch, which has a vertical split at the top. There was a little bit of rock climbing at the end, but it wasn't too bad. There were only two other people there, which also made it enjoyable.

From here we went to Sandstone Arch. The trail itself was mostly sand. Toward the end, it was like walking at the beach.

The description said it was a cool place for children to play on a hot afternoon. We didn't stay long because it was getting late.

The sun was setting as we got to the road that we were going to take to the campground. It was getting darker and darker. I knew the moon would probably provide light and we had our flashlight, but I kept walking faster and faster. I didn't even want to stop for water. The only wildlife we saw on this part of our hike were lizards and beetles. There were some neat lizard tracks in the sand. However, we misjudged our time, and we just barely got back before it was dark. We walked into the talk late by about 20 minutes. The part we saw was a slide show of wildlife in their habitats as found in the park.

Thursday, July 2, 1998

We did one more hike that morning (what we had intended to do the previous night). It's part of the Devil's Garden Trail. We went as far as Landscape Arch, one of the longest arches in the world. The arch is getting thinner. There were warning signs that if you heard popping or cracking sounds, to notify a ranger.

We started to go past here to the Double O Arch, but the trail got rough, and we hadn't worn our hiking boots. So, we went back to the turnoff for Pine Tree and Tunnel Arches. These were very short trails. At Pine Tree Arch, a butterfly—Dick thought it was a swallowtail because it had blue and yellow circles on its black wings—landed on my wristband, which I'd been keeping wet in an attempt to cool my body. We figured it was attracted to the red color of the wristband and stayed to get water. The butterfly stayed with me all the way to Tunnel Arch. It finally flew away, but its visit made our day. We figured that anything else would be anticlimactic.

Capitol Reef National Park, Utah

Saturday, July 4, 1998

We changed our plans again. Originally, we had reserved July 2, 3, and 4 at a private park in Blanding, Utah, so we wouldn't have to be worried about finding a place to stay on July 4th weekend. Instead, there we were, leaving our reserved site a day early and changing to a new campsite on July 4th!

Fortunately, there were plenty of sites at Capitol Reef National Park, and they were *shaded*!

This was once a Mormon settlement, Fruita, a very appropriate name since there are many fruit orchards in the park. Visitors can usually stroll through any unlocked orchards and can sample ripe fruit, but they must pay for any fruit taken from the orchards. Unfortunately for us, all the orchards were closed until Monday because of the holiday.

While we were eating lunch, a mule deer came to within about 20 feet of us and had his own lunch of low plants at the base of a tree. He nibbled for a few minutes, then ambled off. There are supposedly lots of skunks too but fortunately I didn't meet any.

A few minutes later, a tent tried to join us for lunch. The wind came up briefly, and someone's tent started rolling toward us. Dick leaned it against a tree in hopes of reducing its wanderings. Imagine someone leaving an unstaked tent! When we got back at night, I think that tent was set up across the road, quite a long way from us. I don't know if that's where it started out or if the campers moved it.

We checked out hikes and programs at the Visitor Center. We decided we had just enough time to hike to Hickman Bridge before a ranger talk at the Fruita School. The hike was a moderate one—steep in places but no ladders, just a regular trail. It had a trail guide, too, which pointed out various features. Some we were getting knowledgeable on: cryptobiotic soil, and adaptations on desert plants (the flat surface of the prickly pear is its stem and the sharp things are leaves). However, the guide also pointed out an old Native American granary and some Native American petroglyphs.

The bridge was attractive. We got there in time to wade in the stream. That was a *real* treat. It felt wonderful!!

From there we went to the Fruita Schoolhouse. It was a typical one-room schoolhouse. The ranger did a good program. Everyone got parts, and when she held up the corresponding numbers, we read our part. I was a teacher's pet, and Dick got to be a dunce. It illustrated part of a typical school day in the late 1800s.

Then we went to the Gifford House, a Mormon home. There was an exhibit of quilts but not much background on the house itself.

We were back at camp in time to cook a leisurely dinner— yummy pork chops, baked potatoes, and candied carrots. The previous night we had used garlic Melba toast as croutons. It worked well.

We even had time to sit and write before the 9:00 PM program. I saw two more hummingbirds. I had seen one the other day. I had only seen one other one *ever* that I could remember. We saw another one as we were walking to the program.

The program was on the historic settlement of Fruita. The ranger mentioned the trail at Capitol Gorge, which follows the original road, so we decided to do that the next day. We decided (almost as soon as we arrived) to spend a second night at Capitol Reef. It was our favorite park so far on this trip.

Sunday, July 5, 1998

After breakfast, we went on the Scenic Drive. The last 2 miles were a dirt road, through a narrow, winding canyon. At the very end is the trail we wanted to hike. It leads, along the old road, to some Native American petroglyphs and the pioneer register where people signed their names on the rock cliff in the late

1800s. This part of the trail was level, but it was like walking on soft beach sand. The dirt road, the hike, and beyond were parts of the original road through Capitol Gorge. One man with a few volunteer helpers cleared about 3½ miles in about eight days. That was the main road into the area for at least 60 years until Utah Highway 24 was built.

After the pioneer register, we turned off the road and climbed a fairly steep, not too well marked, rocky trail to "the Tanks," an area that had ancient potholes from river erosion. Some of these natural cisterns may have been used by pioneers for water. When we were almost back to the trailhead, it started to sprinkle a tiny bit. We ate lunch at a covered picnic table at the trailhead.

By the time we were almost back to camp, there were huge puddles in the road. There was a lot of lightning and light rain. When we got to the Visitor Center about 5:00, we were told the Scenic Drive was closed due to the possibility of flash floods (good thing we had gone in the morning), and the Weather Service had updated their forecast to predict half an inch of rain an hour between 5:30 and 6:30.

On our way back to camp, an animal crossed the road. Dick thought it was either a coyote or a fox. We had not planned to go to the evening ranger program but at the last minute changed our minds. I'm glad we did. The program started out with a quiz on national parks. We knew quite a few of them but there were some I had never heard of. [47]

---

[47] I bet we could answer all the questions now! Be sure to check out our own quiz at the end of this book.

Bryce Canyon National Park, Utah

Monday, July 6, 1998

The drive to Bryce Canyon National Park was meant to take 2½ hours, but it took us about 5 hours because we stopped for so many pictures. The scenery was spectacular, and it changed several times over the drive. At one point we could see mesas in the distance from where we had come, lush stands of aspen on one side of the road, and desert scrub on the other. At other times it was open range. In fact, we had to stop to wait for some cattle to move out of the road. We also saw a deer on a hillside (thanks to a motorist going in the opposite direction who signaled to us).

We drove up and up and up—to the Aquarius Plateau. At 11,000 feet, it's the highest plateau in North America. I was driving, and I was not thrilled when Dick informed me that we were driving along a ridge with drop-offs on either side. When we came down from the ridge, we could see flat land and dwarf trees that looked like round shrubs. As we approached Bryce, we were back to red sandstone again.

We set up our tent and then went to the Visitor Center for hiking information and the introductory slide show. When we came out, it was thundering.

The previous night, some hikers had told us about the Mossy Cave Trail just outside the park. They had said it was something we shouldn't miss, so we drove there. It started to rain, so we stayed in the car for a while until it let up.

We had been told that the trail had two creek crossings without bridges. I suspect when these hikers did it, it was before the two rainstorms. The creek was very full. The trail was fairly short, but it crossed the stream twice on makeshift bridges.

The first "bridge" was just a big log with a small log diagonally under it. I was scared to death. I really did not want to do this, but I didn't want to let Dick down. With him holding me, I made it. The second "bridge" was a combination of a small log plus rocks, much of which the water was running over. Hikers had to balance on a log barely above the water with nothing to hold onto. We watched two young girls do it, although one took off her shoes to walk on the wet log. This time I just couldn't muster enough courage. I offered to wait while Dick went. He considered going but decided against it.

We came back to eat an early supper so we could go on a ranger-led rim walk. This was just an easy stroll with a ranger explaining geologic time and events—which I still don't understand. The views, however, were fantastic. We were looking down into a pink fairyland. Many formations look like elaborate carved castles surrounded by spires. We looked at one formation and both of us thought it looked like a German castle, such as Neuschwanstein. In the distance we could see the Aquarius Plateau that we drove over yesterday.

Then we drove to the amphitheater at the other campground to wait for the program. It was a slide show billed as "The Hidden World at Bryce: Creepies and Crawlies." Unfortunately, it didn't really measure up. It told a little about insects at Bryce but a lot about other places too.

We did learn that there are fleas that are infecting the prairie dogs and the chipmunks with a disease like the Bubonic Plague in humans.[48] It's especially important not to feed the animals, but the chipmunks are real beggars and very tame. We've seen lots of people feeding them.

Tuesday, July 7, 1998

We drove straight to the end of the scenic drive. This was recommended to us because all sights were then on the right side of the road on the way back. We hiked on the Bristlecone

---

[48] At the time of our visit, scientists feared that the prairie dog population would be wiped out, but they later discovered that prairie dogs can be vaccinated against plague, which almost doubles their chance of survival.

Pine Trail and saw one tree that was 1,600 years old.[49] Clearly, this tree can live under very harsh conditions.

We stopped at a lot of overlooks on the way back. The best was Bryce Point. Then we went to Sunset Point to hike the Navajo Trail down into the canyon. This was amazing. The trail was quite steep with a lot of switchbacks. The bad part (compared to climbing a mountain) was that after hiking down into the canyon, we had the harder task of hiking up at the *end*.

The hoodoos (tall, thin spires of rock), mostly pink limestone, were beautiful. Part of the trail went through a very narrow canyon where there was barely enough room to let sunlight reach the floor for a short while, yet there was a huge Ponderosa Pine growing there. It was about 200 feet tall, and perfectly straight, with barely enough room to fit between the hoodoos. It was an amazing sight. It was like hiking in a fairyland.

---

[49] There are three species of Bristlecone pine, all of which are long-lived. One of the species is among the longest-lived life forms on earth. It includes a tree that is more than 5,000 years old.

I discovered that it seemed harder to find a store near Bryce Canyon than it had been to find one in Alaska. Maybe that's because so much of this area is national parks. There really aren't many people living there.

After dinner we got ready for the moonlight hike into the canyon. We started at 9:00 PM and got back after 11:00. This was an easier trail through a section called The Queen's Garden. We made several stops on the way down to look at the moon and the stars. The moon really provides an amazing amount of light. No one used flashlights at all. We saw the larva of a bug that glows in the dark. Weird! This was definitely a different experience but one I enjoyed.

Cedar Breaks National Park, Utah

Wednesday, July 8, 1998

This park acquired the name "Cedar" because early settlers incorrectly identified the juniper trees growing there as cedars. "Breaks" comes from a term that means "Badlands." We drove up and up. The park is located at more than 10,000 feet. We thought originally that we would just pop in, see a few sights, and leave, but we decided to stay longer when we realized how much there was to see and do. (This was beginning to be a common refrain.)

For a while after we decided to stay, it looked like we had made the wrong choice. We set up the tent and started lunch when it started to thunder. As the rain started, we finished lunch in the car. The rain turned to hail and maybe some sleet, and it got really cold. We went to a brief geology talk at the Visitor Center. The ranger gave a great memory aid: the earth is DUE for a change. D equals deposition, U equals uplift, and E equals erosion. These are the factors that formed and are changing the limestone formations here.

While Bryce Canyon is only 800 feet deep, Cedar Breaks is over 2,000 feet deep. It's a huge red bowl with formations in it.

By the time the talk was over, the rain had stopped, so we decided to hike. The trails were not officially open because of the snow, but we were told it was okay to use them with caution.

We chose the Chessmen Trail. It had a high and low trail, but it was one loop. We made the right choice by starting on the lower trail. Even here there were a lot of snowbanks to climb through, but the snow was solid. Where the trail was hidden, there were tall orange poles stuck in the snow to mark the way. We both loved the snow, although while going from the lower to the upper trail, Dick stepped deeply into a drift—up to his knee. The upper trail was clear. It was fun hiking through snow in July, and I always feel so much more secure on snow than on rocks or logs crossing streams.

Our campground had only been open about a week because of snow. The campground hosts told us that the snow this past winter had been 18 feet deep. The last storm in mid-June deposited 18 more inches of new snow. There was still at least one plowed snow bank on the road that was about 10 feet tall.

The evening program was good. We got there in time to see a colorful sunset and a full moon. The talk was about geology. The ranger explained that Bryce and Cedar Breaks formations were limestone rather than sandstone, and formed in a giant freshwater lake, about 250 miles by 175 miles. It was the same ranger we had heard that afternoon so some of the information was repeated, including "Mother Nature is like an artist (one uses oils, another watercolors)." According to the ranger, Mother Nature uses mostly water for erosion with just a little wind.

Zion National Park, Utah[50]

Thursday, July 9, 1998

We got an early start for Zion National Park. The road into the park, which went through a long, winding tunnel, was on one of Zion's two scenic drives. Zion was as different from any of the other parks we had been to as they had been from each other. One interesting difference was that Zion started on the valley floor, and everything went up from there. The others all started at the top and went down from that.

We were disappointed with Zion. It was very congested, parking was terrible, and there was not that much to see. Their introductory film, however, was the best. It showed where things were and suggested when to see them.

We started up the other scenic drive, stopping for a view of the Three Patriarchs, massive mountains of sandstone. Then we hiked to one of the emerald pools. There are three and we chose the middle one. The hike was fine but not particularly scenic. We saw lots of striped lizards and a view of the river

---

[50] An additional entry on Zion National Park appears in 2014.

below. This is unusual having a flowing river in the desert. The pool itself was not spectacular.

At first, we couldn't find parking at the Weeping Wall or the Riverside Wall, but when we came back to the Weeping Wall, we found a spot. The trail was rated easy and accessible for wheelchairs. I'd say wrong on both counts. It was paved but it was very steep. There were nature signs along the way. They were informative but didn't, in many cases, seem to be in alignment with the thing they were describing.

The Weeping Wall is composed mainly of layers of sandstone and shale. At the base of the wall, there was an undercut portion that made the weeping wall itself an overhanging rock. Water can seep through the sandstone but not the shale. It flows across the shale and ends up dripping through the rocks of the wall to create springs and unique hanging gardens with ferns, wildflowers, and mosses. When we walked under the overhang, it felt like it was raining.

Petrified Forest National Park, Arizona

Monday, July 13, 1998

I was also a bit disappointed with the Petrified Forest National Park. This is probably my own fault for not thoroughly researching the available trails. The petrified trees we saw were not standing up like trees; they were long and short pieces of logs. In a few places, the short pieces are still in their original position, so visitors can see them together as a log. Actually, it looks like a log that has been cut into several cylindrical chunks, each about two or three feet long.

Over 200 million years ago, the trees were washed into a river and buried. Minerals were absorbed into the wood and crystallized. Where there were cracks in the logs, large crystals of varying colors (due to impurities in the quartz) formed.

We hiked on the Giant Logs trail; it was a short, paved path. There were lots of stumps and logs, all petrified. They looked like amethyst and other semiprecious stones. Definitely interesting; this was the best part of the whole park for us. There are also several other trails leading through stands of petrified trees.

What is called the Crystal Forest had been vandalized to such a point that we really couldn't see any crystal (quartz) at all. We only walked a short way on this trail. It was very hot. There must be an awful lot of visitors to the Petrified Forest, because I read a sign that said if each person took only an ounce, the flow of pieces out of the park would equal 28 tons per year!

The overlooks with views of the Painted Desert were lovely. We had seen the Painted Desert years ago, but from such a distance that it didn't look like anything special at all. It looked much better this time. The colors of red, gray, green, and white can be breathtaking. The hills are all different, basically pastel colors.

In retrospect, I wish we had taken some of the other trails. One short trail leads to the remains of a 100-room pueblo from more than 600 years ago. Petroglyphs can be seen along the trail. Another trail leads to Agate House, an eight-room house built more than 700 years ago. Hikes on the Blue Mesa trail lead through badland hills of blue bentonite clay. I want to go back to Petrified Forest National Park for more explorations.

2000

Acadia National Park, Maine

Acadia National Park, Maine

Tuesday, August 1, 2000

Following our son David's wedding, Dick and I went to Canada for a few days. On our way home, we decided to stop at Acadia. We arrived at 5:00 PM and still managed to get a decent walk-in campsite at Seawall Campground. We usually set aside one night to eat out on our trips, and we decided that this night would be a good one. At a walk-in site, campers park at a distance from the campsite and carry in all their gear, so we would have needed to lug the cooler and pots and pans back and forth to the car, which was a fair distance from our site. By eating out, we eliminated this issue. We went into town and had lobster, which was delicious.

We got back just in time to walk over to the ranger program. As usual, it was excellent. The ranger had six volunteers—all young children—come up to be rocks. One child represented volcanic rock and periodically erupted, by jumping up; another child laid flat to represent sedimentary rock, which forms in layers; a third child sort of twisted and curled up to represent metamorphic rock, which forms as a result of heat and pressure. The other three children were bundled together as if they were part of underground magma waiting until the temperature cooled to 800 degrees Fahrenheit. Then one became quartz with shiny (glassy) surfaces and sharp points; one became feldspar with two long, flat sides (here it is pink, but it forms in lots of different colors); and the third became hornblende, which was black. These three together make granite. What a wonderful teaching/learning experience.

Wednesday, August 2, 2000

We set off to find bridges on the carriage roads. These roads, 45 miles of them, were the gift of John D. Rockefeller and family. They are broken-stone roads, built between 1913 and 1940, and aligned to follow the contours of the land and take advantage of scenic views. Native granite was used for much of the construction, and the landscape beside the roads featured native blueberries and sweet fern. There are 16 uniquely designed stone-faced bridges. As part of a high school unit on forces and vectors, Dick's physics students build bridges of balsa wood each year. He wanted to take pictures of the bridges at Acadia to show various possible styles before the students started constructing their own.

The bonus for me was definitely the blueberries. Dick took pictures of bridges while I picked berries, and we both did some walking. We ended our visit with yummy popovers at the Jordan Pond House.

2002

Acadia National Park, Maine

Acadia National Park, Maine

Friday, July 12, 2002

During this trip we were joined by our son Andrew; his wife, Celeste; and their children: Sebastien, age five, and Alexandre, age three.

The previous night, we had taken the boys to a presentation about tidal pools. That day, after a breakfast of blackberry pancakes, we packed lunches and went to a rocky shore, so Sebastien could see some tidal pools. The ones at the base of the rocks were pretty and colorful with all the usual things: snails, mussels, urchins, seaweed, and white slimy stuff along with white branching things.

To minimize the impact of traffic throughout the park, there is now an "Island Explorer" bus, which provides free service between destinations in the park as well as local communities.[51] We took the bus to Sand Beach, where we had lunch. Sebastien and Alexandre had a good time walking, splashing, getting wet, and building sand castles and moats. The water was 50 degrees Fahrenheit, but the boys didn't seem to mind. A seagull took the top bread from the sandwich Alexandre left on his towel. Camping with our grandsons brings back so many memories of our early camping experiences.

We walked to Thunder Hole—a very pleasant walk with beautiful ocean views. The path was bordered on one side by large stones, most of them squarish and blocky. Sebastien loved walking along the tops of these rocks, and sometimes jumping from one to the next. Alexandre had a harder time keeping up because of his shorter legs, but he did really well, being carried occasionally.

Thunder Hole is an inlet with a small cavern that has been eroded out of the rocks by the waves. When waves rush in, air and water are forced out. It makes the sound of thunder, and water

---

[51] http://www.exploreacadia.com/

sometimes spouts 40 feet high. There wasn't much "thunder" at Thunder Hole on that day. We should have been there a couple of hours before high tide. However, we could see the large rock pockets worn into the rock that created the high spray.

Walking through a woody area on our way to the ocean that morning, we had seen some natural features that looked like a beautiful miniature village, so when we got back to camp, Sebastien and Dick built a similar village with stones, sticks, and moss. That evening we all went to the presentation at the amphitheater. Sebastien really enjoyed the ranger programs. He was very attentive and asked lots of questions. He was working hard to earn his Junior Ranger badge, which involves doing a certain number of activities and talking about them with a ranger.

Saturday, July 13, 2002

We hiked partway up Cadillac Mountain and took a spur[52] to Eagle's Crag. It was just the right length and difficulty for the boys. Sebastien hiked all the way; Alexandre did some riding on Andrew's shoulders. On the way up, Sebastien really liked climbing on the rocks. He also pointed out a rotting log that was "turning into soil," a bit of knowledge he remembered from the previous night's ranger program. He doesn't miss much!

Alexandre also liked climbing on rocks, but he didn't have either the stride or the stamina of Sebastien. He both wondered and giggled at almost everything. The smallest pebbles held great fascination for him. Above Eagle Crag, his curiosity helped find a beautiful batch of early blueberries.

When we got back, we went to the Visitor Center, where Sebastien shared what he had learned with a ranger and was sworn in as a Junior Ranger. We were pleased to see him following in the steps of his father and uncle.

---

[52] A trail that branches off the main trail.

2004

Yosemite National Park, California

Sequoia National Park, California

Kings Canyon National Park, California

Yosemite National Park, California

Saturday, July 17, 2004

We sandwiched this trip between a two-day science workshop that Dick gave in Sacramento and a family gathering in New Hampshire to say goodbye to David and his wife, Kristen, who were scheduled to move to Bangladesh for a teaching position at the end of the month. Before leaving home, we bought plane tickets, packed our tent and sleeping bags, arranged to rent a car in California, and made plans to meet with our friends from San Diego, Nancy Orear Bixby and her husband, "Bix," at Sequoia National Park. Nancy and I were classmates at Wellesley College, and she was a bridesmaid in our wedding. We were really looking forward to seeing them again.

After heading out from Sacramento in our rental car, we stopped to buy a few things we hadn't been able to bring on the plane: two chairs, Coleman fuel, a dishpan, and basic food items. The ride to Yosemite National Park renewed all my memories of California: the dried grass on the hillsides, which make this the Golden State, and miles and miles of fruit trees lining the highway, each labeled with what type they are. This time we found stands selling the fruit, so stopped to buy some. Dick bought the largest peach either of us had ever seen.

Once we turned off the highway, the road got steep and curvy. At one point there were instructions to turn off the air conditioner. We guessed it was because it would put too much strain on the engine.

Our campground was the first thing we came to once we entered the park. This was good for arriving and departing but not so great the rest of the time. The sites were not large, but we were on a corner, and would have a neighbor on only one side. Every site had a bear-proof metal container with a complicated latch system in which campers were required to store any coolers, all food, and any toiletries with a scent. Odors attract bears, so it's essential to keep a clean camp. In fact, bears have a sense of smell 100 times better than ours and will break into cars looking for food. Trash needs to go into bear-proof containers, and hikers are also advised to make plenty of noise. Bears do not like surprises and will usually move out of the way if they hear people approaching.[53]

Once we got set up, we drove eight miles down the road to get gas (expensive!) and wood (also expensive!). We hadn't been sure whether we would be able to have fires because of the high fire danger—there were several lightning-caused fires burning in the park—but apparently it was okay in campgrounds.

Our campground didn't have an amphitheater, and the next closest one had only two programs while we were there. We decided to skip our planned walk in order to attend the first program. The ranger had a beautiful campfire, and she talked about bears. She had a bearskin, bear scat, and a bear skull to display. She also had a 10-ounce can of tomato paste to illustrate the size of a bear cub at birth.

It felt so good to stretch out in my sleeping bag when we got back. I love sleeping outside!

Sunday, July 18, 2004

We headed for Yosemite Valley that morning. The road was fine, but views into the valley were very smoky. There were several fires burning that had started from lightning a week or so earlier. They were under control and were being monitored, but they were not being put out because they were part of the natural process. At a few points we could really smell the smoke.

When we saw a sign for Bridal Veil Falls, we decided to stop; we were already too late for the 10:00 AM ranger walk. This was a short hike, but it had a spectacular view of El Capitan.

---

[53] More information on keeping safe around bears can be found at www.nps.gov/subjects/bears/safety.htm.

143

I guess in the spring the waterfall is a real torrent, but in July it did look more like a bridal veil. When the wind blew, it would be swept to one side; it really reminded me of the pictures of Kristen with her veil blowing.

We parked at the Day Use area, took the shuttle to Lower Yosemite Falls, and hiked there. There were a lot of signs warning of danger on the rocks, yet there were many people on the rocks anyway. We could see both the upper and lower falls from there. We initially planned to hike to the Upper Falls as well, but it was much farther than we wanted to do that day.

We ended up at the trail for Mirror Lake. We knew that the name was a misnomer and that it was mostly a mud puddle in the summer. We were pleasantly surprised to find what appeared to be a small stream (which we think was the lake). There was no sign anywhere, but it seemed to be the right distance. We actually took off our shoes and socks and waded across to get a better picture of Half Dome, a 4,800-foot granite dome-shaped rock formation. One side is a sheer face while the other three sides are rounded. All along the trail we had seen evidence of horses; finally, on the way back, we had to wait for 12 horses and riders to pass by. We returned to the stream and agreed that it did appear to be a lake bottom with sand and tall grasses. Coming back down, we missed the trail to our bus stop and walked to the next one, almost an extra mile. Fortunately, it was a pleasant walk.

Monday, July 19, 2004

We headed for Wawona and had a picnic lunch amid a flock of begging birds. Then we took the shuttle to Mariposa Grove, where there is a grove of giant sequoias. We bought tickets for the tram ride: an open wagon (with seats) pulled by a truck. It was crowded, bumpy, and hard to hear the narration. It was worth taking the tram up to the Upper Grove, because it would have been a long, hot walk, but I would have preferred more stops with more walking.

We had one stop at a small museum that was so dark we really couldn't see the exhibits. The next stop was the Grizzly Giant Loop Trail. We got off there and walked back—a very pleasant, albeit somewhat dusty, walk.

I learned a lot about sequoias. They have small cones but don't drop them naturally. They depend on beetles and squirrels, which eat the cones and allow the seeds to drop. For a long time, fires were suppressed until people realized no new trees were growing. They need the heat from fire to help the seeds germinate, and the fire clears some of the underbrush away. The trees have lots of tannic acid in them. The acid acts as a preservative, so even after they die it takes a long time for them to decay—up to 1,000 years. The tannic acid also makes them resistant to bugs, fire, and disease. Some of the living trees in the park are 3,000 years old.

Back at Wawona, we bought ice and ascertained that our cooler was definitely leaking. We figured we'd had it since 1979, so it had served us well.

Wednesday, July 21, 2004

This was mostly an errand day. We went to housekeeping cabins in the park for showers and laundry. They were right next to each other, so we could put the laundry in and while it washed, we could wash. After lunch, we bought groceries. It was a hot day and ice cream sounded good, so we bought a pint of Hagen Daaz—then realized our spoons were back at camp. Dick cut the lid in half and we used each half as a scoop. It worked, and the ice cream was delicious.

One more accomplishment that day: we bought adhesive tape and patched our cooler, which was leaking badly. We'd already had two other cooler mishaps on the trip. Somehow the top got off the aerosol can of whipped cream after we used it for strawberry shortcake. We had cream in the cooler and no pressure left in the can. Dick cut off the top and used what was left for pancakes. The next day, our can of frozen orange juice thawed and leaked all over the cooler. What a mess!

Thursday, July 22, 2004

After breakfast we went to Merced Grove, which was just a few miles away. It had a small grove (six trees) of sequoias, plus a few single ones along the path. It was a 1½-mile hike downhill to the trees (and what goes down must come up!). We went about a mile farther to a little stream. It was a very pleasant walk—mostly shaded, again with pretty wildflowers, butterflies, and a few birds. Dick wrote,

One critter with a lot of evidence was the ant lion—a larval stage of an insect that looks like a dragonfly. They make cone-shaped depressions in the sandy soil and bury themselves at the bottom. If an ant walks along the top edge, it slips and falls to the bottom of the hole, where it is grabbed and eaten by the ant lion. I pointed out clusters of the cone-holes to several groups of people who had apparently never heard of them. Nanc said I was being very teacherly.

We came back to camp for our main dinner at noon. We planned to go on a twilight walk that evening, and the timing made it easier to just have sandwiches later on. We sat the cooler in the shade and used it for a table.

We packed our sandwiches for an evening picnic and headed for White Wolf Campground, where we ate with a giant rock as a table. A squirrel came down the tree about a foot away from us. It had an odd coloration. Most of its fur had a yellowish tinge, and it had a black line outlining its underside and then white inside that outline.

I'm so glad we made the effort to go to the Twilight Stroll (although I got worried when I heard it called a Twilight Trek!). The campground was a beautiful spot with lots of big boulders.

The walk explored different environments. We started in the meadow, where we could see deer footprints and wildflowers. I learned that something I thought was a weed—a flower with purple petals and a yellow center—is called a traveling daisy. At the edge of the woods we looked at grasses, sedges, and rushes. Rushes are round, and sedges have edges. Grasses are hollow inside.

We crossed a stream by jumping from rock to rock and looked at what grows under the rocks, including mosquito larva. Then we climbed up on big boulders. We saw bear scat and what is sometimes a bear den. There are three bears that have been bothering this campground, but we didn't see them. We came back down right at the edge of a wilderness area. The ranger told us that there can only be nine people in a group in a wilderness area.

After the talk, Dick showed the ranger a tree that he had seen while we were eating dinner. It had several lumps and distorted branches on one side for a height of about 30 feet. She said it may have been caused by some sort of fungus.

Friday, July 23, 2004

We drove to Glacier Point and hiked out to Taft Point from there. The brochure stated that this hike was mostly level and slightly downhill. Part of it was quite level—it almost looked like a landscaped park with beautiful fields of wildflowers just a little past prime—but then we came to a sandy, rocky trail, which led to some huge rocky cliffs. The sand made the trail slippery and the rocks made the hiking difficult. Some of the huge rocks on the cliffs had fissures—sort of like a miniature canyon—narrow but very deep. A bit farther was an awesome view of the valley, including Yosemite Falls, which looked tiny from our viewpoint although it's the fifth highest waterfall in the world.

There was another trail from the trailhead, but it seemed to me to be more of the same but without the fissures, so we headed back to camp. After dinner we went to the campfire program at Crane Flat. It was the same ranger as the previous night. She had her guitar and had changed "Roll on Columbia" to "Roll on Tuolumne,"[54] with other details of Yosemite included in the song. We also sang "This Land is Your Land."

---

[54] One of the scenic spots in Yosemite is Tuolumne Meadows near the Tuolumne River.

Sequoia National Park, California

Saturday, July 24, 2004

Although Sequoia and Kings Canyon are each a separate national park, they adjoin each other and are managed as a single park. The road to Sequoia led through more farmland. The closer we got, the more scenic it got—and it was totally different from Yosemite. There were a lot of drier areas with clumps of green trees.

We had a small site, but it was very pretty, with a hilly forest on one side and trees on the other. A man near us said he had seen bear tracks in the woods.

We made s'mores and sat around the fire until dark. And it was *dark*! No lights at all in the bathroom. In the middle of the night we both heard a noise. Dick looked out and was reasonably sure it was a bear. I decided I did *not* need a trip to the bathroom.

Sunday, July 25, 2004

There was a 12:30 talk at Hospital Rock, which we decided we could make. We did—but to get there we had to drive down a long, incredibly steep, curvy road. At one point where we stopped, we could see at least six different parts of the road. I've never been on a road with more switchbacks.

We had enough time for a quick lunch and then joined a ranger for the talk. At first, we were the only ones in attendance, but then two more people joined us. With such a small group, it was easy to get lots of information. We saw some Native American pictographs and a cave used by Native Americans. A white hunter had been treated there after basically shooting himself with his trap. That's where it got the name Hospital Rock.

We saw mortar holes in the rock where Native American women ground acorns. Some of these holes were probably seven or eight inches deep and about four to six inches across. I told the group about making acorn pancakes, which was a project I did with my fifth graders after we read *My Side of the Mountain* by Jean Craighead George.[55] In that book, the fictional Sam Gribley runs away from home and survives in the wilderness of the Catskill Mountains in New York. One of the things he eats is acorn pancakes. Acorns are very bitter, so in my class we cut them open and rinsed them many times with fresh water. After the nut meat dried, we ground it to a powder and used this along with flour to make pancakes. We also made blueberry jam to serve with the pancakes.

After the other couple left, I asked the ranger about easy hikes in the area. She said she was going down to the river, so we went with her. I took off my shoes and socks and waded in the water. It felt great. As we continued talking with the ranger, another ranger literally dropped in (jumped off rocks), and another man joined us. The man was from Massachusetts, and his cousin was a woman who was a neighbor of mine many years ago and who was teaching with me at the time of our trip. And the world continues to shrink.

On our way back to camp, we stopped and left a message for the Bixbys. They hadn't yet checked into the lodge where they would be staying. We got back to camp and apparently drove by them at the ranger station. They found our site and agreed to stay for a supper of hot dogs.

At one point, we saw what we thought was a ferret scamper into a log, but the next day the Bixbys asked a ranger, who said they don't have ferrets here and it must have been a pine marten.

We had a wonderful evening with Nancy and Bix. They brought ingredients for s'mores (we had plenty of marshmallows— now we *really* had plenty), and we enjoyed the fire.

They left about 9:00, and we got into bed. We had barely lain down when we heard a shout: "BEAR!" Then we heard someone run right by our tent. We looked out our tent window

---

[55] George, Jean Craighead. *My Side of the Mountain.* Puffin Books, 1959.

and a man said, "Hi! I'm Joe with Bear Management." He explained that three bears had been bothering the campground that summer. A 60-pound female with a purple tag in her ear had just gone up the tree about 12 feet from our tent. The ranger had shot a pepper ball into the next tree; the ball exploded and would make it unpleasant for the bear. Rangers had been trying to keep the bears wild and away from people. Bears can totally destroy a car if they smell or see food or something that resembles food in the vehicle.

My adrenalin was really pumping now. I wasn't scared—just excited and kind of alert, listening for the sound of the bear coming down. I never did hear her, but I didn't sleep well.

Monday, July 26, 2004

We spent the day with the Bixbys. We used our car and drove to the Crescent Meadow Trail, which was a very pleasant walk. We saw several deer along the way. We walked through a very recent controlled burn to Tharps's Log. This log was hollowed out and had a crude picnic table and bench. Tharp was the white man who discovered the Giant Trees here. A bit farther we found an old tree that had fallen and its roots were now vertical. The spaces between some of the roots looked like picture frames, so we posed with our heads in the "frames."

We posed for pictures in the California tunnel log, which had an opening cut through it big enough to drive a small car through. The roof of the tunnel dripped a brown goo that reminded us of a cross between resin and creosote. This was from the tannin in the tree which had fallen across the road in 1937.

After lunch, Nancy, Dick, and I went to Crystal Cave. The cave had some nice stalactites and stalagmites, but I've been in much bigger and prettier caves, plus the guide wasn't great. He started out saying how each of us would be discovering the cave for him or herself. This was fine, but we all would have just preferred being given some information. The steep walk back up wasn't as bad as I had expected, but I feel so frustrated when I get out of breath.

We improvised another campfire dinner and then went to the evening ranger program—another slide show. We were not terribly impressed with the program, but it was really fun having company.

Kings Canyon National Park, California

Tuesday, July 27, 2004

The Bixbys left that day, so we were on our own. We drove all the way to Cedar Grove, the last half over very twisty roads although not as bad as the one on Sunday. This time we were in Kings Canyon National Park, which was very deep, with mostly rocky cliffs and a rushing stream with lots of rocks on the other side.

After lunch we took the Zumwalt Meadow trail. This had numbered stops and a trail guide. It was a very pleasant walk— not difficult at all, but again I found myself out of breath. Part of this walk was along a river. Some people were swimming and a couple were fishing. Then we took a very short trail to Roaring River Falls. This was a beautiful waterfall.

As we got dinner, several deer were grazing on the hillside near us. Dick built a good fire, which we sat by until it was dark.

Wednesday, July 28, 2004

The deer were back again that morning, even closer than the previous night. After breakfast we climbed Little Baldy. I had been apprehensive about doing it, but it now is at the top of my list of favorite hikes. What a great trail! Although we were climbing from 7,000 feet to 8,044 feet, it was a gradual incline with long switchbacks. There were almost no steep steps. At first there were lots of ferns, then wildflowers. Most of the trail was shaded. We thought we were at the top when we reached some big granite boulders. We climbed up on them and had a snack. We were all set to go back when we heard some other hikers comment that the great view was farther on. So, we continued hiking. I was *so* glad we did. There was a spectacular 360-degree panorama from the rocky summit. It was gorgeous.

On the way up, we had seen a marmot running ahead of us on the trail. Coming down, we saw her in the same place doing the same thing. Dick thinks she was leading us away from her home and babies. On the way down, however, she stopped and posed. There were a couple of other marmots too, and some lovely yellow birds, which I think were western tanagers.

When we got back down, we drove back to Grant Grove. We bought a trail guide and read all about the various trees. Many of the trees are named for early American presidents, generals, and other notable people of the 1800s. We went on another hike, which was supposed to take us to another grove with more solitude. There was solitude, but it was hot and dusty and not at all scenic. We bought ice cream bars and went to find the Big Stump. This was easier said than done. We got to the Big Stump Picnic Area but couldn't see a trailhead. Dick asked someone, who pointed us in the right direction. This area was used for logging and even had a sawmill. Some of the piles of sawdust are still visible since sequoia wood lasts so long. The Mark Twain stump[56] is huge. There are stairs up to it and we were able to walk around on it.

Thursday, July 29, 2004

We got an early start and accomplished a lot. First, a stop to take pictures of some pretty red flowers, then to the Giant Forest for an enjoyable one-mile loop walk. They had made a section of the entryway into an outline of the base of twin trees. With all this, we were still able to get to Moro Rock at 10:30.

This was our goal. There was a ranger talk at the top at 11:00, and they said to allow at least 15 minutes to climb the 400 steps to the top. The steps themselves are a work of art. They are built right into the side of this huge granite dome. They're actually listed in the National Register of Historic Places. They have little rock nooks where we stopped to rest. The view of mountains and valleys from the top is spectacular.

The ranger pointed out various mountains, including Little Baldy, which we had climbed the previous day. She told us that President George W. Bush had visited the park in 2001, climbed

---

[56] The tree was cut, and slabs of the trunk were exhibited in New York and London museums.

to the top of Moro Rock, and given a talk on stewardship. I decided that *stewardship* might be my word of the year for school. It can apply to so many things.

The ranger made me feel better about my breathing. She said it takes her about a month to adjust to the altitude when she arrives at Sequoia each spring, and when she goes home to a lower altitude in the fall, her friends there complain about how fast she is walking! Her lungs get used to having less oxygen, so when she returns to a location with more oxygen, she also has more energy. In addition, she told us that the "bad" ozone, which is a real problem at Sequoia, affects everyone's breathing. It's caused by pollution both from cars and people in the Central Valley.

After climbing back down, we had time for a picnic lunch before joining a ranger for a river walk. Finally, we watched the slide show at the Visitor Center and then went back to the Giant Forest Museum. There was a path on the ground illustrating how high we would be climbing if we climbed Sentinel Sequoia outside the museum. There were some excellent displays, and I started doing a lot more thinking about how I wanted to incorporate the national parks into my curriculum that year.

From there we went to the Congress Trail, which was *very* poorly marked because of the construction they're doing at the Sherman Tree, but it was a good two-mile walk, paved and mostly in the shade with some magnificent trees.

After eating at the barbecue at Wolverton, we went on the twilight stroll with Lacey, our afternoon ranger. This turned out to be *wonderful*. We hadn't gone very far when we saw a bear, about 150 feet away. We watched it for a long time as it dug insects out of an old tree. Lacey did several good activities with us. In one, Dick put on a blindfold (one person in each pair), and I led him to a tree. The object of the exercise was for him to feel the texture of the bark, the size of the trunk, the location of low branches, and the shape of the leaves so he could locate the tree later without the blindfold. He was successful.

As it got darker, we sat on rocks which were still warm from the heat of the day and listened for sounds. As we sat, we saw two deer (after hearing a strange noise, which we thought might have been the bear startling the deer) and bats. Yesterday we saw a bat, which had flown into the Visitor Center. It was actually kind of cute.

Friday, July 30, 2004

We gave all our leftover things, which wasn't much—two chairs, Coleman fuel, dishpan, brown sugar, flour, marshmallows, graham crackers, butter, matches, and a little wood—to the campers in the next site and headed to Sacramento. We both agreed that it had been a great trip.

2007

Congaree National Park, South Carolina

Cuyahoga Valley National Park, Ohio

Congaree National Park, South Carolina

Friday, August 24, 2007

Although Dick had been retired for five years, this was my first year of retirement. I did not want to spend those initial not-back-to-school days at home, so we planned this trip to include the first week of September. After making campground reservations, I discovered a national park I didn't know existed: Congaree National Park. It was 115 miles away from our campground, so we decided to skip a local military park and take a long side trip to Congaree. Part of the ride was on back roads, which made this a very peaceful drive.

The park opened at 8:30. We got there at 11:00 and were the first visitors (and it turned out the *only* visitors) of the day. I guess I wasn't the only one who didn't know about this park. We watched the introductory video. The park was originally called Congaree Swamp National Monument, and it still floods regularly from the Congaree River. It has only been a park since 2003.

We ate lunch in a covered picnic area, where we watched a variety of butterflies. One seemed to be basking like they do when they first emerge, except it wasn't in the sun. Most of them were blue and black, although not all the same. A few were orange and black but different from monarchs.

After lunch we took a 2½-mile walk along a boardwalk trail. It was supposed to take a little over an hour, but it took us much longer because we stopped so often.

We could walk and observe and ponder at our leisure because there was no one else on the trail. The trees here form the tallest deciduous forests in the world and the highest forest canopy. They are mainly bald cypress and tupelo. The bald cypress trees have knees, structures that form above the root and are a foot or two above the ground. Mingled with grasses, the "knees" could resemble elves or wood sprites (if someone had an overactive imagination—like Dick, who claims that he gets blamed for lots of things). There were big sections covered with these knees.

Although we had trouble actually observing this, the moss line on the trees is supposed to indicate the height of the water of the previous year's flooding. We saw lots of lizards of various sizes and colors. As soon as they sensed our presence they scurried under the boardwalk. We also saw a granddaddy millipede—he was huge—several inches long and fat. We watched all his legs moving in unison. At one spot, a butterfly landed on Dick's legs.

Some of the trees had Spanish moss hanging from them. We started seeing some plants that looked almost like our yucca lilies. After Dick said they looked sort of like palm trees, I realized we were far enough south for palm trees. Almost as soon as we made those comments, we got to a sign identifying these plants as miniature palms or palmettos. South Carolina is the Palmetto State.

Near the end of our walk, Dick noticed hundreds of wood chips strewn on the ground. Looking above them, we could see large holes that looked as if they might have been made by a pileated woodpecker. The ranger confirmed this and said that one of the piles had been made only a few days ago.

It was really neat being the only visitors in the park—but a very strange feeling!

Cuyahoga Valley National Park, Ohio

Tuesday, September 4, 2007

As I sat by our breakfast campfire cooking bacon and eggs with Dick on this first day of school, I felt like it was my first official day of retirement. I wanted to call someone to share my experience, but my friends were still heading off to school. Then I thought of our son David, who was teaching in the Philippines. The time there is 12 hours ahead of the Eastern United States, so I took out my cell phone, called his New Hampshire Vonage number, and shared my experience with him. Oh, the wonders of technology!

After breakfast, we headed for Cuyahoga Valley National Park. There were six different Visitor Centers because the park is along the Ohio and Erie Canal towpath route. We picked the two closest to us and headed in that general direction, not being sure which we would come to first.

The first one we stopped at was closed Mondays and Tuesdays. I guess that was true for all of them, but at least the second one—which was hard to find—had maps available outside the building. It was near Lock 29 of the Erie and Ohio Canal Towpath, and there was a good hike for about 2½ miles (one way) along the towpath to Boston (not Boston, Massachusetts, but it made us think of that). It was a pleasant walk along partly paved, partly hard sand paths. There were remnants of a couple of locks and some pretty wildflowers. They needed to trim some of the brush; we struggled to see how it worked as a towpath. There was a really high overpass for the interstate above us. It was interesting to see the juxtaposition of modern travel with the old ways

Near Lock 38 we saw a building that had been operated as a tavern by Moses Gleeson in the early 1800s. Imagine our surprise when we got home and discovered that this Moses Gleeson was an ancestor of our friend, Bill Gleeson.

The Boston Store Visitor Center (which was not open when we were at Cuyahoga—or maybe we just didn't find it) was built in 1836. Settlers could buy and sell goods with merchants who were traveling on canal boats. Today there are exhibits there that illustrate what life was like along the canal. In addition to the Towpath Trail, there are also trails to waterfalls and to Beaver Marsh. The Cuyahoga Valley Scenic Railroad travels for 26 miles through the park. Our visit was relatively short; I want to return and spend more time at this park.

2008

Saguaro National Park, Arizona

Mojave National Preserve, California

Death Valley National Park, Nevada

Joshua Tree National Park, California

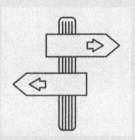

Saguaro National Park, Arizona

Saturday, April 12, 2008

We had never taken a long trip in spring before but looked forward to being in the southwest before the weather got really hot. Saguaro National Park was established to protect local plants and animals, but primarily for the saguaro, which is the signature plant for that part of the country. The saguaro cactus grows really slowly; at the end of their first year they may be only ¼-inch tall. When they are about 75 years old, they sprout branches or arms, and some of the cacti start to look almost like humans. If they live a long time, some get to be 25 to 35 feet tall and may weigh 8 tons. From a distance, the hillside looked to be covered with these tall, straight plants, which all seemed to look the same. However, when we started to walk among them, we noticed all sorts of differences.

There are two parts to this park: east and west. On our first day there, we did the western part. We hiked two trails. The first one went past all sorts of cacti, many of them blooming. The most striking is the ocotillo, which has tall thin branches probably 6 to 8 feet long with 8 to 12 inches of orange blossoms at the end. They are gorgeous against a cloudless, bright-blue sky. There were also barrel cacti, which look like a barrel with flowers on the top, and there were a couple of kinds of cholla. A thin one is called *pencil cholla.*

Our second hike was shorter but led to some ancient petroglyphs, which Native Americans had carved or chipped in the rock.

There were lots of prickly pear cactus plants. Their fruit is made into jams and jellies and probably some other things. We saw lots of palo verde trees with greenish bark and tiny leaves, which help to save moisture.

Tuesday, April 15, 2008

After a couple of days visiting other sites in the area, Dick and I went to Saguaro East. The eastern part has fewer saguaros than the western part and the views are less spectacular. We drove the eight-mile-long loop road, Cactus Forest Drive, stopping for two short hikes along the way. One was a handicapped-accessible nature trail with excellent signs describing the plants we were seeing. The second walk was to the site of a homestead farmhouse. The walls had collapsed completely, so the site was basically a mound of dirt with a few plants and cacti growing on it. The most interesting part was ocotillo trees being used as a natural fence.

We got back to the Visitor Center just in time for a walk through a small garden with a volunteer. Along with more information on all the plants, we saw a pack rat's nest and learned that snakes often winter in the pack rat nests and, in the spring, eat the pack rat babies. This is a form of natural extermination of a pest.

We enjoyed exploring the desert environment that was so different from home.

Mojave National Preserve, California

Friday, April 18, 2008

As we traveled through Arizona, we drove through a variety of landforms. We started in a ponderosa forest and then drove through dry canyons, down to deserts, and back up to mountains until finally arriving in the Mojave Desert. In one place, we drove past a flooded field, while not too many miles away, the ground was bone dry. Arizona is really a big state with lots of variety. While we were in the mountains, there was snow on the hillsides.

When we entered California, we had to go through an agricultural checkpoint. All they cared about were apples, oranges, and avocados—and whether we had come through Illinois. We had oranges, so the agent had to check them. He said we shopped well: they were California oranges. I don't know what the story was with Illinois.

When we had asked directions at Tonto National Monument for the Mojave Desert, the ranger said, "Las Vegas; that's the Mojave Desert." We both thought that was a really weird response, especially from a ranger. Anyway, we made it to the desert—and it wasn't Las Vegas. There are miles and miles and miles of open fields with cactus, and mountains without much vegetation nearby. There's one cattle ranch still left in the preserve. The rancher has to bring in hay because there's not much there.

Dick's notes describe the terrain quite well. He wrote,

I was driving and looked to my left out the window. I felt like I was looking out over the ocean because it was so broad and flat, ending with a slight curvature along the horizon. On a number of occasions, we would see signs indicating dips ahead. To describe what it looked like, try to imagine that the road is a straight, flat strip of pastry, but every few inches you take your finger and press down across the strip. Looking along the strip you will see a series of 'dips.'

We arrived at the Mojave National Preserve, set up camp, and went to the Visitor Center. Just after we arrived, the ranger answered a phone call. The caller was a woman from Delaware who wanted to come out to see Mojave but was apparently expecting more in the way of services (gas stations, stores, etc.) than are actually available. The ranger repeated herself several times, saying essentially "No, ma'am. There is nothing here like that. The closest is 50 miles." And so forth. Eventually, the ranger hung up the phone and shook her head. Then she helped us.

We had a couple of hours before dinner, so we took a short hike, which started at the Hole-in-the-Wall Visitor Center. Our walk was really nice—past lots of colorful wildflowers—except for one very challenging part called the Ring Trail. The ranger said she had taken a group of first and second graders there earlier in the day. I figured that meant I could do it, but it was harder than I expected. The trail went nearly vertical in two places, once for about 10 feet and later for another 5 feet, both in a narrow passage between large rocks. To make it easier for

mortals to climb that part of the trail, there was a series of 6-inch-diameter metal rings on giant eye-bolts fastened into the rock. Standing in a ring and stepping up to the next one allowed us to climb, but it was much more difficult than a ladder. At one point I couldn't lift my leg; I had to switch feet and lift the other leg. It was quite a narrow opening.

There were two sets of these rings. One had indentations in the rock for one foot and rings for the other; the other had only rings. I was close to tears, but I succeeded. Our campground was called Hole in the Wall—named after this formation.

Saturday, April 19, 2008

We started out (after pancakes cooked over a fire) at Mitchell Caverns. This is a state park within the national preserve. We had been told to get there by 9:00 to line up for tickets for the 10:00, 1:30, or 3:30 tours. We arrived at 8:45. A ranger came down to the car and said they were doing a 9:00 tour if we were interested. This worked out perfectly.

The guide gave a very good tour, explaining the geological origin of the caves as well as how the cave tours started. The caves had formed in limestone in the standard way by water running through and/or leaching down from above, but the only water now was a very little bit once in a while after a very heavy rain. We saw exactly three drips of water that have been on the ends of stalactites for a long time. There were some interesting formations—cave mushrooms (limestone that is in the shape of a mushroom), draperies, soda straws, some that look like people, etc. My favorite was called a shield but looked like a polished cross-section of a tree. We were only allowed to touch the formations at one place, where we could see the difference the oils of our hands make. This spot was smooth and shiny.

The caves were originally owned by Jack Mitchell. When he bought the land, it included the caverns, and he staked a mining claim. This gave him some freedom in how he used the property, as long as he was doing some mining (i.e., digging holes once in a while). In the meantime, he and his wife conducted tours of the caverns from 1934 to 1954. In those days, visitors had to crawl through holes to get in. After Mitchell died, the caves were sold to the state parks system, which continued to conduct tours. They also drilled a passage to connect the two parts of the caverns, and in order to eliminate the bats, they closed the cave after the bats left at night. Now the two caves are connected with doors on each end to keep the cave at its normal 65 degrees Fahrenheit. This was our first walk through a dry cave. The others we had been in were still quite active.

Our next stop was the Kelso Dunes. These are the second-highest dunes in the United States at about 600 feet. The hike out and back was through soft, beach-like sand. There were delicate desert rose flowers—white and pink—until we got to the dunes themselves, where there were only occasional grasses. We especially enjoyed looking at dune plants and the circles made by breezes raking leaves and stems in the sand.

We were told that the dunes make rumbling noises when visitors get enough sand sliding down the slope. We tried without success. Maybe if we had gone to the end of the trail we might have found a steep enough slope to produce the effect.

On our way back to camp, we stopped at the Kelso Depot Visitor Center, a former Union Pacific Station. It was very attractively done in Spanish-style architecture, and the green grass landscaping surrounding it made it look like an oasis in the outside desert area. Two rooms are set up with baggage scales, ticket office, etc., and other rooms are museums. At the desk was a vase with fresh purple lilacs. Reminded us of home!

We drove through a Joshua tree forest, the largest stand of these in the world, even more than at Joshua Tree National Park. These trees, which are short with long green needles, were something we had not seen before. Some of them had white blossoms at the end. They are sometimes described as grotesque, and I could see why. Some are straight, and others are very bushy and branching. They start growing straight and only branch after the end either flowers or is damaged (by frost or from being eaten by animals). When it branches, there are two opposite branches, about 90 to 120 degrees apart. These two branches and the original stem are all coplanar, meaning they could be laid on a flat surface. They become grotesque when one of the two branches dies off and two new branches form off the remaining branch, then one of the new ones dies, etc.

A forest fire had burned this area two years before our visit. One campground was really charred and lots of Joshua trees were also burned. However, there were lots of light-purple flowers, which made me think of fireweed in the Northwest.

We went to a ranger talk after supper. I thought it was too long and rambly. Unfortunately, the ranger tried to cover the topic using too much detail.

Sunday, April 20, 2008

It was a very windy night, with gusts up to 40 or 50 mph. It was still cold and windy that morning. The ranger from the previous night led a geology walk that morning. It was better, because he was focused on one topic.

We saw several different rock formations right from the Visitor Center. The first one was a dark rock topped by a lighter rock. The dark rock is a bulge in a conduit of magma formed deep in the earth and the lighter (and smaller) part is what is left of the conduit that continued up to the top of the earth. The rock material the two parts were in was softer than the magma chamber and conduit, so that material eroded away faster.

The second rock formation showed six different layers of rock in a mountain. Each layer came from a different volcanic eruption. At one place the layers dropped (one part went up, one went down, so the layers didn't match anymore), because after all the layers were formed, there was an earthquake.

The third one was called "Glowing Clouds." During the process of formation there was a mixture of lava and water, which produced a cloud of very hot dust and gas. Most of the gas went away very quickly, and the hot dust cemented itself back together to make rock. Traces of the gas that was left produced bubbles in the rock.

We both liked the variety at Mojave National Preserve: from desert plants and dunes to caverns to different rock formations.

Death Valley National Park, Nevada

Sunday, April 20, 2008

As we headed to Death Valley National Park, we discovered that gas in the area was very expensive ($5.00 a gallon) and grocery stores were practically nonexistent. I had to go to two "convenience stores" to find a loaf of bread, and neither of them had eggs.

We drove past flat white land that looked like snow but was some sort of calcium carbonate mixture. The land had weedy-looking clumps of grass and a few bushes. There were rocky, barren hills on both sides of the road.

The previous day we had hundreds of bugs caught in our car's front grille. As we drove, we could see some fly into us. We also drove over lots of washes—dry river beds that fill with water during storms.

There was lots of mistletoe in trees. It grows especially well in acacia trees. The seeds will not sprout until they have gone through an animal's digestive system to remove the outer coating. Birds eat the berries and poop them on acacia branches, which split easily and allow the berries to sprout. The mistletoe eventually kills the tree.

The approach to Death Valley was very unappealing. It was just totally barren. We went to the Furnace Creek Visitor Center and then set up in the Furnace Creek Campground (195 feet below sea level).

Once we took our first scenic drive to Badwater Creek, my opinion totally changed. There's actually water there, which is very salty because there's no outlet. Supposedly a mule long ago refused to drink it, hence the name "bad water." We went out over the salt flats, which had very hard ground that was moist to the touch. There was still water just a few inches below the surface of the lake bed. Coming back up, we took a side drive called The Artists' Drive, with one point called The Artists' Palette. The rocks were all different hues of red, green, white, and brown.

Monday, April 21, 2008

After breakfast (which a raven tried to share), we started out with a trip to Scotty's Castle, 50 miles north, named for Walter Scott, a cowboy in Will Rogers Wild West Show.[57] He was also known as the infamous "Death Valley Scotty," but he did not build the "castle"; it was built by Albert and Bessie Johnson, millionaires from Chicago. The story of their friendship is very interesting.

Walter Scott had left the Will Rogers Wild West Show and was looking for another way to make a living. He decided to sell shares in a mining operation that didn't exist. Albert Johnson was looking for something to invest in, so he bought some of the bogus mine shares. After a few years and no monetary return, Albert Johnson set out to see the mine, which of course he never did. However, he found that his health improved markedly when he was out in the Death Valley area, hiking and camping with "Scotty" as his guide and trip leader. According to the story, Scotty came clean, Albert Johnson didn't press charges, and they actually became friends.

---

[57] Record-breaking rain in October 2015 caused flash floods at Death Valley and caused the closure of many roads. Unfortunately, there was a lot of damage to Scotty's Castle, which is closed for repairs until 2020.

The Johnsons moved to Los Angeles and came out to the Death Valley area to get away from the city. In the early 1930s, they built a large Spanish Revival house—the castle—at a cost of $2 million.[58] Scotty stayed at the house year-round, giving tours of the house to visitors. Johnson liked to say that the house belonged to Scotty and he was just Scotty's banker. The house was beautiful. It had occasional tile tables, huge fireplaces and chandeliers, and a specially designed set of china. Dick especially liked the music room. That room cost $50,000,[59] which was about 5 or 10 times the cost of an average house at that time. One side of the room had automated instruments, including an organ, a drum, and a gong. The drum and the gong each had three sticks, which would hit them at center, off-center, and edge, at different rates and impact. The instruments were all behind a louvered wall, so the louvers could be opened and closed to change the volume of the music. All of the instruments and louvers were controlled in the same way as a player piano: with a perforated paper roll. Our tour guide was a young park ranger, role-playing someone from the 1930s who might have been hired to give a tour of the house for people who visited back then. He clearly enjoyed doing the tours.

On our way back from Scotty's Castle, we spotted a female coyote just walking along the road. We were able to turn around and follow her slowly and get pictures (from the car). We stopped at several interpretive trails. The first one was through Salt Creek. This was particularly interesting because pup fish live there. They have adapted from living in a freshwater lake to the salty creek. They're quite small—about 1½ inches long. There were some birds that were catching them for dinner. One bird had fairly long legs and wide white bands on its throat. We could see deposits of salt where the creek had dried up.

The second trail was to Harmony Borax Works, which showed the ruins of a Borax refinery and some of the wagons

[58] This would be $50 million to $60 million today.

[59] $1 million to $1.5 million today.

that were pulled by 20-mule teams to carry the refined borax to the nearest rail heads for shipment to market. The borax was used for a variety of purposes, including cleaning.

The third hike was the most challenging. It was not really difficult, but it was longer than the other hikes and the sun was hot. This one was the Golden Canyon Interpretive Trail, along the road we had taken the previous day. Most of the walk passed through beige and yellow and brown rock formations, which I assume is the origin of the name for the Golden Canyon. The interpretive signs pointed out rock layers and faults. A flash flood had come through in the 1970s and totally washed out the road that used to be here. Parts of the broken road are still visible. At the end of the trail was an additional ¼-mile spur to a formation called the Red Cathedral. It presented a dramatic view with high, dark-red rocks contrasting with the lighter rock of the Golden Canyon.

We stopped at Zabriskie Point for a short but very steep climb for a view. From there, a 20-mile drive up a steep, curving mountain road brought us to Dante's View at an elevation of 1,669 feet, and a view of Badwater Basin. The view was largely obscured by thick haze, which had been a feature of all views during the past couple of weeks in this part of the country. I'm not sure whether the culprit was pollution, dust, or some combination of ingredients.

I must have been hungry. All the rocks here kept reminding me of food. So far, I'd seen vanilla, chocolate, and strawberry ice cream—the rocks really are white, brown, and pink—and a hot fudge sundae (dark-brown rocks "dripping" down over lighter-colored ones).

We splurged on dinner that night and ate at the very fancy Furnace Creek Inn. We always bring one set of dressy clothes for just such an occasion. I had melon soup for an appetizer. The waitress said it was three kinds of melon blended together. There was something sprinkled on top, which I swear was chopped onion. There was date and nut bread and a *really* good

Asiago cheese bread. Dick had an appetizer of fried beaver-tail cactus. It was green but tasted a lot like French fries. I don't know what my vegetable was: the stalk looked like asparagus, but the flower looked like broccoli so perhaps it was broccolini. I also had halibut and French-fried sweet potatoes. For dessert we shared a mango flan. It was good but didn't taste like mango. We were both overstuffed.

Dick wrote,

Death Valley is my favorite place we visited on this trip so far. It has amazing contrasts and colors. The highest point in the park is 11,049 feet and the lowest is 282 feet below sea level. There are miles when both sides of the road are just rocks and gravel, flat as a pancake, and other areas with steep hills covered with vegetation; hillsides of black rock basin floors covered with white salt; hills of multicolored rocks, including red, beige, brown, white, green, grey, black all on the same set of hills. The many colors, angled layers, and textures come from the faulted blocks of the Earth's crust which spread and tip.

Joshua Tree National Park, California

Wednesday, April 23, 2008

We got to Joshua Tree National Park by mid-afternoon. It's a good thing I had talked to my college friend Lynn and she had mentioned that there are no Joshua trees in the southern part of the park. The ranger at the Visitor Center didn't give us that information.

We set up and drove partway up the road north, stopping at every pullout that had a sign to read. The only one that involved a walk was the cholla cactus garden. It was *full* of teddy bear cholla. Cholla are notorious in having spiked barbs that stick to clothing, skin, and animal fur. There were numbered signs, but no trail guides available, so I have no idea what features they were pointing out.

As we drove along this part of the road, the elevation increased, and the landscape changed from that of the Colorado/Sonoran Desert to that of the Mojave Desert landscape. The Colorado/Sonoran landscape included teddy bear cholla, cactus, and the ocotillo tree (bush). When the teddy bear cholla was dying and brown, it actually looked a bit like a teddy bear. The ocotillos were also beautiful, and one clump was the biggest I had seen so far. The ocotillo is our favorite desert plant, with its bright reddish-orange flowers and leaf-covered stems.

Friday, April 25, 2008

The Thurbers and Bixbys, all college friends who live in California, arrived about 8:30 as planned, and we hiked the Palm Oasis Trail, which started just down the road from the campground. The trail was about four miles one way to the point known as the Lost Palms Oasis. It was a fairly easy, sandy trail to a canyon overlook, where we could see the oasis with one of the biggest collections of fan palm trees in the state. These trees grow to a height of up to 75 feet and have leaves that can be six feet long. The cool shade of a fan palm oasis draws animals to it. We decided to look from a distance and not hike down (and back up!) the canyon. The whole hike took about four hours. I was impressed with how much Dick and I had learned on this trip. We were able to explain several things to the others and knew the names of a lot of plants. Dick and Rich Thurber were behind the rest of us at one point and saw a desert tortoise. They called us to come back to see it. We didn't get too close because if the tortoise gets scared, it empties its bladder and loses its water supply.

Thursday May 1, 2008

So, our "year of the long spring" continued. We had left New Hampshire on March 30, and by the next day, we were seeing spring buds. This continued through the Southwest. We missed the entire month of April in New Hampshire. On the return journey, it was like going back in time, because as we got closer to New England, we began to drive past blooming forsythia and white-blossomed trees.

We began our return journey at 5:45 AM, which was the earliest we had left so far. The farther we drove, the more the topography and vegetation started to look like home. The trees were starting to bud with several colors, much like the leaf colors in the fall. This was the first time I had thought of the fact that spring is, in its own way, as colorful as the autumn.

We both thought it ironic that although we seldom set the alarm to get up in the morning at home, we had set the alarm every morning throughout our vacation. It's nice to set the alarm to do what we *want* to do rather than what we *have* to do.

Another irony is that when we set out at the start of a much-anticipated trip, we proceed at a good clip, trying to fit in all we can, and maybe a little bit more. But at the end of our scheduled time away, we don't dally to extend our vacation to the last possible minute, preferring instead to get home as quickly as possible to get back to our frenetic, nonscheduled days. As we've been told, our desire to get home at the end of a trip is like a horse heading for the barn at the end of the day.

2009

Big Cypress National Preserve, Florida

Everglades National Park, Florida

Biscayne National Park, Florida

Dry Tortugas National Park, Florida

Timucuan Ecological and Historic
Preserve, Florida

Big Cypress National Preserve, Florida

Saturday, January 31, 2009

We had started this trip on Monday, January 26, spending the first night in a motel after a long day's drive because no campgrounds in the Northeast were open yet. We never thought of the bananas, which we had left in the car overnight. They were frozen—kind of soggy when they thawed. The peanut butter was also frozen solid!

Even when we arrived in Florida, the temperature in the morning was surprisingly cold. When I came back to bed after getting up in the middle of the night, I kept my slacks and sweatshirt on! We got up about 6:30, packed up the tent in minutes, and headed for the showers. The air temperature was in the 30s and the bathroom was not heated. Dick wrote,

My shower started very cold, but the water gradually got warmer. But warmer is as far as it went, and the spray was so fine that after a foot or so beyond the sprayer, it was cold again. Even when I soaked the washcloth with warm water, it was cold by the time I got it to my skin. I washed very quickly in little bits.

My shower was hot. It helped as long as my sweatshirt hood covered my wet hair when I got out.

Today was a much longer drive than I had thought—closer to seven hours than four.

I drove all the way. I had not printed out information on the National Park campgrounds where I had planned to stay, and the AAA book only mentioned primitive ones (i.e., pit toilets). The Visitor Center was 20 miles down the road, so when we came to a private campground, we decided to stay. It wasn't ideal, but it did have hot showers. When we finally got to the Visitor Center, we discovered there was a place we could have camped, so I was frustrated since we really prefer national park campgrounds.

When we stopped at the Big Cypress Visitor Center, we watched a 15-minute video about the preserve. The film said the winter was a dry season, which helped explain why so many of the trees looked dead. We signed up for a canoe trip the next day. I hoped we wouldn't freeze.

After dinner we went to a ranger talk at Monument Lake Campground. The talk was about tree snails which are found only in southern Florida. When fully grown they are two to three inches long; they live on land in trees and would drown if put in water. They spend the dry season closed up and stuck to a tree in a state of aestivation.[60] The ranger told us of a walking trail where we could see the snails and their colorful shells.

One of the couples at the program was our former tax collector and his wife! They're permanently RVing. Much as I love camping, I wouldn't want to do that. I like having a home where I can return.

There was a wildfire somewhere nearby. The smoke contributed to a beautiful sunset.

Back at our camp, we dressed warmly for what was clearly going to be a cold night. I had on a shirt and sweatshirt, a set of long underwear, a pair of pants, and socks. Dick had on a T-shirt, warm shirt, sweater, sweatshirt, long pants, and socks.

Sunday, February 1, 2009

It was cold again, but all the warm clothes helped. We slept comfortably for almost 10 hours. By the time we got up, it was less cold, and we cooked pancakes for breakfast. The morning gradually got warmer and warmer, so we started to remove layers. It was probably about 60 degrees Fahrenheit at 10:00 AM, which is when the canoe trip we had signed up for was getting started.

---

[60] Aestivation is a prolonged period of dormancy in hot or dry conditions, similar to hibernation.

I'm so glad we were able to do that trip; it was definitely the way to see Big Cypress National Preserve. The ranger was in a kayak, and there were three couples (including us) in three canoes. We paddled through a mangrove tunnel on the Turner River. The river was quite low—it's near the end of the dry season—and at places it was very mucky. The water was mostly about 12 to 18 inches deep, although there were places where it was about 4 or 5 feet deep. In the mangrove tunnel, we could pull ourselves along by grabbing on to the branches. We saw a poisonous water moccasin curled up on a branch, another snake on the ground, a couple of big turtles, and lots of alligators sunning themselves on the banks. A couple of the alligators were in the water but weren't really moving around.

We ate lunch in the canoes. We saw an osprey sitting on its nest, a small blue heron, big blue herons, and white birds— heron or ibis?? There were also fish in the water. The ranger said they were gar, which are quite bony. Elsewhere in the park we saw people fishing, but I don't know what they were catching. It was a gorgeous day. I actually took off my sweatshirt for the first time on this trip.

After canoeing, we drove the loop road. It wasn't particularly scenic, although we did get some good views of water birds. We had to drive this road to get to the Tree Snail Trail. It only took us 15 minutes to walk this trail—slowly so we could look for snails. I found six on trees. They're aestivating right now, so they have attached themselves to a tree limb for the winter. Dick found one on the ground that had apparently died. They are very pretty with different bands of color.

That evening was warm enough for mosquitoes to be out. We realized that we might need insect repellant in the Everglades!

Everglades National Park, Florida

Twenty-seven years had elapsed since our first trip to the Everglades. It was winter, so we figured the bugs would not be bad. This was correct. However, we managed to time our visit with an unusual Florida cold snap. The wind chill brought the temperature to the 20s overnight, but we still managed to camp in our little two-person tent.

Monday, February 2, 2009

We got to the Shark Valley Visitor Center just in time for a two-hour tram ride. I thought Shark Valley was part of Big Cypress, but it's part of the Everglades. It is called Shark Valley because the Shark River drains to the Gulf of Mexico, and baby sharks live in the saltwater there. The water in the Everglades is fresh. There is hardly any change in elevation there, but apparently it is a slightly lower area, hence a valley.

The tram ride was excellent. There was a ranger narrating the trip, and she was so enthusiastic about everything along the way. There were *lots* of alligators, including one on the sidewalk we walked on to get to an observation tower. We saw a few baby alligators and what was left of an alligator nest. There were a lot of endangered wood storks, along with little blue herons, great blue herons, snowy egrets, and ibis. There was a nest of anhingas, and we could see the fluffy white chicks craning their long necks. Both mother and father were nearby. Another interesting bird was about two to three feet long, with a black head and a long, curved bill. It looked like an ibis but was actually related to vultures.

Because it was the dry season, water levels were very low. One of the things that the ranger pointed out was a brownish, tubular structure that resembled a root, but it was actually made of a combination of algae, fungi, etc. This soaks up enormous amounts of water and provides a place for microorganisms to survive the dry season.

Tuesday, February 3, 2009

We did a ranger-led car caravan today. This included several short walks with the ranger, who had a high-powered "spotting scope" that really brought the wildlife in close, although some we could see just fine with the naked eye. My very favorite was a roseate spoonbill. It is a tactile feeder, which means it has to feel its prey. It wades in shallow water, stirring up fish with its feet. It waves its bill in the water until it touches a fish, then it scoops the fish up with its wide bill. We watched one very close to shore. It never caught anything, but it was beautiful to watch. Another interesting bird is the anhinga. We learned that the reason we kept seeing them with their wings spread is because when they get wet, the water goes right to their skin and they have to dry out. At Flamingo we saw nesting osprey, including the male osprey driving off a seagull that had landed in the nest.

We had a close look at Spanish moss when we stopped at Royal Palms, and we realized for the first time that it was structured like a long, coiled spring with pairs of 1½-inch wings spaced about 4 inches apart. We also noticed that trees called Royal Palms had a lump (or bulge) about halfway up the trunk.

On our walks we learned a lot about plants. Some of them have leaves that are shaped in such a way that dew collects on them during the night and falls off in the early morning to water the plant. We saw the poisonwood tree, which is more poisonous than poison ivy, but more difficult to recognize. It has five to seven oval leaflets which are a glossy, dark green on top and a lighter green underneath. It has a distinctive yellow vein and the outer edge is outlined in pale yellow.

The gumbo limbo tree is very common down here. That's the tree that the tree snails live on. It's nicknamed the tourist tree because it has red, peeling bark much like a tourist's sunburned skin. The tree's bark has a thin, red outer coating and green underlayers, which actually contain chlorophyll. Even if all the leaves have been removed by wind or fire (which would also remove much of the thin, red outer layer) the exposed green layer with chlorophyll would allow photosynthesis to continue.

Most of the "lakes" in the Everglades are manmade "borrow pits" that were made when limestone was dug out to make roads. In the dry season—the time of our visit—wildlife congregates there. From a distance, we saw two crocodiles.

After dinner we did a "starlight walk." I thought we were going to look at the stars, but we were really looking at the animals that are out at night. However, because it was so cold, we didn't see many. The alligators had moved from land back to the water, which was warmer than the air during the cold nights. We saw the eyes of a few alligators in the water and a few birds.

We decided to spend the next day at Biscayne National Park before returning for one more day in the Everglades.

Thursday, February 5, 2009

It was *really* cold at night and when we woke up in the morning. We slept late mainly because we didn't want to be outside until the sun was up, not that it helped a lot.

We had planned to hike on our own, but by the time we were ready, it was time for a ranger walk, so we opted for that. It was on the Anhinga Trail with the same ranger we had for the starlight walk. He pointed out several anhinga nests with young of various ages (infants, toddlers, and teenagers in the words of the ranger). Some were only three weeks old, but they were quite large.

It was quite chilly on the Anhinga Trail. I was still wearing two sweatshirts, a jacket, and gloves. As we looked out over the river of grass, the sawtooth marsh, there was nothing to break the wind. After the tour we watched the birds for a while, then hiked the Gumbo Limbo Trail. This was a wooded hummock (*slightly* higher than the surrounding land). The trees sheltered the wind there, so it wasn't so cold.

We went to a campfire program about the pinelands, which is the part of the Everglades where we were camping. The trees in the pinelands are slash pines, which are hardwood and very fire resistant.

Biscayne National Park, Florida

Wednesday, February 4, 2009

This park almost didn't happen, because a company wanted to set up an oil well drilling operation. Those in favor of conservation won the battle, and we now have Biscayne National Park. It is one of the few parks that is mostly water (95 percent). I had made reservations for a glass bottom boat trip, but the wind was stirring up the water too much. We wouldn't have been able to see the reef, so they canceled that trip.

We walked along the shore and listened to a ranger talk on fish. The parrot fish has a small mouth full of very small, hard teeth. It scrapes food directly from rock surfaces and scrapes some of the rock with it, so it excretes sand along with digested food.

Later in the afternoon we were able to do an island tour to Boca Chita Key. This island was once owned by the Honeywell family, which owns Honeywell International, Inc. They never actually had a house here but stayed on their yacht and had parties for other multimillionaires. The Honeywells had built a lighthouse-styled tower just for an observation point. It had no light fixtures that would allow it to serve as a lighthouse. We climbed the tower for a beautiful view of the island. We had time for a short hike, past coconut trees and a couple of small beaches. There were a few boats around the semicircular harbor, but on weekends there are often 10 or 20 times as many.

On the boat trip back, we saw dolphins. I wish we had been able to see the fish on the coral reef.

In the evening, we went to the "campfire" program. It was a very interesting slide show and talk on birds—but no campfire. We could have used one. It was very cold and windy.

Dry Tortugas National Park, Florida

Saturday, February 7, 2009

We got up early since we had to check in for our trip to Garden Key in Dry Tortugas National Park no later than 7:30 AM. As we waited to board the catamaran, we met a couple from Maryland; they became our saviors at the end of the day.

When it came time to board, the captain briefed us all about the sailing conditions. The trip over would be somewhat choppy, but the trip back would be very rough, and he suggested that anyone who wanted to could jump ship now and get a refund. We didn't have any extra time, so we chose to give it a try. The catamaran took 2¼ hours out. The last part was rough, but I had taken Dramamine and was okay.

The visit started out with one of the boat crew giving us a 45-minute guided tour. We learned that the name of the island group was actually a kind of shorthand or code for navigators. The word *Dry* meant there was no fresh water, and *Tortugas* is the Spanish word for turtles. A navigator reading the name would infer that there was fresh meat for food (in the form of turtles) but no fresh water.

Fort Jefferson at Dry Tortugas is one of the largest nineteenth-century forts in the United States. It was built to protect the coast, initially from pirates. It was never fired on, and no attacks were ever initiated from it. There is a moat around it. Fort Jefferson is made of bricks—one of the largest brick structures in the world. The actual building of the fort was delayed for several years because the first engineer planning the structure felt that the ground of the island was not sufficiently strong to support the weight of a brick fort. He was replaced by another engineer who thought the fort would be stable on the island, and construction began.

The first foundation layers of bricks were dark-red bricks made in Maine. Locally made bricks were actually more resistant to local erosive conditions, so the builders started using them, and the color of the brickwork changed from dark red to beige. That continued until the top few feet, when locally made bricks were unavailable because of the Civil War, so the top few feet are again dark red. The total number of bricks is about 16 million.

Ironically, they might have been better off by not building the fort because the concerns of the first engineer turned out to be correct. The fort has cracked in several places, and it leaks badly. Also, military technology superseded the fort. It was built to withstand cannonballs shot from smooth-barreled weapons, but it could not withstand the projectiles shot from rifled weapons, which were developed during the construction of the fort.[61] Thus, the fort was never finished.

Fort Jefferson was never used for combat, but it was used as a prison. Among the prisoners held there were several people involved in (or, at least, accused of) the conspiracy to kill President Abraham Lincoln. One was Dr. Samuel Mudd, who was sentenced to life in prison for being part of the conspiracy. He had treated the broken leg of the assassin, John Wilkes Booth. While Mudd was in prison here he escaped temporarily but was later apprehended. Then a yellow fever epidemic broke out, and he was released to help care for the sick. He did such a good job that he was eventually pardoned by President Andrew Johnson.

Right after the tour, lunch was served on the boat. We took ours outside to eat but it practically blew away. We also had to be careful of frigate birds, who are neither hunters nor fishers but thieves. They steal food right out of other birds' mouths. There were also some ruddy terns. Two of the neighboring islands are closed because of nesting noddy terns, which were very noisy.

After lunch, we walked around the outer perimeter and around the inside of the fort. A lot of Cuban refugees have

[61] A rifled weapon has spiral grooves on the inside of the barrel, so projectiles fired leave the barrel spinning, which makes them able to travel faster and straighter and have a stronger impact on the target.

made their way to Dry Tortugas.[62] Walking around the outside, we saw a display of a "chug," which was the slang name for a homemade boat that people used to escape from Cuba, which was only 90 miles away. They were made of scraps of whatever people could find. This particular boat was shaped something like a zodiac that we had ridden on during our trip to Antarctica. On the "chug," however, the sides were made of a material that resembled plasticized canvas, and it was then filled with foam material, which would expand and harden so that it could be unsinkable. The motor was in the middle of the boat, with the propeller shaft poking through the floor. The rudder was made of galvanized sheet metal, and the rudder handle was made of galvanized pipe. The total length of the boat was about 30 feet (maybe less) and probably carried 15 to 20 people. Inside the fort was another chug, about the same size, but made of sheet metal instead of fabric and foam. I can't imagine how bad conditions must have been for people to attempt this 90-mile trip.

---

[62] This continued through 2016. From 1995 until 2017 there was a policy known as "wet foot, dry foot," which said that if refugees were intercepted in the water they were sent back, but if they made it to land, they were given asylum.

The snorkeling at Dry Tortugas was supposed to be really good, but the weather was still cool and windy. Some people went in the water. We considered it until a woman came out and said all she had seen were two fish because the water was so stirred up. So, we walked all around on the moat—some places were *very* windy—and around on the inside of the fort.

They had warned us that the ride back would be rough, and they weren't kidding. I took another Dramamine, but it didn't help. I was *so* seasick. The crew helped me out to the back of the boat and were very helpful with paper towels. I had taken off all my sweatshirts on the boat, which I guess may have been a good thing. They eventually brought me a jacket from one of the crew members. I was soaked to the skin and freezing but couldn't move except to get sick. Dick came out shortly after I did. I couldn't even turn to talk to him. There were several others out with us. When we got to shore our teeth were chattering, and we were miserable. This is when our saviors from Maryland stepped in. They were staying at a near-by motel and invited us to go there to take a hot shower and change into dry clothes before driving back to camp. This was a *huge* help.

So often on our travels we have seen The Golden Rule, "Do unto others as as you would have them do unto you" exemplified. We have sometimes helped people we have met, and other people have helped us. Whether we are on the giving or the receiving end, the experience adds something special to our trip.

Timucuan Ecological and Historic Preserve, Florida

Wednesday, February 11, 2009

We ended up going the long way around but finally got to Fort Caroline and the Timucuan Ecological and Historic Preserve. Fort Caroline National Memorial is a National Park Service replica of what they think the fort looked like. It was originally built by the French in 1562 in an attempt to challenge the Spanish for control of Florida. The settlement was called La Caroline. The French fort only lasted a few years. A French force led by Jean Ribault sailed from the fort to attack a Spanish settlement, but the ship was wrecked by bad weather. The shipwrecked French force was found by the Spanish, and almost all were killed at a place the Spanish called *Matanzas*, which means *massacre*. This was the last time that the French strongly challenged Spanish claims in North America.

After seeing the "fort," which was made up of earthworks and a fence surrounded by a moat, we went on a very good nature trail. It had great informative signs, but in most cases, we couldn't see the thing being described anywhere near the signs. The Spanish moss here was particularly beautiful. However, it's neither Spanish nor moss but rather a tropical American bromeliad that grows on larger trees. It doesn't put down roots in the tree it grows on or take nutrients from it. Instead, it gets moisture from rain and fog and nutrients from the air and from debris accumulating around it. There was also a red lichen on some trees—a combination of a fungus and algae.

Thursday, February 12, 2009

We didn't leave camp until almost 10:30. This gave us enough time to visit the Kingsley Plantation, which is the oldest existing plantation in Florida. The National Park Service has been working for quite a few years to restore the buildings. There are good informative exhibits in the building that was once the kitchen.

Kingsley, the plantation owner, married his 13-year-old slave and eventually freed her. He was a slave owner who was almost an anomaly. He allowed his slaves to have time for their own pursuits once they had finished their day's work quota. He was very open-minded, but once Florida became a U.S. territory, blacks were not treated well, and he eventually moved his family to Haiti, where conditions were better. (It's interesting that Haiti is so poor and undemocratic today.)

The Spanish attitude toward slaves and slavery was very different from the British approach. Slaves in Spanish territory would gradually improve their status, have possessions, and eventually get freedom. They had upward mobility and legal status. Under the British rule and later American rule, slaves had few if any legal rights and little or no chance for freedom. Throughout history the British were not very kind to others, and they were especially nasty to those enslaved or conquered.

We read a sign with an explanation of how sugar was made—a very labor-intensive process. At this plantation, sugar was made only for personal use; their big cash crop was cotton.

The slaves' cabins are still standing—in various states of disrepair. They were made of "tabby," some sort of mixture with lots of shells in it. There are about 20 or 30 cabins in a semicircle some distance from the main plantation house. There was one slightly larger cabin that was used by the foreman.

The plantation is located on the St. John's River. It's a beautiful setting but was chosen not for beauty but for ease of shipping.

2010
(APRIL AND MAY)

Little River Canyon National Preserve,
Alabama

Guadalupe Mountains National Park, Texas

Little River Canyon National Preserve, Alabama

Friday, April 9, 2010

The sky cleared up, but that made for a cold night. Actually, the night was okay, but morning was frigid. When we got up there was also a fairly strong breeze. My fingers—even with gloves—were so cold. I had forgotten that we were moving toward the western end of the time zone. We ate breakfast by starlight—and a lantern.

From Russell Cave National Monument, we drove to Little River Canyon National Preserve. This is one of the deepest and most extensive canyon and gorge systems in the eastern United States. Many endangered and threatened species are found in the preserve. Little River flows for most of its length on the top of Lookout Mountain.

We took the 11-mile scenic drive along the canyon rim. The Little River Falls Boardwalk was our first stop. There we took a short walk to an overlook with a nice view of the 45-foot Little River Falls, which is where the canyon actually begins. There are several other overlooks providing different views of the canyon. The Beaver Pond Trail leads through a wetland habitat with a variety of wildlife.

We did not spend a lot of time here but enjoyed the scenic views.

Guadalupe Mountains National Park, Texas

Saturday, April 17, 2010

It rained very hard during the night and was still raining when we woke up. We packed up everything inside the tent, and when the rain let up a bit, we took down the tent and packed the car.

We drove through heavy rain off and on all morning. We debated and finally decided to go to Guadalupe National Park, which had not been on our original itinerary. As we drove, we wondered if we could see enough of it to justify our saying that we had been there. We decided that if we could see the Visitor Center and take a short hike, that would legitimize our claims to have visited Guadalupe. What a good choice! I wished we had planned to camp there, although it would have been damp and chilly. We'll have to come back again to camp and explore more of the 80 miles of trails.

We looked around the Visitor Center and watched the slide show before going on a nature walk. The trail led us to the ruins of the Pinery Station on the Butterfield Overland Mail Stage Line, which provided the first regularly scheduled mail route between St. Louis and San Francisco. Their contract was canceled because of the Civil War, but the route was the predecessor of the Pony Express and Overland Rail. The Butterfield Stage Line helped the development of the West.

We made a short stop at the Frijole Ranch. This area was a popular place for early settlers because there were five springs with fresh water within a two-mile radius of the ranch. The Frijole Ranch House was built in 1876 by the Rader Brothers. They left in the late 1800s, and the Herring/Wolcott family moved in and stayed until 1895. In 1906 the Smith family filed a claim on the vacant land, settled there, and stayed for 36 years. They expanded the Frijole Ranch House in the 1920s. In 1942,

John Smith sold the property to Judge J. C. Hunter, who was an early conservationist. He tried unsuccessfully to make the region a park in 1925. His dream was finally achieved when his son, J. C. Hunter, Jr., sold the property to the National Park Service in 1966. The Frijole Ranch House is now a history museum.

Wednesday, May 5, 2010

After visiting Guadalupe National Park, we visited friends in New Mexico and Arizona before spending one night at a motel in Tucson, Arizona. We parked our car in the motel parking lot and left from there for a group tour to Copper Canyon, Mexico. On our return, we spent one more night at the motel and then began the drive home. It was good to be sleeping in a tent again, although we could hear highway noises.

We had set the alarm for 4:00 AM, but we woke up about 3:30 and decided to pack up. We were *so* ready to get home.

Except for a brief stop to buy a few groceries, we just drove. For the second day in a row we had amazingly clear blue skies—not a cloud in sight.

We got to the campground about 6:30 PM and had just enough time to set up, cook dinner, and clean up. We were the only tent campers there. There was plenty of wood for fires, and we considered making one just for s'mores, but we decided against it in favor of getting up early again.

It's kind of funny: we *love* sitting around a campfire, and it was a perfect night for it; we *love* camping, and yet we felt so anxious to get home that we were willing to pass this up. We decided we could make it home in two more long days and agreed to try.

2010

(AUGUST)

Acadia National Park, Maine

Acadia National Park, Maine

Sunday, August 22, 2010

This visit to our favorite park was part of a trip to Canada, which was our birthday present for our grandsons, Sebastien and Alexandre, who were now 13 and 11 years old. En route to Canada, we stopped for one night at Acadia.

In keeping with our family tradition, we asked the boys to keep journals. It was interesting to see how similar their observations and their behavior were to those of their dad and uncle at the same age. Each day Sebastien included a weather report:

August 22—Weather partly cloudy to cloudy with some sprinkles. August 23—clear, almost no clouds, no rain.

Both boys commented on the license plates we saw, with Alexandre keeping a detailed list in his journal. (Dick and I still keep a list of the ones we see on each trip.) Sebastien was precise in recording time:

We drove 4 hours and 20 minutes to Acadia National Park. We drove to our campground, and arrived at the site, after picking up a bundle of wood at just about 5:15.

Alexandre wrote,

I found some blackberries and tried one. They were very sweet ... After the fire was low enough, all four of us roasted some marshmallows (most of us torching them, but most were quickly extinguished). It took me a while to fall asleep because Sebastien kept annoying me with his flashlight.

I had forgotten all about those nights of pillow fights and flashlight wars and constant reminders that it was quiet hours. Some things just don't change!

The boys did go to bed—voluntarily—and Dick and I sat by the fire. My idea of heaven!

2010

(SEPTEMBER)

National Park of American Samoa, American Samoa

National Park of American Samoa, American Samoa

Thursday, September 16, 2010

We spent a week in the Philippines with our son David and his family before going to Hawaii for a few days and then on to American Samoa to try The National Park of American Samoa's unique program where visitors can arrange to stay with a local family.[63] This meant we did not need to bring camping equipment on the plane, and it seemed like a wonderful way to learn more about the local culture. I had spoken with the family directly two months prior to our trip, but as we soon discovered, I should have reconfirmed those plans before we left home.

After leaving Honolulu about 5:00 PM, we arrived in Pago Pago, American Samoa about 9:30 PM local time. We checked through and found the Avis car rental office, a small room that was open only from 8:30 PM to 11:30 PM. Sounds in the room echoed, and there were lots of kids making lots of noise. We tried to call our host family, but neither of our phones worked. The Avis clerk called on his phone and got through to someone, but because of the general chaos, Dick couldn't hear what was being said. The Avis clerk had trouble too and actually had to repeat the call several times.

When Dick finally spoke with Jaden,[64] the husband in our host family, Jaden tried to give us directions of where to meet them, but we were totally bewildered. The Avis clerk took the phone again and spoke in Samoan. When he finally hung up,

---

[63] The National Park of American Samoa acts as a facilitator for the Homestay Program and is not responsible for the Homestay families or the guest experience.

[64] For privacy, the names of the members of our host family have been changed.

he said he would take us to meet our hosts, who would take us from there to their house. It was clear that the clerk wanted to get home and was going out of his way for us.

We went out to the parking lot and tried to get into the car we had been assigned. Dick unlocked the driver's door but couldn't get the passenger door (or any other door) unlocked so I could get in. He also couldn't find any way to turn lights on so he could see what he was doing. He was very frustrated. He asked the clerk for help, but the clerk didn't show us how to turn on lights or unlock other doors. Rather, he just gave us a different car.

With the second car, Dick managed to get all the doors unlocked, but he still couldn't find the lights. He also had a hard time using the brake lever because the lid of a compartment between the seats wouldn't stay closed. And last—but not least—the car stank. I said it smelt like urine, but Dick thought it was something that had died and rotted away. The car was drivable, and it was late, so we just went with it and tried to ignore the smell. To use a Japanese phrase from a recent adventure we'd had in Japan, it was definitely "not a preferred car."

We followed the clerk from the airport to and through the city of Pago Pago (pronounced Pango Pango, but with the *n* providing only a slight *ing* sound). As we left Pago Pago and neared the town of Aua, we noticed a very strong fish smell coming from a Starkist cannery. We came through at what must have been a shift change because there were lots of people outside with hairnets on. Some looked like they were going in, and some looked like they were coming out.

The Avis clerk stopped on the side of the road near the cannery, and we pulled over with him. One more phone call and Jaden came out. He explained that our phone call had caught them off guard. He said that they weren't expecting us and that his wife was inside playing "pinko," which we later discovered was the local pronunciation for bingo. I told him that we had called two months ago to say that we were coming, but it didn't seem to register with him. A few minutes later, his wife, Baylie, came out; she also said she hadn't known we were coming. When I mentioned that we had called two months ago, she gasped apologetically and said that she had forgotten to write it down.

Jaden invited us in to play "pinko," but we declined, so he told us where to wait for them. A few minutes later Baylie came out again to be sure we didn't mind waiting. There were *lots* of kids running around on the street. One girl came up and spoke to us; another asked for money.

It took about half an hour for their games to finish, and it was after 11:00 when they finally came out. We followed them to a gas station and then to their house. The drive took another half hour, maybe a bit more, and even in the darkness, we noticed a lot of dogs and people. The dogs seemed to be strays and hung around in groups of two to eight. As far as the people, we concluded that the Samoans just seem to keep different hours than we do, staying up much later.

The drive itself was something else. It was one of the steepest, curviest roads we've ever been on, bringing back memories of Fluella Pass in Europe and Bear Tooth Pass in Montana. Keep in mind it was dark and—oh yes—there were both speed bumps and potholes. Dick said the road over the ridge to our hosts' house was among the very steepest he'd ever driven on. It was comforting to finally reach the shoreline on the other side.

We finally got to their house around midnight—and discovered that their six-year-old daughter, Azul, was with them. She has to leave for school at 6:30 AM. She was still in the backseat while they put sheets on our bed, swept, and made a vague attempt at cleaning the bathroom. Jaden said not to use the bathroom sink; we could brush our teeth in the tub. I was extremely glad I had brought some bottled water.

All the furniture was covered with large pieces of cloth. Another piece of cloth covered the doorway from a sort of sitting room to our bedroom, and one covered a window between the sitting room and our bedroom. Our bedroom had a double bed and a large wooden cabinet, also covered with cloth, that we could set things on. The ceiling in our room was covered with strips of cloth that bulged down. The windows in the sitting room had "curtains" that looked like they were made from the skirt or petticoat of a wedding gown. The walls were stucco. Many of the daughter's school papers were posted on one of the sitting room walls; two of the bedroom walls had leaflets about prophets in the Bible.

Our bathroom had a square tub with a shower. There was a faucet on the shower and another, sort of wobbly one, lower down. The handle on the toilet was also extremely loose. The floors were all a variety of linoleum.

Jaden and Baylie brought in a fan and a large nightlight in the shape of a religious statue. They told us they had two dogs—who apparently stayed outside—and seven puppies that were one or two months old. They couldn't remember, which seemed very strange. These puppies made squeaking noises most of the night.

We didn't get to bed until 1:00 AM and then were kept awake for a while by the dogs. We had to get up at 6:00 so we could follow our hosts to the National Park Visitor Center.

What a day!

Friday, September 17, 2010

We had set the alarm for 6:00, but we didn't need to. The church next door had a *very* loud bell at 6:00, plus the puppies were squealing.

Azul got ready for school and left before 7:00. Baylie said she gets breakfast there.

We followed Jaden and Baylie for miles and miles to the park's Visitor Center. As we drove, we were very confused because we weren't going in the direction where the Visitor

Center was marked on the map. Since we were very close to the airport, Dick concluded that maybe they thought we wanted to go to a park on another island. We had just about decided to make our way on our own when we turned in at a sign that said Park Visitor Center.

It turned out that the Visitor Center on the map had been destroyed by a tsunami about a year ago. Consequently, this one had offices only—no displays. They told us that they were working on rebuilding close to where the original Visitor Center had been.[65] They had postcards for sale—well, on display. No one knew where the key was, so they said we would have to come back later in the day to buy cards.

Since we were already at the southwestern end of Tutuila, the largest island on American Samoa, we decided to explore there. We found a restaurant for breakfast—I was starving! Then, at a grocery store, we bought food for lunch and the next two breakfasts. (When I had inquired about breakfast, Jaden had suggested McDonald's or KFC.) Before we left the grocery store, we asked for directions. The clerk said, "Oh, you can't get lost here. There's only one road." However, that was not entirely true. What *was* true was that there were no signs when we came to an intersection. A map (which, fortunately, I had printed on the computer before leaving home) was essential.

Our first stop was at the Turtle and Shark Legends Site. Here is the legend.

> During a famine, a local village cast out a grandmother and her granddaughter. They threw themselves into the ocean and were transformed into a turtle and a shark. They traveled together to find a new home but were rejected at many locations. They were finally

---

[65] The rebuilt Visitor Center now has exhibits in Samoan and English that describe the national park's recovery efforts and showcase the significance of the island's tropical rainforests, coral reefs, fruit bats, and the Samoan culture. There are interactive exhibits with models of islands, sea life, forest birds, fruit bats, and cultural handicrafts and tools.

welcomed by the people of Vaitogi, and they turned back into human form. However, the grandmother eventually decided that they should return to the sea as a turtle and shark. She promised to make these waters their permanent home, and she gave the villagers a song to sing to summon them back to shore.

The villagers still sing this song, and many claim to have seen the turtle and the shark. On the day of our visit, there was high surf breaking over the black lava rock, and the water was a beautiful shade of turquoise. We walked a little bit there. The shore view was lovely, helped by the rich aqua-colored water and the deep-blue sky. However, the sky did not stay blue; clouds would gather and then it would rain briefly and clear again.

From there we drove to the village of Vailoatai. We walked along the shore for a little bit before it started to rain. We believed this was the Leala Shoreline National Natural Landmark, but it wasn't labeled. We continued up the western coast almost to the end of the road. It got very steep and curvy, and we weren't quite sure where it was going to end, so we turned around. The view from the top was spectacular. This park is the only one in the National Park System that is south of the equator, and it is almost all tropical rain forest. There are a lot of high islands totally covered with tropical vegetation.

We drove back to the Visitor Center to get our postcards and back to the grocery store for more water. Baylie had given me her extra phone; she called me and said they wouldn't be home until 10:00 or 11:00 PM. This was fine with us.

We made our way back to the mountain road and stopped at the scenic turnout—a good decision. There were informative signs about the island and the wildlife. The only native mammals are three kinds of bats. One is the White Naped Flying Fox, or *Pe'a vao*. It is a fruit bat, and it is active during the day. Right after I said I wished we'd see one, we did. I concluded that the "birds" I had seen earlier were probably bats as well. These bats have a three-foot wingspan. They flew low enough for us to see the webs on the wings. The other two bats are the Samoan fruit bat and the sheath-tailed bat.

From here we went back to the house and decided to take a short walk. We passed the elementary school, which has several separate small buildings, perhaps for separate grades. Then we got to a National Park Trail. At 6:00 PM we were near the church, and the bells started to chime the Westminster Quarters like our grandmother clock at home, and then it struck six. We were going to walk on the trail, but a woman came out of her house with her three children and said we couldn't go down there right now. She said something about a curfew, which we didn't understand. She told us that when the bells ring at 6 PM, everyone is supposed to stop walking or driving on the road until the third bell rings, at which point it is okay to resume normal activity. Apparently the first bell is represented by the set of 6:00 chimes; the second bell occurs a few minutes later, and it's not as loud. I had heard that one also but didn't know what it signified.

During the few minutes between the first and third bell, people are expected to take time for prayer and meditation. It's kind of like a 10-minute sunset sabbath.

"It's spiritual," the woman said.

All three kids shook hands with us and introduced themselves, although the youngest had to be prodded. We never figured out why we couldn't continue our walk, but the woman said her 12-year-old son, Iosefa, would walk us home when the "sabbath" ended. We had to wait until we saw traffic moving. In a couple of minutes, we heard the third bell, along with cars moving in the distance, so we were able to go on. As we walked, Iosefa pointed out his school and told us that there were eight kids in his seventh-grade class. After we got home, he continued to his grandparents' house.

Saturday, September 18, 2010

We used the fan in our room at night to blow air across us. There was also a good wind that blew through the house on a regular basis. When we got up that morning, Dick noticed that the cloth covering the doorway to our room would blow into the room and then, several seconds later, blow out of the room. The fairly frequent changes in direction surprised him because he thought that ocean breezes would be more uniform. He decided that perhaps the frequent changes were being caused by the same effects that produced the frequent rains.

We gave Baylie the maple syrup we had brought from New Hampshire, and she gave us a coconut Samoan bread, which had been wrapped in a banana leaf and cooked over hot stones.

Baylie and her daughter went hiking with us that morning. We left about 8:00 AM to drive to the hiking trails. On the way, Baylie told us about the tsunami that had reached the island the previous year.[66] First, she felt the earthquake; then she heard the warning alarm. They picked up an elderly neighbor, who couldn't drive, and headed to high ground, which also happened to be where we were driving that day. I experienced a deep sense of urgency and fear as she described the event and pointed out places on the side of the road where people had slept on mats and in sleeping bags. I still get chills writing about it.

Baylie told us that their house had been flooded with water, and a lot of their items had been destroyed. After the flood FEMA came by, recorded damages and measurements, and, a month later, sent them a check for $20,000, which allowed them to replace and repair damaged items. She said that FEMA also came back to check that the money had been properly spent. Apparently, some people had spent the money improperly, such as for a vacation, and got themselves in trouble. She also said (and we saw) that some people were still living in

---

[66] Tropical storms occur occasionally in American Samoa. Tropical Storm Gita caused widespread devastation in American Samoa in February 2018.

tents a year later. We couldn't tell if there was any connection between people living in tents and people who had misused their FEMA money.

The two hikes which Baylie suggested weren't ones we had planned to do. The first one was shorter, but it was difficult—mainly because it had rained *very* hard overnight and the trail was muddy. Being with Baylie was like having my own Sherpa. Almost the whole way down she had me keep my hand on her shoulder. There were a couple of places with really lovely views.

Baylie alternated between telling her daughter to hurry up or to wait for us. We finished the first hike at 9:30. I could see the sweat dripping off me and felt like I had done a day's work.

After a short break, we took the second hike, which started about 100 yards up the road from the first. The trailhead was at a scenic lookout where we had parked the car. This trail went downhill and wasn't as long. But the most impressive thing was the fact that Azul decided to go the whole way barefoot. I would not attempt that. The *thought* of doing it was painful. There were a few informational signs telling about the early settlements here.

I was still soaked with sweat, so I was very glad when Baylie suggested we return to the house to shower. We didn't do the really scenic hike along the ridge. Instead, we decided it was more important to spend time with Baylie and learn more about their culture. She is from Western Samoa; Jaden is from American Samoa.

Baylie told us that the only cemetery on American Samoa is a Korean fishermen's cemetery and a spot where some other foreign sailors may be buried. Practically every house has tombs (the kind that look like stone caskets) in their front yard. At one house, a child's swing set was set up on the same foundation. Most homes also have open buildings with lots of pillars. Baylie said they are used for funerals and nothing else, but I saw clothes drying in some of them and people sitting in others.

Later in the day we drove into town with Baylie and Azul. We drove over the hills, around the harbor, and through Pago

Pago, stopping at the village of Utuloi to do some shopping. I bought a few things woven from local material that appeared to be coconut palm. Then we treated everyone to ice cream cones. We were just finishing the cones when Jaden called. He had finished work at the cannery and came to meet us. We then followed him to several places.

First, we went to Coconut Point, which we had seen on the map but hadn't yet been to—partly because we weren't sure if we could actually find it due to the inadequate signage we had encountered (or, really, *not* encountered) everywhere. Coconut Point was at the end of a narrow peninsula that went south from the village of Nu'uuli. To the southwest was the end of another peninsula, which was used for a runway of the Pago Pago International Airport. Those two points surrounded (except for the small gap between them) a body of water called Pala Lagoon.

Coconut Point itself was very scenic, and there were hundreds (maybe thousands) of coconut trees, which makes sense, considering the name of the place. There were also many upscale homes along the road, which also makes sense, considering how quiet and scenic it is there.

Our next stop was near the top of Mount A'oloaufou. The outlook point where Jaden took us included the ruins of a large house. It struck me as ironic that the property had probably belonged to someone with a lot of money. Now it was serving as a scenic outlook for everybody, including poor people. While we were there, Jaden spent several minutes talking with Dick about Samoan culture and the importance of respect. This included respect for others and a respect for nature.

We wanted to try a couple of things on our own, so we thanked them for the tour and said we would meet them back at the house in the evening. We were looking for Tisa's Barefoot Bar, which our daughter-in-law Kristen, who spent a college semester in Western Samoa, had said we should try to find. We were not sure exactly where it was, so when we drove past the general area without finding it, we figured that we would look more carefully on our way back, when it would be closer to dinner.

We drove about halfway down the east end of the island, which was very different from the western part. The eastern part had fewer houses and businesses, and it felt decidedly more rural. We learned later that people and villages on the eastern part tended to be more traditional.

Geographically, the east is also different from the west. Driving along the western coast, the roads were fairly level, but we were not always near the water. On the eastern part, we were usually right near the water, but the road went up and down quite a bit. There were places where the waves hitting the coast lapped against the face of the cliff, and the most direct way to get past that point was to go up and down along the edge of the cliff.

On our way back toward the western part, we found Tisa's. It was still a bit early for dinner, but the bartender/waiter offered to prepare us swordfish. Needless to say, I jumped at this—my favorite dinner. The whole meal, which was served on a banana leaf, was delicious. It included plantain (sort of like potatoes) in a sauce of coconut cream and onions, coleslaw, and a slice of papaya. Papaya is not usually my favorite, but this was sprinkled with cinnamon and was quite good. The swordfish was excellent.

When we got back to the house, Jaden was out in the yard with a friend. Their front yard is made up of smooth pieces of coral, and the sea is directly across the street. Jaden and his friend were using long sticks to knock coconuts down. They brought them in and removed the outer shell. Then they brought us each one to drink. There was *so* much liquid inside. It was very watery. We had to stealthily pour some into a glass and hide it to have later. Then they cracked the coconut open and brought us spoons to eat the meat. It was totally different from any we've ever had. There was only a thin layer of meat, which was soft and sort of slimy. It tasted good but didn't have a strong coconut flavor.

Sunday, September 19, 2010

I woke up to the smell of fire. Dick couldn't smell it, but he could see it out back. I think Jaden was cooking some of the food for after church. I don't know when he ever sleeps. When I got up at 1:00 AM he was working in the kitchen.

We did most of our packing before it was time to go to church with Jaden. As soon as we walked out the door, we saw Samoan ladies in bright-colored dresses and white brimmed hats walking down the street. The outfits—at least the hats— were reminiscent of the 1950s.

The interior of the church was beautiful. The wall at the front had colorful patterns of light blue, pale yellow, and white fragments of colored porcelain. From back to front were four or five pairs of columns, approximately one-foot square from floor to ceiling and covered with hand-carved wood. The ceiling was also very dark wood, but just as narrow boards, not hand carved. The walls were white. The side windows were plain glass with a cross dividing the panes. During our visit, everything was clean and in good repair. It looked as if it had been built fairly recently.

Jaden said the church was Catholic (CCSA), but I think he meant Christian.[67] There were no icons, no crucifix, no mention of the pope, no one crossing themselves, no communion. The service lasted 1½ hours.

About 75 people were in church. There were approximately 20 rows of pews divided by three aisles into four sections: far left, far right, center left, and center right. The front third of the center left was filled with women wearing white broad-brimmed hats and very colorful dresses. The front third of the center right was occupied by men in colorfully printed shirts. There were about half as many men as women. It turned out that those two groupings in the front were the choir; they just weren't robed in the manner to which we were accustomed. The choir seating apparently affected overall seating, because all women were on the left side and most men were on the right with a few exceptions, including Jaden and Dick.

The service started at 9:00 with choir singing and organ accompaniment. The choir sang four or five times during the service; the songs were beautiful. They sang several lively songs in Samoan. All ended with "amen."

All the readings and the sermon (which had many loud emphatic comments) were in Samoan except for a few phrases such as *Jesus is the Messiah* in English. The sermon reminded us of "fire and brimstone," but that may have been partly due to the volume settings on the church speaker system. Parts of it were very loud. At the end of the sermon, which had been entirely in Samoan, the pastor said a few sentences in English. I wondered if that was for our benefit.

Near the end of the service, two men spoke. One welcomed us—we stuck out like sore thumbs—and people turned and stared at us.

The other man gave what Jaden described as a kind of financial summary for the two types of collections that occur. The first is done as parishioners enter the church. They stop at

---

[67] I looked this up later—it's part of the Congregational Christian Church in Samoa.

a table in the back and pay some amount, which gets recorded. The money collected in this way goes to pay the pastor. The other collection is referred to as a donation and is done during the service; people put money into purple velvet bags, which get passed around. Jaden and Baylie had both told us to put one dollar in the bag. According to Jaden, the money collected in this way goes toward maintaining the church building. When church was over, everyone left *fast*—no shaking hands, no conversation.

Immediately after the service, we went back to the house for a traditional Samoan Sunday dinner. Baylie had stayed home to cook; they said that the previous week, Jaden had stayed home. We both thought this was going to be a big gathering—sort of like a church potluck—but it was just us. There were just enough chairs; Baylie's was quite broken. She cooked on a two-burner "stove" that sat on the counter and was powered by a big metal jug of something—maybe propane. She had a small oven sitting in the corner, covered with a cloth. Her refrigerator was a normal height but still fairly small.

We had fried chicken, taro leaf with onion and coconut milk (this was all wrapped in foil which was twisted at the top), and another dish they called "chop suey". It consisted of noodles cut into one-inch pieces in a broth that reminded me of miso soup. There was also something they called chow mein, but it just looked (and tasted) like noodles in broth with turkey (which was very bony) and cabbage. Baylie had made her favorite dish: baked unripe bananas. They were very dry, were tough in texture, and did not have much flavor. They also offered baked ripe bananas which were served with some sort of coconut sauce. They had tried to buy breadfruit, a starchy fruit used as a vegetable, but they couldn't get it. Azul had white sticky rice, which is not traditional. The drink with the meal was a coconut full of liquid, like we had sampled the previous night. The volume of liquid was about three cups in each coconut. This time we drank the liquid but didn't eat the meat.

We had spoons and forks but no napkins. Traditionally, Samoans just eat with their hands. At the end of the meal, Baylie brought out a small plastic dishpan filled with soapy water and a cloth for drying our fingers.

It sounded like this Sunday meal is the only big meal they cook. They eat leftovers for a couple of days. For breakfast they usually had bread and tea. Azul got breakfast and lunch at school. They gave the dogs leftover bones.

When we were done eating, we finished packing and took pictures. Baylie gave me Samoan earrings and the two lava-lavas she had given us to use. Lava-lavas are big pieces of cloth in pretty patterns that people wrap around themselves after a shower or swimming; some people also wear them as clothing.

I tried to ask questions about their American citizenship but didn't get too far.[68] The government takes taxes out of any earnings. Jaden worked only a couple of days a week. Baylie, who didn't work, had taken care of Jaden's grandmother until her death the previous year; now she planned to stay home for her daughter until Azul entered high school. It didn't seem like there was any work closer than Aua, a 30-minute drive over Rainmaker Mountain's curvy roads.

We really enjoyed staying with a native family, and this approach gave us access to a lot more information about Samoan culture than we might have learned exclusively on our own. If we had been staying in a hotel, I doubt that we would have experienced the evening "Sa" when the villagers stop for prayers nor would we have drunk coconut milk from coconuts that had just been knocked down from a tree. Staying in the home of native Samoans provided a good introduction to their daily life and an opportunity to sample many foods that were unfamiliar to us. We highly recommend the homestay program.

---

[68] Later research helped me understand the complexity. American Samoa is an unincorporated territory, and its citizens are called U.S. nationals, not U.S. citizens. They pay American taxes but cannot vote, run for office, or serve on a jury.

2011

Badlands National Park, South Dakota

North Cascades National Park,
Washington

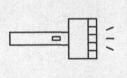

Badlands National Park, South Dakota

Sunday, August 7, 2011

Returning to our campsite from a visit to Minuteman Missile National Historic Site, we took a side road rather than the interstate and drove through a chunk of Badlands National Park. The Badlands didn't look the way we had remembered it, but it was very pretty, and we stopped for some pictures.

According to one bit of information we read, the Badlands are eroding away at about one inch per year. Considering that it had been more than 30 years since we were there last, the features had all lost close to three feet, and they all looked somewhat different now than they did then.

After dinner we walked to the amphitheater for a program. It was an excellent presentation, but the mosquitoes were brutal. The ranger said this was because of the very wet weather they'd been having. He had a slide that suggested renaming the Badlands as the Greenlands. That summer, there were wildflowers and green grass, which was *very* unusual. The ranger had planned to use a laser light to point out constellations, and three telescopes were available, but we— along with a lot of other people—left during the program's intermission about 9:15. No one was sure whether they'd really be able to see anything because of the cloud cover.

North Cascades National Park, Washington

Saturday, August 27, 2011

We began our day at the Visitor Center at North Cascades National Park. Ross Lake National Recreation Area is included with the park, as is Lake Chelan National Recreation Area, which is only accessible by boat. The ranger gave us suggestions for overlooks and easy trails.

From the Visitor Center, we continued east on Route 20. Our first stop was at the Gorge Creek Falls, where Gorge Lake empties into Skagit (rhymes with *gadget*) River. Gorge Lake is actually a wide part of the Skagit River.

After a long day's drive with stops at many scenic overlooks, we got to Diablo Dam just in time to drive over the dam before it closed to visitors at 4:30. The dam is a bit unusual because it was

built on top of a rock base. We tried to imagine what the falls and rapids must have looked like as a river flowed over and around the rocks before the dam was built. The water everywhere is quite green, reminding us of Innsbruck, Austria, and some of the mountains are snow-covered. How they built this dam is totally beyond me, but it's quite an impressive structure.

We also walked a short trail to the Gorge Overlook. Adding to the views was a clear, bright-blue sky. Clear weather was predicted for the next couple of days.

In addition to those two specific sites, we also stopped at several pullouts to view the scenery and take pictures. At all the points where we stopped—and during the drive in between the stops in both directions—the scenery was absolutely spectacular. We both agreed that it was one of the most (if not *the* most) scenic drives we had ever been on.

Sunday, August 28, 2011

I hated to pack up and leave this lovely site, but we did. Dick wrote,

Last night was our best sleep so far and topped off a truly perfect day yesterday. The best scenery, the best campsite, the best dinner (because of the best corn), and the best night. It must have been an early present because my birthday is tomorrow. All the days Nanc and I spend together camping are wonderful, but yesterday was truly special.

On our way out this morning, we decided to continue farther up the road past our campground and get into National Park territory. We were told that the road would come to a dead end, but we didn't find it. The road went from two-lane paved to two-lane dirt, then to one-lane dirt, and then to narrower and rougher one-lane dirt. At that point, we decided to turn around, even though there were other cars continuing farther out along the rough, narrow dirt road. There was actually (in our opinion) a fair amount of traffic on such an out-of-the-way road. But the scenery was worth the trip.

We made a few more stops as we drove through the park. First was Gorge Creek Falls. We had done a short walk there the previous day but had not crossed the street, which actually gave a better view of the gorge and the falls. The Diablo Lake Overlook had gorgeous views of the lake. The water was bluish green, caused by the silt carried by glaciers. The ranger said there are 300 glaciers in the park. There was a white boat that added to the scene. The air was clear and the sky a brilliant blue with some white, wispy clouds.

Dick saw a bear on the side of the road. He turned the car around so I might see it, but the bear was gone. We also missed the Ross Lake Overlook, but there were plenty of other scenic views.

We stopped outside the park on National Forest land where there was old, granular snow on the side of the road. Dick outlined a snowman with a stick and added features. We have seen snow in several parks in the summer, but it always seems to surprise and delight us.

Monday, August 29, 2011

We celebrated Dick's birthday with a boat trip to Lake Chelan National Recreation Area. Lake Chelan is the third deepest lake in America. We had a three-hour stop at the village of Stehekin which has 85 year-round residents and a one-room school with 17 students. I liked what seemed to be their simple way of life. While at Stehekin we took a ranger-led bus tour to Rainbow Falls and a short hike around the village. A shop was selling crafts made by the residents. I especially liked the ones made by children—long marshmallow sticks, snowflake ornaments made from melted crayons, and papier-mâché piggy banks.

North Cascades National Park offers glacier topped mountains, hiking trails, scenic drives with spectacular views, and a variety of ranger-led programs. We found this to be a relaxing place to explore.

2012

(FEBRUARY)

Channel Islands National Park, California

Channel Islands National Park, California

Thursday, February 2, 2012

Dick was giving a science workshop at California Polytechnic University, so we decided to take advantage of our time in California and spend a day at the Channel Islands National Park. After checking out information from the Visitor Center in Ventura, we selected Anacapa, the easternmost island in the cluster (or string) of eight small islands, which were once inhabited by the Chumash Native Americans.

Because of the isolation of all of the Channel Islands, there are a lot of animals and plants there that are found nowhere else. There are also some that were almost wiped out but have now returned, including a kind of fox and the bald eagle.

We boarded the boat a bit after 9:00 AM and took seats on the top deck in the back. The top offered a better view, and the back was calmer than the front, which reduced the chance of seasickness during the one-hour trip.

Before we docked, we spent a little time watching sea lions, and we also saw the beautiful 40-foot-tall sea arch, which was formed when waves eroded a volcanic island and created sea cliffs and sea caves, as well as natural bridges or arches.

When we docked, we had to climb a few steps on a metal ladder with very narrow steps and then the equivalent of 13 flights of stairs. I think there were 154 steps. Once we reached the top, the ground was relatively level. The quiet was disturbed by a helicopter, which was bringing in big items. During our visit, the picnic tables had been removed for replacement, but the new ones had not yet arrived.

The Chumash Native Americans lived on Anacapa 10,000 years ago. How they got up the steep cliffs is beyond me. The Spanish settlers brought in disease, which reduced the Chumash population. The Spanish also brought glass beads, which were more desirable than the ones the Chumash made from shells and used for trade. This changed their economic and social structure, and by the 1820s, the remaining Chumash had moved to the mainland. One of the areas where we walked had fragments of shells—an old midden or garbage dump.

We walked first with Kathy, a volunteer naturalist. There were lots of ice plants, which had succulent type leaves and beautiful reddish flowers. Apparently, the ice plant was brought in from Africa as a groundcover to help prevent erosion. However, it has become invasive and, since it's nonnative, it is being removed. The other plants that we saw a lot of were yellow coreopsis. I thought these were flowers that grew on slender stalks, but these were on thick woody stems and were more like a bush. There were also a buckwheat grass and a type of low morning glory. The morning glory was not flowering on that day, but when it does flower, it is usually white. Occasionally it has pale pink veins.

Dick was struck by one plant, which was different from any we remembered encountering before. It had soft green leaves that looked like pieces of felt. Actually, the top of the leaves looked like dried felt, but the bottom of the leaves looked like fuzzy material covered by dewdrops. They weren't actually wet, but they did look like it. After about two hours, the guided part of our walk was finished at Inspiration Point. There were benches, so we sat there and ate our packed lunch.

This is a major breeding ground for seagulls. The mating/nesting season was just starting, and there were seagulls everywhere. A few were competing for mates, but not as many as there would be when mating season was in full swing. Since there wasn't much action, it was a challenge to get a picture of the gulls that showed how many there were, how scattered they were, and how each was proclaiming its own territory. Some sat in hollow spots, some perched on rocks, others perched on trees, and others were still looking for a place to stay.

The Anacapa deer mouse is found only on this island. One of the other islands has a silver fox, which is the size of a cat. We saw a couple of brown pelicans in the air. The bald eagle is here too, although we didn't see any.

Near the end of our walk, it got very noisy, and I looked up to see a large flock of gulls flying and squawking. I wondered if that was part of their territorial maneuvers.

We walked toward the lighthouse but couldn't go all the way because the fog horn was sounding every few seconds. We were told that visitors who got too close could actually damage their hearing.

The trip back was great. It seemed smoother than going out, plus we were in the middle of a huge pod of dolphins. They swam on both sides of the boat for a long time and did some amazing jumps. The man speaking on the intercom estimated there were about a thousand of them.

We only had time to visit Anacapa Island, but the other four sound equally interesting. All offer primitive camping, but no water or food services are available. There are small Visitor Centers on Anacapa, Santa Cruz, and Santa Barbara Island; ranger-led programs are usually available on each island on days that the concessionaire boats run to that island. The description of all the wildlife that can often be seen at San Miguel Island—seals, sea lions, dolphins, porpoises, gray whales, killer whales, and blue whales along with many different varieties of birds—makes that island sound particularly enticing. Perhaps we will plan a trip there on our next visit to the area.

2012

(MARCH AND APRIL)

Shenandoah National Park, Virginia

Mammoth Cave National Park, Kentucky

Shenandoah National Park, Virginia

Friday, March 23, 2012

Once again, Dick and I found ourselves driving on Skyline Drive. There were lots of red bud trees with their pretty purple flowers and some white flowering trees as well. There were hazy views of the valley, and Dick took lots of pictures. He wrote,

One of the pictures I took showed the countryside from the bridge down to the valley. I actually took that picture twice. The first was nice and clear, but while taking the second picture I was swarmed by gnats. There were so many bugs that the second picture looks like the lens is covered by dust specks, which were actually pictures of the bugs buzzing around.

Mammoth Cave National Park, Kentucky

Sunday, April 8, 2012 Happy Easter!

After getting information at the Visitor Center of Mammoth Cave National Park, we got a site in the national park campground. It was very quiet. At dusk there was a deer across the street from us.

Monday, April 9, 2012

There were three deer near our campsite this morning. It had been a clear night and consequently a cold morning.

Mammoth Cave is not only a national park but also a world heritage site. We got to the Visitor Center right when it opened and bought tickets for the 9:00 AM "Historic Tour." It was billed as moderate difficulty but wasn't bad. It led through some very-high-ceilinged rooms, past a couple of drop-offs equivalent to an 11-story building. There were a few places where we had to stoop down, and one area called "Fat Man's Misery," which was a wiggly, narrow passage.

When we came to Mammoth Cave about 30 years ago with our kids, we went to the part that had all the typical cave features, like stalagmites and stalactites. For some reason we can't find any journal entries documenting that visit. To see stalactites or stalagmites now, visitors have to take the "Frozen Niagara" tour.

There were some surface walks that sounded interesting, as well as other cave tours. This time we took a tour that focused on 4,000 years of cave history, from early Native Americans through mining and saltpeter-making in the 1800s until the present day as part of the National Park System.

In the late 1800s and early 1900s, most of the visitors touring the caves were wealthy men and women. The guide told us that those people would wear their finest clothes in the cave: top hats and suit coats for the men, fancy dresses and hats for the women. Considering the casual clothes we were wearing, we might not have been allowed on one of these tours. We also learned that those tours took 8 to 10 hours (short tour) or 14 to 16 hours (long tour), which is understandable since those tours involved walking and crawling over fallen rocks—not walking on paved walkways or up and down stairs.

Mammoth Cave has more than 365 miles of surveyed passages, which makes it twice as long as any other known cave. It's been a scenic attraction since the 1800s. A lot of the early tours were conducted with oil lamps, and the soot blackened the ceilings. There is a lot of old graffiti written with this soot; it is still visible today.

The bat disease called White Nose Syndrome has killed lots of bats in recent years in the United States. To prevent its spread, visitors can't go into the cave wearing clothes that they have worn in another cave and they must walk on bio-security mats when they leave the cave.

Before I had ever visited a cave, I thought of them as all being the same—underground, dark, and having stalactites and stalagmites. Now I know that each one is unique and special. They are well worth visiting.

2013

Virgin Islands National Park, Virgin Islands

Virgin Islands National Park,
Virgin Islands

Friday, April 5, 2013

This trip included Puerto Rico and several islands in the Virgin Islands. We spent several days staying in hotels and bed and breakfasts while visiting national monuments and historic sites; Virgin Islands National Park on the island of St. John was the only national park we visited on this trip. It had a campground called Cinnamon Bay that provided floored tents and cots, so we didn't have to bring our camping gear.

We rented a car on St. John, stopped for gas at the only gas station on the island, and shopped for groceries at the only grocery store. It was hard to figure out what to get since we really didn't know what facilities we would have at the site.

By the time we got to Cinnamon Bay, it was dark. We had to park away from the site and carry everything down in a wheelbarrow cart. The only flashlights we had brought were our two little ones, which were in the duffel bag. At least I knew where they were, and Dick was able to find them.

Our tent had four cots in it, so we used two for spreading things out. The campground provided sheets and towels, but it was a challenge making the beds in the dark. Then we had to go buy ice for the cooler at the camp store. Dick went through a lot of matches trying to light a lantern, but the matches wouldn't stay lit. I was glad we had bought cold food for dinner so we could eat without further preparation. It was after 8:00, and I was very hungry.

Saturday, April 6, 2013

It was wonderful to be sleeping outside—we could hear birds and tree frogs and gentle surf on the bay—but mosquitoes kept me awake. Finally, Dick found the bug spray, and I slept. It was hot!

After breakfast, we drove to the east end of the island. Dick wrote,

The drive was a challenge because of continuous ups and downs and frequent sharp switchbacks. Every so often there would be a sign with a wiggly arrow on it, indicating "curvy road ahead." Every time, I thought it was actually very redundant and simply a restatement of the obvious. However, the first time I saw the sign I wondered and asked myself: "How much curvier can it get?"

As we approached the end of the road, the pavement went on vacation to some other place and left a stretch of dirt road that was seriously potholed and grooved with rocks. We drove a short way and turned around. We stopped for lunch on a rocky beach, which was covered with rounded gray rocks, smooth and slightly flattened, and varying in size from golf balls to footballs. The beach was quiet, and it provided a pleasant respite from driving on steep, wiggly roads.

Our plan had been to see a beach that the car rental clerk had said was her favorite, but we missed the turn and ended up back in Cruz Bay. So, we stopped to buy more groceries and went into the National Park Visitor Center in town. The person at the desk couldn't suggest much more than what we had done. She said the beach we had missed was very nice, so we decided to try to find it the next day, along with Trunk Bay, which is supposed to be one of the most beautiful beaches anywhere.

We came back to camp for a short swim in Cinnamon Bay. The water was crystal clear and a beautiful shade of turquoise, but it was not as warm as I had expected. After swimming we took showers—cold ones, where we had to hold the water on.

We had decided not to cook, so we ate at the campground restaurant. When we got back, Dick managed to light the lantern, so we sat outside writing postcards and journal entries.

Sunday, April 7, 2013

I slept much better, although I woke up once because I was very hot. At some point we were awake because we heard animal footsteps. In the morning, Dick found the tracks of a large lizard and guessed it was about two feet long

After breakfast, we headed to Trunk Bay to snorkel the underwater trail. My only previous snorkeling experience had been in Hawaii, where I was a dismal failure. I did a little better this time. The trail had three buoys: one white, one red, one blue. In between them were underwater signs, which I had trouble reading, but I could see the fish and plants. First there were lots of little white minnows, then several larger fish. There were some spiny-looking plants and some thin purple ones. I couldn't really identify any coral.

Dick was less successful the first time and did not use the underwater camera. I took the camera and went out again. He came too and managed to see some things. Even after this experience, neither of us is particularly excited about snorkeling.

Our next stop was Francis Bay. We had to hike in past an abandoned house of the Francis family. There were lots of big termite nests in trees. The beach was about the same as the others: narrow with trees for shade along the back. I swam for a bit; Dick didn't get in past his waist.

Back at camp, we took a hike to the Cinnamon Bay factory ruins, which are right across the street from the campground. The walk was a bit of a challenge because the map we had didn't seem to match the roads and paths on the ground. The path was fairly flat and not too difficult, and we did finally figure it out. The estate house here was in ruins but was actually lived in until 1968. Things deteriorate quickly in a tropical climate. A sugar mill was better preserved. The loop walk started at the mill and then went up a fairly steep hill, across the end of the valley, and back down. There were good informative signs describing various flora and fauna along the way. When the huge termite nests fall and decompose, they provide nitrogen for the soil. We saw two deer, which seemed as interested in watching us as we were in watching them. Bats are the only native mammals here.

Another inquisitive creature today was a bird at Trunk Bay, where we were eating our lunch. He came right up next to me and stayed for a long time, hoping—futilely—for a handout. His eyes reminded me of a penguin whose picture I have in my slide show of Antarctica: big white circles with darker pupils

We enjoyed the picturesque beaches and learning about sugar production which was once an important industry on St. John. Four years after our visit, the park was closed due to damage from hurricanes. Hurricane Irma in September 2017 brought destruction to the island of St. John. Most of the trees were knocked down, trails, beaches, and roads all needed to be cleared of debris. Shortly after Hurricane Irma, more damage was done by Hurricane Maria. The Navy, the National Guard, and many other groups worked hard to restore the facilities in the park. By the end of December 2017, Virgin Islands National Park, which comprises two thirds of the island, had reopened. When we visit again, the island will not look the same, but we will still be able to enjoy the restored national park.

2014

Tallgrass Prairie National Preserve, Kansas

Mesa Verde National Park, Colorado

Zion National Park, Utah

Great Basin National Park, Nevada

Pinnacles National Park, California

Lassen Volcanic National Park, California

Redwood National and State Parks,
California

Tallgrass Prairie National Preserve, Kansas

Saturday, August 2, 2014

In our quest to visit all the national park sites, we stopped at the Tallgrass Prairie National Preserve in Strong City, Kansas. We didn't spend much time looking at the exhibits inside because we wanted to see the prairie itself. The ranger suggested the Southwind Nature Trail with a spur to a one-room schoolhouse, the Lower Fox Creek School. We actually drove to the schoolhouse, which had been nicely restored, and then walked on the Nature Trail. It was HOT, and although it shouldn't have been a difficult hike (1¾ miles), I found it strenuous. There were no signs to indicate what we were seeing, so it was basically just a hot walk!

There are ranch buildings that can be toured but the ranger didn't mention this, and we didn't discover them until the end, when we were too hot and tired. We decided we've seen other ranches, so we didn't really need to see one more.

Mesa Verde National Park, Colorado

Wednesday, August 6, 2014

We camped at Mesa Verde for two nights in 2014. When we were there 34 years ago on our first cross-country trip with the kids, there was no campground in the park. Now it is quite well developed: a little village with laundry, showers, store, etc. We decided to set up camp and catch up on things in the afternoon, then go to the campfire program at night. Many of the sites now require tickets and guided tours to visit them, but these were the places we had visited in 1980, so we didn't need to go back.

It was a long drive (not that far, but on slow, curvy, mountain roads) to the Chapin Mesa Archeological Museum and Visitor Center, where we watched the introductory slide show. A ranger suggested that we should see Spruce Tree House, which is the best preserved in the park.[69] The trail started right

---

[69] In August 2015, there was a rock fall at Spruce Tree House, and it was determined that to protect the safety of visitors, it would not be open to the public for the foreseeable future. Visitors can still see it from overlooks.

outside the building. According to the brochure, it "is one of more than 600 cliff dwellings within Mesa Verde, but it is much larger than most." It was named Spruce Tree House not because it was made of spruce trees (it was adobe), but because of the Douglas Fir trees (historically referred to as spruce trees) in the canyon bottom below it. It is a well-preserved site, and there were several rangers there to make sure it stayed that way (as well as to answer questions).

I'm glad we were able to do this hike, although I found the return trip *very* difficult, partly because of the elevation (7,000 feet). There was a kiva, rooms with windows and doorways, some walls that had remnants of decorations (designs and color), and three sets of mano and metate[70] used for grinding.

On our way back, we stopped at a geologic viewpoint. It explained that the type of sandstone and the way it eroded provided the cave-like shelters for the cliff dwellings.

At the evening campfire program, we watched an excellent slide show and talk about the CCC (Civilian Conservation Corps), which did a lot of work here as well as at other national and state parks. The CCC was started by President Franklin Roosevelt as a way of providing jobs for young men during and after the Great Depression. The men earned $1 a day and usually sent $.75 of this home to help the rest of their family. Housing and meals were provided for them. The whole setup was a lot like the military. They built trails and roads, fought forest fires, and built Visitor Centers and other buildings. The CCC ended when World War II began, and the men went into the Armed Forces. One CCC worker who was at Mesa Verde was very talented in art. He made most of the dioramas, which are still on display at the Visitor Center. Years later he came back as superintendent of the park.

---

[70] A metate is a large stone with a smooth bowl-like depression that has been worn into it by a mano, a smooth, handheld stone used for grinding.

Zion National Park, Utah

Monday, August 11, 2014

The road toward Great Basin National Park in Nevada continued through Zion National Park. When we were here in 1998, it was my least favorite of the parks in the area (Bryce, Arches, Canyonlands), but it was also the last one we visited. I think I was on rock formation overload, the same way I felt after seeing so many castles in Germany and cathedrals in France. Anyway, this time I loved it. The views were spectacular.

Great Basin National Park, Nevada

Tuesday, August 12, 2014

On the way to Great Basin National Park, we bought ice, gas, and some food. In the heat of August, ice has a limited life, so we bought it every morning and packed it into clean gallon milk jugs with the tops cut off, and into various pitchers. Then we drank the melted ice every night.

We made the turn for the park and saw a sign indicating "no services for 85 miles." Right. Just a very straight road through ranchland. There were signs indicating cattle might be crossing the road, but we saw no cattle until we were almost there. I just can't imagine living in such wilderness.

The topography of Great Basin is called basin and range. Basically, this means there are alternating mountain ranges and valleys (basins), all parallel to each other. It is caused when the earth's crust stretches, creating faults. Then the pieces between the faults either tilt or alternately rise and sink, causing the basins and ranges.

We got to the Visitor Center about noon, checked on the various campgrounds, and bought tickets for a cave tour for the next day. I also bought my own National Park Pass.[71] The cave tour only gave the discount to the cardholder. In this case it was a wash: we saved $10 on tickets and spent $10 for my pass. If the situation ever arises again, we are covered.

We set up camp at Upper Lehman Creek, which was a very rocky, wooded area with quite large sites. After lunch there we

---

[71] Most National Parks sell these passes for U.S. citizens or permanent residents age 62 or older. Passes allow free access to more than 2,000 federal recreation areas for the pass owner and three others in the same vehicle. Pass holders can get half-price camping at National Park and Bureau of Land Management campgrounds. In 2018, the cost of a lifetime America the Beautiful Senior Pass increased to $80. A twelve-month senior pass costs $20. Free annual passes are available for U.S. military personnel and for every U.S. fourth- grade student. These passes also cover up to three companions in the same vehicle.

headed back to the Visitor Center. We watched the introductory movie and then a program on meteors. The Perseid meteor showers occurred that evening, and the park would have been a great place to see the event, but there was an almost-full moon (just past) and lots of clouds.

Wednesday, August 13, 2014

Our tour of Lehman Caves began at 9:00. This cave tour was one of the best we've ever had. The ranger did a really good job of explaining things clearly and slowly enough so we could really understand them. The cave itself was beautiful. Many of the stalactites had reached the floor and joined with stalagmites to form columns. Three features I didn't remember seeing elsewhere were shields, helictites, and balls. The helictites were sort of wormlike structures coming out horizontally from other formations. The balls looked almost like Christmas decorations.

The walk was level enough and the cave was small enough to make it possible to easily see all of it. The features within the cave were basically small scale and fairly near, which made the tour feel up close and personal, especially with the excellent explanations provided by the ranger.

In one room they used to hold dances and have lunch meetings of Elks and some other groups. The entry used to be via a ladder. The original entry is closed except for a special bat entry there. The National Park Service made a tunnel entry. The ranger told about a friend who was in a cave during an earthquake and heard a sound like banging on the tunnel wall, which he demonstrated. Small, tunnel-like passages in caves are relatively safe places to be during a tornado or an earthquake. In general, the deeper underground, the safer the location.

After the tour, we took the Wheeler Peak Scenic Drive up (and down) a steep mountain road. There were some good views of the basin below. At 7,000 feet (where our campground was), there was lots of sagebrush. We think that may have been the source of the sweet smell at our campsite. At 8,000 feet there were pinyon pine and juniper. Juniper has what looks like blueberries but are really tiny pinecones. We ate lunch at an overlook and continued to the end of the trail, which is more than 10,000 feet in elevation. There's a trail to a grove of bristlecone pines that I really wanted to see. Bristlecone pines are the oldest trees in North America. They can live for 3,000 to 5,000 years, and they grow in weird shapes. Unfortunately, the hike was 3 miles roundtrip. At this elevation that's quite strenuous, so we decided against it. We came down and took the much shorter nature trail, and even that was difficult.

Dick made a fire for us so we could sit beside it and write before dinner. We usually do that after dinner, but that night we planned to attend a 7:00 program on camp cooking.

The program was interesting but really not anything we would use. Much of it involved a Dutch oven banked with coals. The only thing the ranger made that we might even consider was an apple crisp of sorts—all the ingredients wrapped in aluminum foil and cooked in the coals. She also did a demonstration of peeling garlic three ways. Dick got to shake it in a covered plastic jar for 30 seconds, which worked well.

Thursday, August 14, 2014

We stopped very briefly at another Great Basin Visitor Center and at a ranching exhibit. The latter had an edging of carved metal along the roof edge showing a ranch scene. Many of the ranchers started out west to look for gold. When they didn't find any, they stayed to ranch. Except for the use of motorized vehicles, the ranching hasn't changed much.

Pinnacles National Park, California

Saturday, August 16, 2014

The drive to Pinnacles National Park took us through a very remote area, but it was prettier than some of the others, especially the last part of the drive through a hilly region on curvy roads. The land is all very brown, but there are splotches of green trees.

We got information on hikes at the Visitor Center. The ranger suggested two hikes but said that because of the heat, we should do them only in late afternoon or early morning. So, we set up camp in a partially shaded spot and decided to read and write until 4:30 when we could hike.

We took the Moses Spring Trail. The hike took us about 1¼ hours, with about a 500-foot change in elevation as we went along. It was a more strenuous hike than I had anticipated. I let Dick go ahead for a while and I waited, but even he didn't go all the way. We did see a lot of big boulders all jumbled together, and we walked through a cave tunnel. We expected the hike we had planned for the next day to be flat, although not shady.

As evening settled in, we watched two deer grazing about 100 feet from us, and later a flock of about 15 quail moved through the campsite next to us. They went from the campground down to a dry stream bed, back up again, and then farther away into the woods. It was fun to watch them.

Sunday, August 17, 2014

When I got up at midnight, the stars were spectacular. I even saw the Milky Way.

We were at the trailhead for Old Pinnacle Trail at 8:30. Although we had left camp with sweatshirts on, we left them in the car; we definitely didn't need them as the day went on. Going out was pleasantly cool, but the return was much warmer. It was not intolerable, but it was less comfortable than the earlier part of the hike. The trail was 5.3 miles round trip but, as we had been told, it was mostly flat. It was a pleasant walk except for my hip[72] and the heat on the way back. This was definitely my limit.

When we started out, a cute, white-tailed bunny posed for us. Along the trail we saw lizards, butterflies, and birds (including several wild turkeys). During our walk out and back, we enjoyed the scenery and the solitude. We could see why someone might choose to live in such an environment. We also took lots of pictures of rocks, bugs, birds, and bushes. There were a lot of interesting things to see. Pinnacles was formed by long-ago volcanic action that, along with earthquakes, caused huge boulders to fall into narrow gorges and form caves. Dick compared them to Lost River in New Hampshire. While they are definitely pinnacles of rock, I think this park could more aptly be called Boulders.

---

[72] I had replacement surgery in January 2015.

We got as far as Balcony Caves. Dick climbed over the rocks to look inside, but we both decided I shouldn't try this. Partway back we sat on a log to eat lunch. We were by ourselves for almost the entire time, although we began seeing more people during the last hour of our four-hour trek. We both wondered why people would want to attempt a hike like this during the hottest part of the day.

The sign at the Visitor Center said that the temperature would reach 101 degrees Fahrenheit. To cook dinner, we set the Coleman stove on a low wooden curb next to our site because it was in the shade; we moved our chairs over there for dinner.

Monday, August 18, 2014

As we drove out that morning, we noticed a lot of animals. There were 20 to 30 deer in several small groups along the road, and they seemed to be very contentedly enjoying the local greenery. We also saw a flock of quail, some turkeys, and a few squirrels. It was really fun to slow down or stop and watch them. The deer especially tended to watch us—rather nervously and suspiciously I might add.

Lassen Volcanic National Park, California

Sunday, August 24, 2014

Visiting this park was my favorite part of the trip. To begin, we stopped at the Visitor Center for brochures, information, and suggestions. A short walk in a section called Devastated Area sounded interesting, but we decided to do that the next day.

Lassen Volcanic National Park is isolated but really beautiful. Lassen Peak is one of the volcanoes in the Ring of Fire (along with Pinatubo in the Philippines and Fuji in Japan). It formed 27,000 years ago as a volcanic vent on Brokeoff Volcano, and it is one of the world's largest plug dome volcanoes. The park has examples of all four kinds of volcanoes: plug dome (or lava dome), cinder cone, composite, and shield. We watched the introductory film and then set out to explore.

Just up the road from the Visitor Center was Sulphur Works. It was a very short walk from a parking lot to a vigorously boiling—and stinky sulphur-smelling—mud pot. After this we made numerous stops for the views. The road was very steep and curvy (again!) with elevation of 7,000 to 8,000 feet. I was certainly feeling the effects of elevation, and between that and my aching hip, we decided to skip the hikes, which promised to be steep.

We saw a few deer and two lovely lakes. The first one, Emerald Lake, was very green due to algae on the bottom, and the second, Lake Helen, was very blue. There were more mud pots and fumaroles, which we've seen in other places. We stopped when we got to Summit Lake North Campground, where we had reservations, and decided to see the rest of the park the next day on our way out.

All of the sites at the Summit Lake North Campground had special metal boxes to store food and "anything that smelled" (such as deodorants and other toiletries) to keep them away from bears. At this campground, we were told that keeping such things in the car was not an option. Maybe the bears there were more aggressive.

When we had been driving earlier that afternoon, we had heard several funny noises. Once we got to camp, Dick asked me if I had opened the new bag of potato chips. I hadn't, but apparently the elevation change made the bag pop open.

Monday, August 25, 2014

It was cold that morning—definitely the coldest of the trip. The oatmeal tasted good!

Our first stop was The Devastated Area. It is not devastated anymore, but in 1915 it was flooded by a layer of lava, mud, and water. The hike in and around the area provided descriptions of just what happened. This was a half-hour loop walk with excellent panels explaining the devastation that occurred when Lassen Peak erupted on May 19, 1915 and again on May 22, 1915. B. F. Loomis documented the eruption and the changing landscape with photographs and journal entries. Trees were swept off the hillside, leaving them bare, and huge boulders rolled miles away. There were explanations of the hot rocks and how they cooled. Dacite is a rock formed from lava.

We drove past piles of rocks called Chaos Jumble, and that's exactly what they looked like. We considered hiking at Manzanita Lake but decided we really didn't want to take the time, and my hip didn't need any extra walking. The scenery in the Devastated Area was quite barren, with trees blackened and defoliated from recent forest fires and piles of rock debris from volcanic eruptions, while the hydrothermal area we had seen the day before featured green forests as well as sulphur springs.

Redwood National and State Parks, California

Tuesday, August 26, 2014

We drove on curvy, steep roads to get to Redwood National and State Parks. We stopped at a Visitor Center to get maps and information on what to see. Our campground was just seven miles farther up the road and seemed to be in a good location for a lot of interesting things. Our site was compact but private. It was a good thing we had made reservations because the campground was full.

Lyndon Johnson made Redwood a national park in 1968, and his wife, Lady Bird, came here to dedicate it. There were already several state parks in the area protecting the trees. The state and federal governments now work together here.

Wednesday, August 27, 2014

We wanted to be at Lady Bird Johnson Grove at 10:00 AM for a ranger-guided tour, so we had limited time to see some of the other attractions before that. We headed north to see Corkscrew Tree and possibly Big Tree before we had to head south for Lady Bird Johnson Grove. We both missed the stop for Corkscrew Tree the first time we passed it, so it took us 10 to 15 minutes longer than we had planned on. The Corkscrew Tree was either two or three trees that had become twisted around each other as they grew, or a single tree that forked and twisted as it grew. We photographed it, and then we set out directly for the tour at Lady Bird Johnson Grove.

We got to the grove just in time for the ranger-led walk, "The Beauty That Comes with Age." The path is 1½ miles long. We did about half with the ranger and the rest on our own.

On the way, the ranger explained some of the dynamics of the redwood forest. He showed trees where the top had broken off and the top end was like an elevated bit of the forest floor with ferns and seedlings growing in it. He told us about branches that supported ground-level growth, and he described one where the understory was a few feet thick. He also described the forest as having multiple canopies—ground-level shrubs, top level of trees, and some in the middle. He pointed out lots of different plants in the understory and some of the same ones growing on bits of dirt on limbs. We saw old-growth and new-growth trees.

The redwood is the world's tallest tree, but prior to 1948 they were logged extensively. The new-growth trees have grown since logging, so they are almost 70 years old. There is much less growing under them. The Native Americans used to burn the understory to open up pathways, and the tall trees never burned like they sometimes do now. However, even after a tree has burned, it can send up new shoots. These shoots often grow in a circle around the original tree and are called cathedrals or fairy circles.

The brochure explained that fire was not only a natural occurrence but also actually essential for new life and for the forest to be maintained. The ranger had commented that Native Americans had occupied the area for approximately 10,000 years, and they had done repeated burns of the ground-level vegetation.[73] The National Park Service has adopted a program of controlled burning of protected areas.

A man who climbs the redwoods every two years to measure them has discovered animals living their entire life in a redwood, even creatures that usually live in water. The redwood vole is one animal, but there's also a salamander and some sort of crustacean.

There were a lot of varieties of ferns. The deer fern has two types of fronds: some that are evergreen, with normal-looking fronds, and some that are sort of spiky and die off in the winter.

---

[73] Native Americans in the eastern part of the continent also did repeated burnings to help with hunting and travel.

254

After lunch we drove down a very dusty, very hilly, very curvy dirt road, Davison Road, to Gold Bluff Beach. The cliffs to the side were gold-colored. Dick walked down to the beach, but I stayed near the car. This road and the meadow by our campground were said to be prime areas for viewing Roosevelt Elk, but I spotted a herd lying in the grass on the side of US 101. At first, I thought they were big woodcarvings. They were very still. One really big bull had a large rack of antlers. There were also a couple of smaller bulls, and we guessed that the rest, which had no antlers, were female. There must have been 20 to 25 of them. Quite a few cars stopped, but the elk didn't seem to care.

Our final stop of the day was the Big Tree Wayside. It was a very short walk. The tree is over 300 feet tall and is 1,500 years old. We felt like dwarfs standing next to it!

In addition to the scenic drives and ranger-led walks which we did, visitors can also explore tidepools, watch Tolowa and Yurok Native American dance demonstrations, and go on ranger-led kayak tours of the Smith River which is part of the National Wild and Scenic River System. In November, December, March, and April there are opportunities for whale watching. Redwood National and State Parks offer much more than just tall trees!

2016

(APRIL)

Big Thicket National Preserve, Texas

Jefferson National Expansion Memorial
(now Gateway Arch National Park),
Missouri

Big Thicket National Preserve, Texas

Thursday, April 14, 2016

While visiting Dick's brother and sister-in-law in Texas, we were able to take a day trip to Big Thicket National Preserve. The mosquitoes there rivaled those of the Everglades in August. At the Visitor Center, we watched a really good video about the park. However, the video suggested that visitors should stop and stand still to see and hear the birds and animals. There was no way we were standing still. On the first trail there were lots of benches where visitors could sit and observe—and get eaten alive! Fortunately, there were fewer mosquitoes on the second trail, so it was much more pleasant.

The Big Thicket was the result of different biomes coming together and meeting there over thousands of years. It is unique in that it has habitats, pushed here by the glaciers, that are more commonly found elsewhere. There are oaks like those found in the Northeast, prickly pear and yucca like those commonly found in the Southwest, and alligators like those found in Florida. It also includes bogs, swamps, and wetlands. Four of the five carnivorous plants found in the United States grow there. We took the Sundew Trail in hopes of seeing two of them, the sundew and the pitcher plant. We didn't see the sundew but

did find some pitcher plants. They were on much longer stems than ones we've seen before. We also saw bald cypress knees.

The area was so lush and wet that Native Americans and early white settlers did not consider it a good place to live. However, it was considered a good place to hide, particularly by Texans who didn't want to fight in the Civil War. The Alabama and Coushatta Native American tribes settled there when they were pushed west, and they are now on a reservation together located very close to Big Thicket National Preserve.

Jefferson National Expansion Memorial (now Gateway Arch National Park), Missouri

Thursday, April 21, 2016

I had loved the museum at the Jefferson National Expansion Memorial when we visited it in 1980, so when I realized we were driving right past it again, I suggested we stop. However, there was major construction going on, and the museum was closed. A temporary Visitor Center and a few artifacts from the museum were in the Old Courthouse, which itself was extremely interesting. It was originally a national historic site before it merged with the Arch to form the Jefferson National Expansion Memorial. We talked with a ranger who directed us to a room with a very informative video and exhibits on Dred and Harriet Scott. The Dred Scott Case started as a suit for freedom for Dred, Harriet, and their two daughters because Dred had been taken by his owner, Dr. Emerson, from the slave state of Missouri to the free state of Illinois and then to the free territory of Wisconsin. He married Harriet there, and they lived as slaves.

There were several trials with verdicts being overturned. The case eventually went to the U.S. Supreme Court, which ruled against Dred Scott. His owner, Dr. Emerson's widow, remarried and transferred ownership to Taylor Blow, who freed them in this courthouse. Dred Scott died a year later. One of his descendants was in the video that we watched.

Upstairs in the Courthouse were two courtrooms and lovely views down into the Courtroom rotunda on the first floor. We decided that this visit was well worth the stop, even though we didn't get to see the museum that we had originally expected to see.

2016

(AUGUST)

Glacier Bay National Park and Preserve, Alaska

Katmai National Park and Preserve, Alaska

Aniakchak National Monument and Preserve, Alaska

Noatak National Preserve, Alaska

Kobuk Valley National Park, Alaska

Bering Land Bridge National Preserve, Alaska

Lake Clark National Park and Preserve, Alaska

Wrangell-St. Elias National Park and Preserve, Alaska

Yukon-Charley Rivers National Preserve, Alaska

Glacier Bay National Park and Preserve, Alaska

Monday, August 1, 2016

We set a new goal for the summer: to visit all the hard-to-reach parks in Alaska. Most are accessible only by bush plane. To prepare for the trip, I used the national park website,[74] to research each of the parks in Alaska. The basic information for each park includes options for commercial air providers. We contacted several different providers and decided to use Pen Air, Back Country Flying Service, and Katmai Air.[75] We also decided not to camp since most of the parks had only wilderness camping. Campers get dropped off by bush plane with no guarantee of when they will be picked up since all flights are dependent on weather conditions. A wilderness area also offers no protection from the wild animals who live there and no on-site personnel to provide help.

We flew from Boston to Anchorage and stayed overnight at the Puffin Inn.[76] Their shuttle provided transportation to and from the airport. Breakfast was included at the inn, and we were within walking distance of a restaurant. It seemed like a great jumping-off point, and we planned to return to Anchorage as needed over the next few weeks to get flights to other more remote places.

Tuesday, August 2, 2016

Our first flight left Anchorage on time at 12:20 PM and got to Juneau before 2:00 PM. We then had to wait until 4:30 PM for the

---

[74] www.nps.gov.

[75] www.penair.com; www.arcticbackcountry.com; www.katmaiair.com.

[76] www.puffininn.net.

half-hour flight to Gustavus (long *a*). For the last 45 minutes or so there were nine passengers in the waiting area. The incoming flight with a full load of passengers deplaned, and the nine of us boarded. The plane was practically empty.

The Glacier Bay Inn bus, which looked like an old school bus, was waiting to take us to Bartlett Cove. We stood outside to get our luggage and boarded the bus for the ride to the inn, which took about 30 minutes. We arrived about 5:30. Both the buildings and the environment seemed increasingly rustic as we got closer to Glacier Bay Lodge. The buildings were rugged and made to withstand harsh environments. We were told to make reservations for dinner immediately, which I did, but the earliest I could get was 7:45 PM. I was very hungry, but this actually worked out well.

We went to our room, which was close to the bay with a beautiful view, and then went back to the Visitor Center, which is on the second floor of the inn. We looked at the exhibits and got suggestions from a ranger until it was time for a 7:00 PM ranger program about Glacier Bay, which included the geologic history of Glacier Bay and the human history of native Tlinget, who lived in the area. That night the program was given by a Hoonah Native American woman, who told us about the tribal house that was being built here. It was a $3 million project and would be dedicated on August 25, the 100th anniversary of the National Park Service. The tribal house will serve two purposes—one for the natives as a place to keep their traditions alive, and the other to educate the public.

When we went to dinner, the table we sat at was rustic, like all the other tables around us. The tops of the tables were made of wood and included knots, cracks, and bug tunnels. The edges of the tables were finished with bark-covered strips of wood.

Wednesday, August 3, 2016

Right after breakfast we headed to the boat, *Baranov Wind*. We were on the water from 7:30 AM to 3:30 PM. It was somewhat foggy although not enough to obscure views of wildlife and glaciers. When we started moving, the guide, who was a park ranger,[77] explained that for the first few miles we would be going slowly, about the same speed as the whales. This was to reduce the risk to the whales and make it safer for them.

After a little way up the bay, we started seeing increasing numbers and varieties of animals. Among the first were large colonies of sea lions. Most were on the slopes and rocks of the shore; very few were actually in the water.

We saw sea otters off and on all day. Apparently, their numbers were in the single digits 20 years ago and now there are 9,000.

We had a good view of a brown bear on a beach. The boat stopped, and we watched for quite a while as he walked along, turning over rocks to look for barnacles and other food. Later we spotted a brown bear mama and two light-colored cubs high up on a mountain.

There were several white mountain goats, again high up on a mountain. I saw the blow of a whale several times and its tail once. There were eagles on several beaches and also on trees.

There was a great variety of birds including puffins, seagulls, black-legged kittiwakes, and cormorants. One bird was described as a small bird that did better flying underwater than flying in the air.

As we continued up Glacier Bay, the ranger explained the history and present condition of ecology, environment, geology, glaciers, and human habitation. Not surprisingly, all of these things were interconnected.

---

[77] In addition to giving talks for passengers on ships leaving from the National Park, National Park rangers also sail out to cruise ships in Glacier Bay to give talks for the passengers.

One of the first stories was about the Tlinget history in the region. The Glacier Bay area actually used to be land with a gently flowing river. The Tlinget farmed and fished in the area, and there were a few thriving villages. Uphill from the area was a glacier that had been there for hundreds of years. According to Tlinget stories, about 250 to 300 years ago, the glacier started moving down the valley "at the speed of a lame dog running." Scientific evidence indicates that this actually happened. The advancing glacier wiped out the farms and villages and carved out the present Glacier Bay.

The movement of a glacier creates friction, which produces enough heat to make the bottom of the glacier melt. The melting water forms a river, over which the glacier moves quickly. Our map showed where the edge of the glacier was in various years. It has definitely retreated a lot.

The ranger also told us about a time a whale beached itself and died. The bears had a feast. Prior to this, a group of scientists had attached some barbed wire to a tree to snag fur so they could use the DNA to identify which bears had been there. After the bears' feast, their fur was all greasy from the whale blubber, and when the fur was tested it came back 100 percent whale DNA!

A related story explained how one of these whale-eating bears used a barnacle-covered rock to comb its fur to remove some of the grease. When a rock got too greasy, the bear would throw it away and get another one.

Glacier Bay is sort of Y-shaped. We went up the westernmost part of the Y to the John Hopkins Glacier. We saw the Margerie Glacier from a distance and got up very close to the John Hopkins Glacier—we sat there for about 30 minutes. We heard some very loud crashes and splashes and watched one small piece calve. The face of the glacier had some deep wrinkles and indentations, so a lot of calving was happening in places we couldn't see. The glaciers were still spectacular, but there was more dirt and rocks in them than the beautiful glacial blue that I remembered. We were next to the Lamplugh Glacier. The mountains here are the Fairweather Mountains.

Our boat went right up to the shore to pick up two campers. The crew put out a ladder and the men climbed aboard. We also circled by another beach where they had dropped off campers some time earlier. They weren't scheduled for a pickup, but the captain wanted to check to make sure there wasn't a problem.

Lunch was included with our boat trip: a huge sandwich, chips, lemonade, and an apple. When we finished, I said to Dick that all I would like was a chocolate chip cookie. He bought me a bag of Famous Amos cookies, which were fine. Then about an hour before the end of the trip, a crew member came around with a tray of chocolate chip cookies. They must have read my mind!

We were almost to the Canadian border. We were also the farthest visitors can be from a road anywhere in North America. On our way back down the bay, we watched the progression of the landscape along the sides of the bay. When the glacier suddenly advanced, it scraped off all vegetation down to bare rock. As soon as the glacier stopped advancing, it began to recede. As it receded, the ground on the sides of the bay were exposed and became reseeded (from *receding* to *reseeding*). The sides nearest the glacier were the most recently exposed and had vegetation that reminded me of a tundra: basically, grasses and some small shrubs. Gradually, as we went farther from the glacier, we passed by slopes that had been exposed longer. They had larger shrubs and more deciduous trees, with an occasional small conifer. Near the lowest end of the bay, where the slopes had been exposed the longest, there was a mature evergreen forest of Sitka spruce. It was interesting to see the transition.

Gustavus is flat because it's a glacial moraine. Bartlett Cove is on a hill where the moraine got pushed up. The cabins were on different levels with lots of steps and no easy way to move luggage but with beautiful views of the bay

When we got back from the boat trip, we had just enough time to get to the 4:00 PM talk with a ranger. She talked about the movement of glaciers and the rocks that get dropped. At 5:00 PM, we watched the movie, *Reflections of Glacier*, about underwater life in Glacier Bay. Just as there was an above-ground ecological progression, there was also an underwater ecological progression. The movie described how simple sea life enters first into new areas and then progresses until it includes kelp, barnacles, anemones, plankton, fish, and more. There was a comparison with the above-ground forest growth. In both cases, it starts with very simple things, and then it grows to include complex mixtures of life. The movie said that the underwater flora and fauna of Glacier Bay is very rich.

After the movie, we went to supper, and then we went to one last presentation, which was basically a talk that provided an overview of the history and ecology of Glacier Bay. We didn't learn anything new, but it was a good summary.

Thursday, August 4, 2016

After breakfast we went out to walk along the shore during low tide. It was very foggy when we started, but gradually the fog lifted for some beautiful views of the bay and the mountains beyond. Parts of the shore had grass growing in areas that were right next to very wet tidal areas. When I asked a ranger later, he said even those areas are covered whenever there is a very high tide. As we walked along the beach, we noticed an abundance and a variety of rocks, kelp, moss, grass, shells, and soggy beach sand. We also noticed an increasing abundance of sunlight and diminishing clouds. When we reached the dock where we had taken the boat the previous day, the air was very clear for the half of the bay closest to us and gradually foggier toward the other side. The boats close to us had a very clear reflection in the water, but those near the middle of the bay showed little or no reflection.

We walked by the new tribal house but couldn't go inside. The Tlinget had considered the Glacier Bay region as their homeland, but they had to leave and live elsewhere after their land was covered by the glacier. A recent agreement between the Tlinget and the National Park Service involved the building of a Clan House for the few Tlinget clans that had been here before they were forced out. Traditionally, each clan had their own clan house, but this one was being built to serve four clans.

Because this plan was less traditional, the approach needed some modifications. Usually, the decorations on the front of a clan house were related to that clan, but since four clans were now involved, the decoration on the front had to be more generic. Inside the house, each clan would have its own post with its own clan symbols. The house was set to be dedicated on August 25, which is when we would be on our way home. I wished we had realized this was happening. We could have done some of the other parks in reverse order and been at Glacier Bay on August 25.

There were signs identifying some plants. Devil's Club has the huge leaves we've been noticing. Baneberry has bright-red berries that are very poisonous—eating them can be fatal. The start of every ranger presentation warns about these.

We saw the bones of a whale named Snow, who was hit by a cruise ship in 2001. The rangers let animals eat the flesh. Then they allowed the whale to decompose in nature before scrubbing the bones and setting them up in an exhibit. The skeleton is huge. There was also a dugout canoe that was made in the traditional way about 20 years ago.

After lunch we watched a movie titled *Forever Wild*. It described very well the changes we learned about and saw the previous day with respect to Glacier Bay.

Our last activity was a ranger-led hike on the forest loop trail. The sun shining on all the green of the forest floor was beautiful. One of the first things the ranger pointed out to us was what he called a "squirrel midden." It was basically a large pile of scraps from nut shells and seed coverings. It reminded us of the pile of wood chips left by a pileated woodpecker in the woods at Congaree National Park.

Dick wrote,

The rain forest features we saw as we walked along (moss, mushrooms, decaying trees) reminded me of the arch-based trees we saw in Olympic National Park. I remember seeing trees with an arched opening at their bases, where the arch was about three feet high and about three feet wide. For the arch to form, a tree had to start growing on top of a downed tree, and then have the downed tree rot away to leave the arch-shaped opening. I'm guessing that the process needed to form an arch like that could take 500 to 800 years: 200 to 300 years for a tree to grow and then fall down; another 100 to 200 years to partially rot away; and then another 200 to 300 years for a new tree to grow on top of it and support itself. The Glacier Bay rain forest was 250 to 300 years old, so it was probably too young to have arches of that size. There could have been some smaller arches, but I didn't see any. The walk gave us a detailed look at what one would find in a temperate rain forest. This is actually a part of the temperate rain forest that extends from southeast Alaska, along the western coast of Canada, down to the coast of the northwestern United States. There is green growing everywhere—on branches, on rocks, on the ground. There were a couple of ponds, one of which had pond lilies growing in it.

We got back to the lodge in time to get the shuttle to the airport. It was a 13-minute flight from Gustavus to Juneau. Again, we flew over the Mendenhall Glacier—interesting to see it from the air. From Juneau we flew back to Anchorage. I thought we were going to be able to buy food on this second flight, but it wasn't available. We could have bought a box lunch at the lodge. Obviously, we should have.

Katmai National Park and Preserve, Alaska

Friday, August 5, 2016

This was a long day after a short night. We had granola and juice in our room this morning because we had to leave so early, but when we came downstairs, breakfast was set out, so I had half a muffin and more juice. We had about an hour's flight on a two-prop plane. They served juice (in a bottle, so I saved it) and Famous Amos cookies (which I also saved).

It was a short flight to King Salmon. When we got to the King Salmon airport, a Katmai representative met us. He took us to their office, where we stored our luggage. Then we weighed ourselves and our backpacks so they could determine how many people could go on a flight, and how best to distribute the weight on the plane. Weather didn't allow a trip to Aniakchak that day, but we were able to go to Brooks Lodge at Katmai National Park. What an experience!

It started when we boarded a five-passenger seaplane, which involved climbing up a thin-runged ladder. Surprisingly, I really enjoyed the flight to Brooks Lodge. We flew over the Alagnak River with many small islands and little ponds. When we landed on Naknek Lake, workers from Brooks Lodge pulled the plane to the beach. Getting off involved walking on a plank (maybe one foot wide) over the shallow water before stepping onto the muddy shore.

First order of business was "Bear Orientation," a mandatory film and talk. We had to leave *all* food in a special bear-proof cache, so we couldn't have any snacks as we walked. This meant that we had to find all our granola bars, which we had scattered in waist packs, backpacks, and Dick's camera bag. We kept one package of granola bars, which we took across the path to a picnic area surrounded by an electric fence. It was too early to eat lunch, but a snack seemed like a good idea.

Katmai was first declared a national monument to preserve the area where there had been a huge volcanic eruption in 1912. This is the Valley of Ten Thousand Smokes. The eruption was from the Novarupta Volcano, which was 10 times stronger than the eruption of Mount St. Helens in 1980 and one of the world's largest in the last few thousand years. I would have loved to take the tour to The Valley of Ten Thousand Smokes, but visitors have to stay overnight at the *very* expensive Brooks Lodge.

Now it's become equally important to protect brown bears there. For this reason, it became a national park and preserve in 1980. Bears we got to see! Alaska's brown bears and grizzlies are now considered one species. Grizzlies are those living 100 miles or more inland. Brown bears are bigger than grizzlies because of their rich fish diet. We saw our first bear of the day as it walked down the path behind the food cache.

We had to check in at the office to confirm the time of our flight back: 6 PM (so we had to be back there by 5 PM). We then started down the path but hadn't gotten past the trading post on the back side of the office when we were stopped by a ranger who said we had to wait for a "bear jam" to clear. A group of about 20 people was gathered on the hill because a sow and her two cubs were right near the path, and people are supposed to stay 50 yards away from any bear. After we had been there a few minutes, the rangers decided to try a detour for 10 people. We were in that group. We walked down to the beach—very narrow and rocky, with shrubs—but partway along, another ranger reported that a bear had "popped up," so we had to turn around and go back to the hill. We waited a while longer. Rangers were still radioing information when suddenly the bear and two big cubs ambled across the path in front of us. Ironically, they came to within about 30 yards before they passed by and headed toward open territory. Apparently, the bears are not aware of the rule to stay 50 yards away from humans. As they moved out of the way, we went partway down the path, where we had to wait again because of bears close to the bridge.

We were cautioned that both ends of the bridge had to be clear of bears, and we were not supposed to stop on the bridge to take pictures or pause for any other reason because bears can get on the bridge; we walked quickly. Just before we got to the bridge, we had to wait again for a short time, but then we were able to cross. The rangers kept in touch with each other constantly with a fairly sophisticated communication system.

To get to the bridge, we had to get our shoes a little wet. The entry (and exit) points go under the water, especially if someone heavy is in front. Once across the bridge, we climbed up to an overlook and watched a couple of bears about 100 yards away swimming in the river. We watched for a few minutes and then walked to the falls.[78]

Although I think it was just over half a mile from the river to the falls, it seemed like a long walk. There were two viewing points at the falls. We did both, but the upper falls spot was definitely the place to be. There were two bears actually at the falls and one a little farther down. One bear was sitting in the water near the base of the falls; the other was standing and was a bit more active. The falls are not particularly high, but the

---

[78] A live webcam allows the public to watch bears at the falls. Check out www.explore.org.

salmon were struggling to leap up. Some of them made it, and a couple were grabbed by bears.

Between the two viewpoints, there were informative exhibits about bears. Cubs stay with the mothers for two years; the mothers can reproduce again in the third year. The bears eat 90 pounds of salmon a day during the summer months. One five-pound salmon has 4,500 calories.

When we headed back, we were stopped by a staff member who is a wildlife biologist working on his PhD. He was on a tractor but had gotten word that there was a bear on the path. So, we hung out with this man until he got word that we could get to the viewing platform at the river. The bridge was closed because of bear activity but reopened shortly after we got there.

We got back to the lodge about 1:00 PM for lunch. This was a good thing since it closed at 1:30. Dick had soup and salad and I had the buffet—salmon, mac and cheese, vegetables, and salad. We both had lemonade and bars for dessert.

We bought postcards and then headed to the Visitor Center for a guided cultural walk to see evidence of past dwellings. This area was apparently well-populated because they showed us a map that marked hundreds of dwelling sites. Archeology indicated that the dwellings were partially underground, which helped keep them warm in the winter. The walk involved stops at places that showed something about the people who lived here 4,000 years ago (e.g., plants they might have eaten, places they might have lived). There are 900 places that have archeological significance, but most have not been excavated. Artifacts are still being found right on the ground.

On our walk the ranger pointed out a plant called watermelon berry. It has bright-red seeds, which are found in abundance in bear scat. There were depressions in the ground that might have been places for homes or meeting places. The people who lived here would have worn waterproof clothes made of animal intestines. The cultural site has the framework of a house that was reconstructed on the site of an original house. The entry was lower than the living space, which was a way of keeping out cold air.

The ranger who took us on the cultural walk opened the theater building to show us a tapeworm from a bear (huge—yuck) and some skeleton heads of animals.

After the guided tour, Dick asked some rangers about something he had seen and photographed. On the side of the road to the waterfall outlook, he had seen two places that looked like they had been clawed by bears. The rangers agreed with him and added that the gray layer that showed the claw marks was a deposit of volcanic ash from an explosion of the volcano Novarupta in 1912.

We were both exhausted at this point, so we went to the lodge to read and write, even though we would have had time to hike for two more hours. While we were there it started to rain fairly hard. We went out on the porch and met another couple, Kathy and Eric Johnson, who were also trying to visit all the national park sites.[79] They were about 20 behind us. They were are also trying to go to Aniakchak and Alagnak, so we discussed sharing the cost of the plane with them. Our 6 PM flight back to King Salmon didn't leave until about 6:45.

The Katmai Air tour people brought us to the inn where we were staying. They said they probably wouldn't know whether we'd be able to do Aniakchak the next day until about 12:30 PM, but they promised to call us either way.

---

[79] Travelers can buy a National Park passport and get it stamped at each park. We never did this because we had started visiting the parks years before this program was initiated. There is also a National Park Travelers Club: www.parkstamps.org/index.php.

Aniakchak National Monument and Preserve, Alaska

Sunday, August 7, 2016

Due to poor weather, we hadn't been able to get to any parks on the previous day, but as soon as we got to the Katmai Air office that morning—after picking up Eric and Kathy Johnson, whom we had met at Katmai—we were able to leave for Aniakchak National Monument and Preserve. It was great to share stories with people who had similar interests and similar experiences. The plane had room for five passengers. I sat in the back, which was very hard to get in and out of, but I managed. As soon as we got on the plane it started to rain, but within a few minutes the sun was shining.

The scenery on the way to Aniakchak was beautiful, and somewhat different from anything we had seen before. Probably the biggest difference was the fact that we were seeing it from 500 feet up in the air. It allowed us to see more of the overall geographical details than we could have seen from the ground. One thing that struck us was the different shades of green. There was bright green from new growth (maybe grass), dark green and blue green from other growth, and brownish green, probably from moss. I was impressed by the many small lakes.

There were also lots of patterns, shapes, and textures. The land was very flat, so any flowing water followed a meandering path. We could even see places where the meanders had broken off and become oxbow lakes. Some of them had dried and filled, and now those had bright-green, new grass in them. There were also places where the ground had frozen and cracked and thawed, leaving patterns like a mosaic. Other places showing deposits of dirt and silt were brownish orange, which added to the color drama because it contrasted so strongly with the greens. Dick commented that he really enjoys Nature's artwork.

Aniakchak is a caldera formed by the collapse of a 7,000-foot volcanic mountain. It was unknown until 1920. As we approached the caldera, we could see the rim, which had very tall hills with snow on them. A low spot in the rim, called The Gates, is where the water drains from Surprise Lake, which is the lake in the caldera.

When Aniakchak erupted 3,700 years ago, the eruption was far larger than any of those we were familiar with, including Fuji, Krakatoa, and Mount St. Helens. After the eruption, the mountain was surrounded by a deposit of ash and tephra that extended about 20 miles in all directions. This effectively separated tribes on the northern peninsula from those on the southern peninsula, so they developed differently, linguistically and culturally.

Two of the largest eruptions on earth were on the Alaskan Peninsula: Aniakchak about 3,700 years ago and Novarupta in 1912. About 2,000 years ago, the lake in the caldera breached the wall and flooded the area southeast of the volcano, creating a new river (the Aniakchak) in the process. The flood was so huge, it carried truck-sized rocks seven miles down the slope. This enormous flood is what created the notch in the caldera wall, The Gates.

En route Kathy and Dick each saw a bear. We landed on a black sand beach. Once we were on the ground, we hiked up a hill. Our pilot joined us in picking raspberries, blueberries, and huckleberries, all of which were abundant—and delicious! We also went a little way up the slope of Vent Mountain, the small volcano now inside the caldera, so we could get a wider view. It was all very pretty, and it was amazing to think of the history of it. The views were spectacular.

Apparently Aniakchak is THE hardest park to get to. Only 2 out of 20 parties that wanted to go to Aniakchak so far that summer had actually been able to get there, so we were really lucky. As we flew out, we got one last look at the inside walls of the caldera, and then we exited through The Gates.

We flew back to Anchorage that night and planned to leave for Kotzebue, 35 miles north of the Arctic Circle, the next day.

Monday, August 8, 2016

We got to the airport more than two hours early—it was either sit in the hotel lobby or the airport. Fortunately, the flight left on time.

Our arrival at the airport in Kotzebue was chaotic. The terminal was very small, and it was jam-packed with people coming and going. There wasn't even a sign showing where the baggage would come out. Bags were pushed out through an opening in the wall—no moving belt. The first bunch seemed to be big packages: toilet paper, paper towels, and a large-screen TV. Once our bags came out, we didn't know how to get to the hotel. Someone pointed it out to us and said it was about a mile walk, but we knew that would be hard with luggage. After standing outside for a while, we finally got a cab.

We shared a salad at the hotel restaurant, which overlooks water—Kotzebue Sound—and then walked to the grocery store. We bought enough for our three breakfasts here and lunch the next day (we even bought two peeled, hardboiled eggs!).

It was still light when we went to bed. I think sunset is 11:40 PM.

Tuesday, August 9, 2016

After breakfast we walked to the office of Arctic Back Country at the airport. Originally, we had planned to go to Cape Krusenstern National Monument, Kobuk Valley National Park, and Noatak National Preserve that day and Bering Land Bridge National Preserve the next. However, they told us that someone who was coming in that night wanted to go to the first three parks, plus Gates of the Arctic, which we had been to in 1995. We could do all four the next day by splitting the cost with him. We were told to come back at 11:00 AM to see about Bering Land Bridge.

We went across the street to the Northwest Alaska Arctic Heritage Center, which is the park headquarters. They had some interesting exhibits and a small gift shop. There was a beautiful "picture" made of fabric, which I loved. It wasn't for sale, which is probably a very good thing. I would have bought it.

We went back to the airport and were told that we could do all four of our original parks the next day (Wednesday). The other person wasn't coming, but Arctic Back Country was short a pilot on Tuesday. Stacy, the woman at the desk, suggested a small gift shop to check out and told us where we could go blueberry picking.

We looked at the gift shop—a couple of large dioramas that were lovely, expensive, and impossible for us to transport and some lovely birch-bark baskets that we didn't need.

After leaving our backpacks at the hotel, we headed out to pick blueberries. Once we got out of town, we walked past Swan Lake and over two bridges. We walked about 2½ miles from the hotel without seeing any berries, primarily because we expected to be able to see the bushes from the road. After another few hundred feet, we went off to the side into a bushy, tundra-like field and found lots of them. We picked for most of an hour and got about three cups. There were plenty to pick. It must have been right at the end of the season, because I didn't see a single green berry, and a few were overripe. Fortunately, no bears were blueberry picking in that area.

When we got back to the room, we divided the blueberries into three batches. We were planning to eat one batch as our dessert after dinner that night, and each of the other two for breakfast over the next two days. After dinner, we walked to a nearby store and bought a small container of vanilla ice cream to have with our blueberries. There was just enough ice cream for each of us to have one serving with some blueberries. The blueberry/ice cream mix was very good.

Wednesday, August 10, 2016

We had blueberries along with the rest of our breakfast food. I had mine with yogurt—delicious!

We walked over to the Arctic Back Country office, and they were ready for us. It seemed almost like cheating—four national park sites in one day with lots of short flights.

The first stop was Cape Krusenstern National Monument, which is on the Chukchi Sea. On the way to our stop, we saw a herd of musk ox. The area where we landed was flat tundra. We walked around for a few minutes and took pictures, but there wasn't much to do.

Noatak National Preserve, Alaska

It was a short trip to Noatak National Preserve. En route our pilot, Eric, pointed out a moose, which I never would have seen on my own. We flew over the Noatak River, which was a beautiful braided, meandering river.[80] From start to end, it is probably 600 miles as the crow flies, but because of the meandering, the water probably travels more like 1,200 miles.

We landed on a gravel beach, one of Mother Nature's few paved "runways," beside the Agie (short for Agasbastok) River. The rocks on the beach were very rounded and colorfully textured. I loved the views here—mountains, river, stones. Coming in, I noticed some of the skinniest trees I'd ever seen. Eric said they were black spruce. The river floods in the spring, all the way up to the trees. He told me that if this land wasn't protected by the federal government, miners would be in here digging it up for valuable minerals. It probably would never be settled, but the wildlife and beautiful scenery would certainly be disturbed.

Visitors can get dropped off at any of these parks to camp, but I'm not ready for wilderness camping with bears. The rivers and ponds that we saw as we were coming in were beautiful.

---

[80] A braided river starts as a single stream but gradually splits into several streams that intertwine with each other.

Kobuk Valley National Park, Alaska

It was very foggy much of the way as we flew over the Kobuk River. On the way in, we could see large ranges of sand dunes, and we landed on top of one—something I never expected. The sand was created by the grinding action of glaciers and carried to the Kobuk Valley by wind. There were small grasses and flowers growing here.

When we got out of the plane, we walked around to look at the dune features. Dick wrote,

One thing I noticed were small plants that looked a bit like grass and were a few feet apart from each other. I soon realized that I could tell which plants were very new and which had been there the longest. The "older" plants had a trail of sand pointing downwind behind them. Newer plants had a smaller, shorter sand trail, and those with no sand trail were the newest. As I was looking at the plants with sand trails, I noticed that there was steady wind blowing, and it was in the direction that would form the existing sand trails. That implied to me that the wind in that area was quite steady. Along with the sand trails behind the plants, the whole top surface of the dunes had ripples perpendicular to the direction of the wind.

Bering Land Bridge National Preserve, Alaska

After a brief break for us to use the bathroom at the office and for Eric to fill the gas tank, we took off again, this time to Bering Land Bridge National Preserve. When we arrived, the pilot did an almost-landing. He touched down on a narrow sand beach, rolled a short way to leave some tire tracks, took off again, and then circled around to actually make a landing. He explained that the tracks he left in the sand gave him a reference point for the best way to land the plane.

This is apparently a very active beach. Just after we landed, we saw a caribou atop a ridge above the plane. As we walked along the beach, we noticed lots of animal footprints, but we couldn't be sure what they were. Some were seagull footprints, and some looked like they might have been bear. A little further down, there were three sets of parallel footprint tracks. Each trail was about 12 to 18 inches apart, and these were clearly identifiable. One trail was bear prints, one trail was caribou, and one trail was seagull. Not far from there was a trail of just bear prints that ran clearly for 100 to 200 feet. We climbed a little way up the dune, which had the usual tall grass but also some very low, very green plants.

The spot where we landed was about 100 miles from Russia; Russia is 40 miles from the end of the beach. Eric said that any trash that washes up is almost all Russian. The land bridge was here about 13,000 years ago, when the sea was at lower levels. One theory, which had been discredited recently, was that early man had walked to North America over this land bridge.

When we left, the takeoff was as different as the landing. Eric wanted to take off in the same direction as we had landed, so he taxied back to the point of touch down. The only problem was that the higher, flat part of the beach where he had landed was very narrow, and he had to taxi back on a more sloped part of the beach, which was closer to the water. When he got to the point where he would start his taxi for takeoff, he had to get back up from the sloped beach to the flatter part of the beach. The ridge between the two parts was soft, and he really had to gun the engine to get back up to where he needed to be. Taxi and takeoff were okay, and we were soon back to Kotzebue.

All of the parks we visited that day were wilderness areas. We never saw another person or even another bush plane. From Kotzebue we flew to Nome, where we had arranged to stay for two nights. Although no national parks are located in Nome, the Visitor Center for Bering Land Bridge is there, so we wanted to stop in to get a brochure. One line in that brochure struck me: "The park is difficult for the average traveler to reach." I guess we're not your average travelers.

Lake Clark National Park and Preserve, Alaska

Sunday, August 14, 2016

We had flown from Nome to Anchorage on the previous evening. The shuttle from our hotel took us to the office of Lake Clark Air. Fortunately, I had brought the address, because it was hard to find. We sat out front for a few minutes before Dick figured out that we had to go around back. Another couple, Lorena and Bill, was there waiting. The four of us were on time for the 7 AM check-in but had to wait a few minutes for the office to open. Workers weighed us and our bags, and then we waited again. More and more people crowded into the little room. I was glad the four of us had seats.

Around 8:00, they called for those going to The Farm Lodge in Port Alsworth. There were eight or nine of us on a slightly larger bush plane than we had been taking on previous trips. The flight took about an hour. It started out over flat tundra with mountains in the distance, some poking up through clouds. Then we got to Lake Clark Pass, and the scenery was spectacular. We were very close to the mountains and the glaciers. We could see rivers and lakes, steep hills, snow-capped mountains, glaciers coming off the mountains, and streams from melting ice flowing down steep hillsides. I don't remember glaciers at Gates of the Arctic National Park, but the mountainous scenery was very much the same. We landed on a dirt runway right at The Farm Lodge,[81] where we would be staying for two nights. Port Alsworth was homesteaded in the early 1940s by Leon "Babe" Alsworth and his wife, Mary, and The Farm Lodge is still run by members of the Alsworth family.

A teenage girl met us and walked us over to the cabins. Ours wasn't quite ready, so we waited in the lodge until she

---

[81] www.thefarmlodge.com.

came to get us. It was a very simple cabin—just our style. There was a porch with chairs in front, a boardwalk, and then the lake. There was also a seaplane docked right in front, and a flock of ducks huddled around it. We had a beautiful view not only of the lake but also of the mountains. There are several large cirques[82] on the mountains.

We were just finishing unpacking when a young man came with our lunches. They were huge. We each had a sandwich, chips, an apple, a homemade cookie, a candy bar, a chocolate mint, apple juice, and water. Oh, also more gorp, in addition to the two bags that were in our room when we arrived.

We took some of the lunch with us—later we realized we should have brought more of the liquid—and headed out. We walked across the two runways and up one of them to get to the Lake Clark National Park Visitor Center.

The ranger was wonderful. He gave a little talk just for us at three exhibits outside the Visitor Center. The first exhibit was a boat about 30 feet long that had been used for salmon fishing. The salmon were caught in nets and hauled up onto the boat. Two men would stay on the boat for about eight weeks, sleeping under a tent/canopy at one end, right next to the bins of fish. When the boat was full, they would sail toward a barge, where they would unload the fish using a short pole (about five feet long) with a curved point. In a single motion, they would swing the pole down, poke the fish with the curved point, continue the motion to lift the fish up, and stop at the top of the swing, allowing the fish to slip off the hook and onto the barge. When the barge was full, it would then take the fish to a cannery.

These boats were hand-powered and wind-powered craft, so they became less useful for fishing when the fishing boats were allowed to use motors. The boat was then repurposed to be used for collecting firewood.

The second exhibit was a steam engine that was brought by dog sled, in pieces, for sawing lumber. The ranger explained that

[82] Cirques are large hollows formed by glacial erosion.

the natives could get boards cut from trees they had harvested. Because theirs was not a cash economy, they paid for this service by bringing extra trees, which the sawmill would keep and then cut and sell.

The third exhibit was a fish cache and drying rack. The salmon cache was a block-shaped structure made of square logs with spaces between them, and the drying rack was made of horizontal sticks. The ranger explained that the fish had to be dried before it was put into the cache. To dry it, they would cut off the head, then cut the fish vertically in half up to the base of the tail. They would then clean out the insides and turn the fish inside out, draping it over a stick on the drying rack. When the fish was dried, it could be smoked and then stored in the cache. Each layer of fish in the cache would be separated by a layer of sticks to ensure proper air circulation so the fish would stay dry. We were told that the cache could hold 3,000 fish. These would be eaten not only by the family but also by the sled dogs. The cache roof was sod on top of copper, but at one time it would have been sod on top of old gas cans that were cut apart. The cache had been reused and rebuilt a few times. Dick liked the way the ends of the logs were cut at angles so they would fit solidly together without the need for pegs to hold them.

We ate lunch on the front porch of the Visitor Center. Dick cut the sandwich in half using the clip part of the top of a Bic pen.

Then we set off to hike. We decided to go to Tanalian Falls. It was billed as moderate difficulty, but it was really hard. The first part of the trail was very muddy in places. Sometimes we had to walk on the very edge of the path to avoid the water. There were several fairly steep inclines. At three places along the trail there were benches—much appreciated, especially on the way up. At times I wasn't sure I could make it, but I got to the Lower Falls. We decided not to go the extra 0.8 mile to the Upper Falls and Lake Kontrashibuna. On the way back, Dick found me a branch to use as a hiking pole (I had left mine in the cabin). The pole definitely helped, but my legs were exhausted when we got back—according to our pedometers we had each walked about 21,000 steps.

The Lower Falls was beautiful. There was a huge boulder at the base of the falls, and the water really sprayed up around it. Views of mountains from the trails were great too. At one point we could actually see the lodge of The Farm Lodge.

It sprinkled briefly while we were hiking, but by the time we got back the sun was shining. We enjoyed sitting outside and looking at the lake, the mountains, and the ducks while we wrote.

Dinner was served in the lodge. There were only seven of us that night. A grandson of the owner came over to say grace. He was going to be a senior in high school.

Monday, August 15, 2016

Right after breakfast, we hiked to Beaver Pond. Although this hike was also billed as "moderate," it was a much easier moderate than what we had experienced the previous day. For one thing, it was much more level, although there were some ups and downs and quite a few muddy spots. The path varied among packed dirt, a dirt trench several inches deep, muddy puddles, sections covered by networks of exposed roots, boardwalks, and one section that looked like a rocky trough. The latter section had rocks in the bottom with the sides supported by large, flat rocks about a foot across, placed vertically. Between the side rocks, the path floor was covered by golf ball to baseball-sized rocks to provide solid footing. It must have taken a lot of work to make that section, but it was stable to walk on.

On the trail we saw Lorena and Bill, whom we had met the previous day. They were hiking further to Tanalian Mountain. A friend of their daughter works at The Farm Lodge and thought she could arrange a tour of the greenhouse for 3 PM, so we agreed to meet them a little before 3. The beaver pond was particularly tranquil, with a lovely, clear reflection of the mountains in the water. A *huge* dragonfly landed on Dick's back, and we watched one bird skittering across the water. Dick got some pictures of that bird flapping its wings slightly to raise itself a bit, and then running along the surface of the pond. The bird would flap-run left to right, then float back to the left to about the same starting position, and flap-run again.

We didn't see any beavers at the pond, but there was abundant evidence that they had been there at some time, including a dome-shaped mound of what looked like sticks and mud. I couldn't see it well because it was way on the other side of the pond, but it definitely looked like a beaver-made structure.

The strongest evidence of beaver habitation was several short stumps that looked like they had been gnawed off by beaver teeth. The stumps appeared to have been there for several years; they were all gray or rotting. None had been freshly cut or chewed.

We also saw a large clump of fireweed that had gone to seed. Each flower stalk was covered with cottony clumps. I don't remember seeing any cottony fireweed during our trip to Alaska 20 years ago. At that time in July they were all full of fresh blossoms.

When we came down the trail, we went to the Visitor Center again and watched a film on the history of the area from 1900 to 2000. The first white settlers brought diseases—measles and something else—that wiped out 25 percent of the native population. If we ever return, I plan to go to Dick Proehneke's cabin. He built it himself and lived in the wilderness for 33 years. We could have watched several long videos about his life and/or bought several books of his journals, but we decided to save that for next time. This is a place we'd both be happy to visit again. I probably wouldn't hike, but I'd go for the scenery and go to Proehneke's cabin.

We ate the bag lunch we had picked up at breakfast in the lodge. Then we tried to use FaceTime with our 11-year-old granddaughter Hannah in Venezuela. I suddenly got a connection to Comcast, so I was able to send some more pictures and read email.

FaceTime worked—sort of. We had to reconnect a couple of times. Today was their first day of school, so we were able to get firsthand reports, which I loved. They got to see a seaplane take off from the lake in front of our cabin, but the noise made it hard for us to hear each other.

The kids here—at least the Alsworth grandchildren—learn to fly at an early age (around 11), although they can't get their license until they are 17. However, they can drive ATVs at any age.

Thinking about the previous day, I decided that the hike to Tanalian Falls ranked third in difficulty after Fuji and Machu Picchu. I was sorry we couldn't get all the way to the lake, but I just couldn't go any farther.

We returned to our cabin to sit outside on our porch. The view was *so* beautiful and peaceful. Bill and Lorena came to get us just before 3:00, and we all went on a tour of The Farm Lodge's gardening facilities. Some of the plants were being grown outdoors, and some were being grown in what the workers called "tunnels," which were essentially plastic-covered greenhouses. They grow until the first frost, about the first of October. The greenhouses are about 10 degrees Fahrenheit warmer than outside temperatures, which were in the 60s and 70s when we were there. They seemed to have everything imaginable growing: tomatoes, zucchini, corn, asparagus, strawberries. Outside there were *huge* rhubarb plants (stems and leaves about three or four feet long), along with potatoes and other things. The young woman who gave us the tour had just graduated from college with a degree in horticulture. It was her first year working at The Farm Lodge. They raise a lot of their own food, and they are even able to sell some.

Three young women came in to the lodge today. When they heard what we are doing with national parks, one of them called us her "heroes." They said we should create a blog, but I told them a book was more likely.

Tuesday, August 16, 2016

It was a spectacular trip back to Anchorage. Even the pilot said it was one of the best ever—jagged mountain peaks, snow, glaciers, sun until close to Anchorage, when we were flying over a bed of clouds.

Wrangell-St. Elias National Park and Preserve, Alaska

Saturday, August 20, 2016

Wrangell-St. Elias is the largest national park in the United States; it is six times the size of Yellowstone. In 1995, before we were visiting national parks in earnest, we had driven by the entrance to the park but decided the drive in would be too difficult.

This time we had rented a car for the last few days of our trip. The drive from Palmer to Copper Center was very scenic. We stopped multiple times to take pictures. We stopped at the Wrangell/St. Elias National Park Visitor Center (which is actually outside the boundaries of the national park) at 5 PM and found out there would be a ranger-led walk at 6:00 and a PowerPoint talk at 7:30, both of which we wanted to do.

We set out to find the bed and breakfast but had to go back to the Visitor Center to ask directions. It turned out that Sawing Logzz B & B is on the *Old* Richardson Highway, which turns off from the Richardson Highway. We got there with just enough time to drop our bags and head to the Copper River Princess Lodge, where the walk and talk would occur. Apparently, this lodge works with Princess Tours and the National Park Service (sort of like Glacier Bay sends rangers out to cruise ships).

We got to the lodge with enough time to make a reservation for dinner and get to the walk, which was along an easy trail. At one point there was a view where we could see a couple of local rivers, a major road/highway, and part of the Alaskan pipeline. Ranger Joseph was excellent. He was a former teacher, and he used a lot of teaching skills. He divided us into four groups and asked trivia questions. Our group won—Wrangell/St. Elias stickers. One question we got wrong was Alaska's state insect: the dragonfly.

After dinner we went to Ranger Joseph's PowerPoint talk, "Bite Goes the Weasel," which was really well done. The largest weasel is the wolverine. The ranger gave an example of a wolverine catching prey and carrying it a long distance, equating it to us picking up a large dog with our teeth and running with it for four miles. Smaller weasels have been known to jump on the back of a bird and fly with it, biting the back of its neck and holding on until the bird drops. They also kill rabbits significantly larger than they are by jumping on the rabbit's back and biting the back of its neck.

Ranger Joseph also explained the origin of the old rhyme that ends in "Pop goes the weasel." In the rhyme, the word *weasel* usually referred to a fur coat, possibly because fur coats could have been made from weasel relatives, including ermine. The word *pop* referred to having to sell the coat to borrow money, with the intent of repaying the "loan" and getting the coat back. If money was tight, even a series of small expenses could add up to more than the coat's owner could pay and create the need to borrow money by pawning the coat. Part of the rhyme goes like this:

A penny for a spool of thread,

A penny for a needle,

That's the way the money goes,

Pop goes the weasel.

The first three lines describe expenses, and the fourth line says basically, "We had to sell the coat."

On the way back to the B & B, we had a gorgeous view of Mount Drum. We actually drove all the way down, turned around, and went back up to find a place where we could get out to take a picture.

Sunday, August 21, 2016

We got back to the Visitor Center for a short program centered on the relief map of the area. Ranger Diane (also a former teacher) talked about the various mountains and glaciers. Mount Wrangell is a volcano that still sends up steam, which people can see in the winter.

After the talk, we watched the movie about the park and then went on a guided walk through the boreal forest with Ranger Kate. She identified low-bush cranberries[83]; pumpkin berries, which are small and orange; and rose hips. The other name for a boreal forest is taiga; I remembered teaching about that in our old science book. Taiga is made up largely of willows and black spruce.

Along the path there was an overgrown hole that was used thousands of years ago either as a home or a food cache, and also a squirrel midden, which was basically a pile of pine cores and stripped scales left after the squirrels nibbled the cones. Along the walk we noticed aspen leaves with insect tunnels inside them from the aspen leaf miners. The patterns were similar to those we have seen in the leaves of plants in our backyard. The paths the insects use are completely random, but sometimes they produce interesting patterns.

Spruce broom rust, a fungal plant disease, was on a lot of the trees. We had seen it on other walks, and it reminded me of mistletoe; both are parasitic.

Ranger Kate also showed us a fish wheel, which was used for catching salmon in buckets as they swam against the flow of water. To understand how it works, picture some baskets on the edge of a wheel positioned so that they go just below the surface of the water. They are also positioned so the open end of the basket is pointed downstream. Because of this positioning, the salmon, which are heading upstream, swim into the open end of the basket and are caught. When the basket starts to get lifted up, the fish fall to the bottom of the basket and then out the side into a larger and stationary basket. The flow of water turns the wheel and it does not need human attendance, so someone could set up several and then go do something else for a few

---

[83] Because these cranberries are growing in permafrost, the ground is soggy, so it's similar to a bog.

hours, coming back only to collect the captured salmon. This device was not developed by native Alaskans, but it was adopted by them, and they became expert at using it.

After the walk, we went back to the Visitor Center, opted out of a ranger talk on coyotes, looked around the exhibit room, and went back to the B & B briefly before returning to the Copper River Princess Wilderness Lodge for dinner. We had decided to eat in the slightly less fancy restaurant, but there were no seats. A couple we had seen the previous day at the evening program invited us to join them, and they immediately asked whether we were the couple visiting all the national parks. Yup—that's us! We lingered at the table, enjoying the conversation.

After dinner, we sat in the car and wrote until it was time for the evening ranger program. This one was on climate change, and it was very well presented. The evidence of change was obvious and especially so in the last 50 years. The ranger who gave the talk was a single mom who had lived in the wilderness for 27 years. She told a story about one of her kids seeing a bear in their barn. She went out and talked calmly to the bear, and it left. The next day it was back. Again, she did something to shoo it away. The third day she took more drastic measures and threw firewood at it. This time it left and didn't return.

Monday, August 22, 2016

Today was the day for us to actually get in to Wrangell-St. Elias National Park: number 59 out of 59 for us![84] A van picked us up at the B & B at 7:15 AM and got us back about 7:45 PM. The McCarthy Road is a 60-mile-long gravel road, and it's very bumpy. It's not recommended to drive an ordinary car on it

---

[84] In 2018, Jefferson National Expansion Memorial became Gateway Arch National Park and Indiana Dunes National Lakeshore became Indiana Dunes National Park, making the national park total 61. Since we had visited both of them on previous trips, we decided that counted for national park visits!

and definitely not a rental car. We made two stops on the way. The first was Liberty Falls, where we walked over to see a pretty waterfall. The second stop was at the Gilahina Trestle. The CR & NW Railroad[85] (nicknamed Can't Run and Never Will) was built specifically to carry ore from the mines to Cordova. Fifteen percent of the track was on truss-style wooden trestles like the Gilahina Trestle.

On our way we passed by the town of Chitina, which was once considered as a possible site for the capital of Alaska. I'm guessing that may have been because it was in or near the region of copper mining and transportation. The Alaskan map shows Chitina as the only inland town near Wrangell-St. Elias National Park that has an airport.

After Chitina, the road to McCarthy became mostly dirt, especially below hillsides, although there were some paved parts. The driver said that dirt frequently falls down onto the road from the hills, so they have to plow it about once a week to keep it smooth and clear. Much of the road is on an old railroad trail, possibly part of the route that took copper from the mines to the coast to be shipped out. The town of Strelna had an airport runway that was parallel to and very near the road. We made a quick stop at the Gilahina River to see a large wooden bridge and trestle which was made for the railroad.

When we got to the Kennicott River, we had to walk over a footbridge and get the Kennicott-McCarthy shuttle. The tickets were included in the price of our trip from Copper Center; otherwise it cost $10 for the round trip. The shuttle dropped some people off in McCarthy, but we decided to go to Kennicott first. The river and town are spelled Kennicott (with an i) but the mining operation is spelled Kennecott (with an e) because someone misspelled it on the original deed. The only tour of the mine was at 1:30, and it was scheduled to take more than two hours. That would have left us no time to explore on our own, so we skipped the mine tour.

---

[85] Copper River and Northwest Railroad.

We arrived around noon, so we went for lunch at the Kennicott Glacier Lodge. From the upper level, where the restaurant was, we could see the Root Glacier and the Kennicott Glacier, which is now essentially a glacial moraine covered with rocks and dirt, although visitors can still see ice in some places.

After lunch we went to the National Park Visitor Center. Then we walked down the main street of what was once a "company town," The National Park Service is working to preserve the buildings. From the looks of them, it won't be an easy task. We could see where the railroad tracks ran through the town and under a small overhang next to the Mill Building. Parts of the road that still had tracks were paved with boards to bring the level of the road up to the top surface of the tracks.

Some of the hillsides that were serving as foundation support for the buildings were becoming less stable and needed reinforcement. They had diagrams to show how they anchored rods into the ground and then bolted them to the buildings. We saw several places where these rods were installed.

We went into the power plant, where there is still a lot of equipment; we also went into a cottage that would have been the home for a family during the heyday of the town and mill. It was built in the early 1900s and has cabinets very similar to some we have in the original kitchen area of our house. It was really neat to see them and realize this must have been a common style at that time. The cottage is completely restored, but the rooms are empty.

We also looked at the school. The top (second) floor was at street level, and the bottom (first) floor was below street level. We couldn't get into the building, so we just had to use our imagination to picture what it might have been like. A brochure described it as being cold in the winter and noisy because of the mining operations.

The copper mine was discovered in the early 1900s by two prospectors with the help of Ahtna Chief Nicolai. He sold information on the world's highest concentration of high-grade copper ore in exchange for much-needed winter supplies. The financial backing to develop the mine came from the Havemeyer, Guggenheim, and J.P. Morgan families. These three families formed the Alaska Syndicate, which later became the Kennecott Copper Corporation, which still operates mines in other parts of the world today. By 1938 there were more than 100 buildings in the camp, but prices started to drop so Kennecott closed that year. In total, it produced $200 to $300 million of copper and silver.[86]

Kennicott, as a company town, had wholesome activities like movies and dances. When the men wanted something less wholesome, they went five miles down the hill to McCarthy, a wild town with women, dance halls, and saloons.

We got the shuttle back to McCarthy and walked around there for a while and then went to the museum where we spent a short time. I read quite a few things there about a female teacher who came to work in McCarthy during Prohibition. She was a member of the Women's Christian Temperance Union and not afraid to make her opinion known. This was definitely a challenge to the town, but because she was an excellent teacher, they kept her. Federal agents were never able to find any liquor in the town because whenever agents were on the train, the engineer blew the whistle twice to alert the town to hide the liquor.

Overall, there was less to see in McCarthy than in Kennicott, so we decided to walk the half mile to the footbridge to meet our shuttle and head back to Chitina and Copper

[86] $3.4 billion to $5.1 billion in today's money.

Center. On the shuttle, the driver, Cutler, frequently wove from side to side along the road to avoid some of the potholes. After about 1¼ hours, we paused at a rest stop near the Kuskulana River Bridge, which is a one-way bridge constructed during the winter of 1910 as a railroad bridge. We walked across to get a great view of the river below, and Cutler picked us up on the other side. A little farther along, there was a large dip in the road that Cutler said was caused by a fault line. He also said it had moved two or three times already that year.

Seeing an active fault line across a road made me really appreciate how much geological activity there is in southern Alaska. We had already seen on our trip evidence of volcanic activity along the Aleutians and the Alaska Peninsula. That range includes some of the most active and powerful volcanoes in the world, but people almost never hear of them.

Yukon-Charley Rivers National Preserve, Alaska

Wednesday, August 24, 2016

Right after breakfast we headed to 40 Mile Air for our trip to Yukon/Charley River. We were early but so was the pilot, so we were able to leave early. It was a one-hour flight over terrain different from every other flight we had been on. It started out over flat tundra but then changed to rolling hills with little vegetation. There were lots of rivers, which we could recognize because there was a narrow band of trees along the riverbanks.

The sparse foliage seemed to be rapidly changing to yellow. Fall was on its way! There were also patches of red and yellow lichen. Initially there were quite a few ponds, but then it became more rivers. We flew over the North Fork of the 40 Mile River, the Charley River, and then the Yukon River before landing at Coal Creek, which got its name from coal that was discovered there. However, it was not high-quality coal, and thoughts of mining it ended when gold was discovered.

The pilot parked the plane near the start of the trail so we wouldn't have to walk so far. We started out walking to the dredge, which was a two-story-high floating mining machine that extracted gold from sand, gravel, and dirt using water and mechanical methods. We expected to be gone about an hour, but it turned into more like three hours. The trail was easy, on an ATV track.

We met two national park workers on ATVs several times. Initially when they saw our plane land, they thought it was their supervisor's plane.

On both sides of the trail there were piles of dirt that looked like tailings. We took pictures of some of the piles and continued walking. We did not expect—but kept finding—streams repeatedly crossing the trail. The streams were too wide to jump over, and the rocks weren't always in the right places, so Dick laid down some sticks to walk on and keep our feet drier. They weren't great, but they worked most of the time, although we left with wet sneakers and socks. There were several places where the trail crossed a stream several inches deep.

We got to the dredge and looked around the outside. We decided against going to Slavens Road House, another mile down the trail. A road house was an inn for travelers; most were used extensively by miners. Just as we turned around to go back, a ranger came and asked whether we'd like to go inside. Of course, we did. Dick was especially interested in how it worked. I told him the extra time we spent on the ground (about $200/hour) could be his birthday present. The ranger explained that the dredge was in need of repair, but they didn't expect to have the money until 2018, so they were doing some stop-gap work to prevent the roof from leaking. The two men whom we had met earlier on the trail were part of the crew working on the dredge to repair and upgrade it so it would be more accessible and safer for people coming to see it. The ranger cautioned us about risky places as we walked along.

The dredge was built in San Francisco, taken apart, and shipped to Alaska. It was reassembled and pulled over the ice to its starting point. It started in 1936 and worked until the early 1970s. The dredge moved forward through bedrock, digging a pond as it went. A string of buckets was attached to a slanted conveyor belt. The buckets were brought down to scoop rocks and dirt, and then brought back up carrying the material. The ranger explained that the buckets even went a little way into the bedrock. The upper part of the bedrock became cracked and loose enough to be scooped up. This was important to the process because any gold dust that had been deposited on the bottom of lakes and streams could also sink into the cracks of the bedrock, so scooping up loose bedrock brought up more gold. Of course, the leading edges of the buckets wore out regularly because they were constantly scraping against rocks. Because of this, the leading edge of each bucket was replaceable so they wouldn't have to stop production to replace the entire bucket.

As the dirt and rocks got carried up into the dredge, they dropped into a rotating cylinder with a lot of holes in it. The large rocks tumbled along through the cylinder and onto a conveyor belt that carried them up through the tail and out onto the ground. This is why the dumped material is referred to as "tailings."

The dirt and rocks smaller than approximately one inch got sifted through the holes in the cylinder. Then they fell into troughs that had grids in the bottom and sat on top of what is referred to as a "carpet," which is similar to moss. The gravel and small rocks got rinsed so the dirt and sand would sift through the grid and down to the "carpet." The material in the carpet had the greatest likelihood of having gold (dust) in with it. The rocks and gravel on top of the grid got sorted by hand in case there were any gold nuggets, and the sorted gravel got tossed. The dirt got processed, and mercury was added, which bonded with the gold. The compound was heated, the mercury evaporated into the air, and the gold melted and got cast into ingots.

In addition to explaining how the gold was processed, the ranger showed us a couple of other interesting things. One was a gear that had been put on backward and needed to be blown off with dynamite so it could be turned around and mounted correctly. Another was a set of tools that had been handmade because there was no convenient hardware store. A third thing we noticed was permanent graffiti. The words, names, and comments were written by using an arc welder to leave trails of metal that formed letters on the metal floor.

Both the bucket ramp and the tail were permanently and rigidly fastened to the dredge. In order to keep the buckets digging into fresh ground, the entire dredge had to be pivoted. That caused the dredge bucket ramp to move sideways in one direction, and the tail at the back end of the dredge to move sideways in the other direction. After the dredge bucket ramp had been moved from one side of the stream to the other, the whole dredge had to be moved a few feet forward to provide new material for digging, and then the pivot process repeated, but going the other way. The side-to-side pivoting motion and the forward movement were accomplished by two tractors, one on each side of the stream and tied to the dredge. Because the dredge was constantly pivoting, the tailings formed arc-shaped deposits. We got a better understanding of the dredging and tailing process from this visit.

The ranger told a story about road houses where prospectors might stay and take a bath. When they were done, roadhouse workers would scrub the tub and scrape gold off the tub edges.

After the tour, we hiked back to the plane. The pilot very nicely flew over the area of the dredge several times so we could be sure to see it well. Dick was able to get some pictures that clearly showed the arc-shaped tailing deposits.

We ate a late lunch and then worked on drying our sneakers with the hair dryer. My feet were so cold from being wet that I finally turned the heater on for a little while.

I also checked email. There was an appeal from the National Parks because they were trying to raise $100,000 in 100 days, culminating the next day, which was the actual 100th birthday of the national parks. A postscript at the end of the appeal said we could celebrate the addition of a new park. It happens every time we take a trip. At least this new one, called Katahdin Woods and Waters National Monument, is in Maine, a drive of only a few hours from our home in New Hampshire.

Thursday, August 25, 2016

We were on our way home from a successful trip to Alaska. I had worried about this one for a long time, wondering how we could ever get to these hard-to-reach parks. There had been no guarantee that we would actually be able to reach all the parks there. We had allowed for extra days because of possible weather delays and we needed every day we had planned. We had flown over glaciers, mountains, meandering rivers, and ponds. We were impressed with the pilots who had landed small planes on both rocky and sandy beaches, tundra, sand dunes, and gravel runways. These pilots had also provided a wealth of information. It was an amazing trip. Years ago, a friend had remarked, "Have you ever wanted to do something but just never got around to it?" and my answer was "No. If I want to do something, I find a way to do it." I wanted to get to all the parks and I found a way to accomplish this. It turned out that with research and planning, it wasn't so difficult after all.

Happy 100th Birthday, National Parks!!

2017

Valles Caldera National Preserve,
New Mexico

Valles Caldera National Preserve, New Mexico

Friday, August 11, 2017

Valles Caldera National Preserve became part of the national park system in 2000. It included an historic ranch inside a volcanic caldera. Since it was a relatively new park, we knew that the infrastructure was still being developed, but since we were close to the end of our goal to see all the national park sites, we wanted to stop there. We were pleasantly surprised to find that a tour was being offered.

On the way in to the preserve, we drove along part of the rim and could see a huge hollow spot, which Dick thought looked like the main part of the caldera. The size perspective was enhanced because there were some buildings down in the center of the hollow spot. The buildings were actually fairly good sized, but they appeared to be really tiny in comparison to the size of the hollow spot. We learned later that the portion we saw was actually only about one fifth of the entire caldera.

This caldera is the result of a volcano that erupted most recently 40,000 years ago. This volcano ejected enough material to cover a 400-square-mile area with volcanic ash up to 1,000 feet thick. The caldera is now grass covered.

Dick had a lot more notes on the caldera:

The amount of material that got ejected in the process of forming the Valles Caldera was about 600 times the amount that was ejected from Mount St. Helens about 30 years ago. The ejection from Valles Caldera took place about 1.2 million years ago, but that didn't end the volcanic activity. There have been a few more eruptions during the last 300,000 years or so; eruptions were taking place about 50,000 years apart. Since the most recent was 40,000 years ago, it is likely that another might happen relatively soon.

The original eruption that formed the caldera actually provided future building materials. The ash deposit was very deep and covered a huge area. Over time, the ash hardened into rock. During the last few thousand years, the natives of the region would cut the rock into chunks and use it as construction material for building their dwellings. But the process wasn't easy, and the material was "tuff."

The caldera floor was good for farming and ranching. The floor was all grassland because the ground was too wet, and the winters were too cold, for trees to survive. The winter temperatures were about 10 degrees Fahrenheit colder than on the higher ground in and around the caldera. Looking around the edges, we could see a clear demarcation between the areas with grass and the areas with trees.

While we were waiting for the ranger-led tour, Eric and Kathy Johnson, who had gone to Aniakchak with us in 2016, came over. What a surprise! They hadn't known about the tour either, but they were able to join at the last minute, so the four of us were once again in the same vehicle on the same tour.

The guide took us to see several buildings, mostly related to farming and ranching. Over the years, the land within the caldera was owned by five different ranch families, but it was eventually owned by several with marital and familial relations. As the story goes, ownership became very contentious and family members were suing each other. It seems like the final solution came when the land was sold to the United States government for $100 million.

Several movies, including *The Lone Ranger* and *Buffalo Girls*, were filmed there; we saw some buildings that had been erected for that purpose and some farm buildings that had been repurposed for movie sets. There were even a few buildings that were put up for a resort.

When we left Valles Caldera, we had 11 more national monuments, national historic sites, and national memorials to visit, 8 of which we did on our trip home. I was beginning to feel the way I do when I'm reading a really good book: I'm anxious to see how it ends, but I don't want it to end.

September 9, 2017

When we got home from our trip in August, we had only three sites left to visit: Harriet Tubman National Historical Park in New York, Katahdin Woods and Waters National Monument in Maine, and Saint-Gaudens National Historic Site in New Hampshire, all within a day's drive from our home. We had deliberately saved Saint-Gaudens in our home state of New Hampshire to be last. Initially, we planned to save it for our fiftieth wedding anniversary celebration in June 2018, but I couldn't wait.

On September 9, 2017 we visited Saint-Gaudens, our 416th national park site. Now we are just waiting for Honouliuli National Monument in Hawaii to be open to the public.

What a journey this has been, and one that we have enjoyed sharing with family, friends, and you, our readers.

2018

Waterton Glacier International
Peace Park,[87]
Alberta, Canada and Montana

Glacier National Park, Montana

Theodore Roosevelt National Park,
North Dakota

Indiana Dunes National Lakeshore
(now Indiana Dunes National Park)

---

[87] This park includes Waterton Lakes National Park in Alberta, Canada, and
Glacier National Park in Montana.

Waterton Glacier International Peace Park, Alberta, Canada and Montana

Friday, August 17, 2018

We spent three weeks in August visiting national parks in the Canadian Rockies. These included stops at Kootenay, Yoho, Mt. Revelstoke, and Glacier National Parks in British Columbia and Banff, Jasper, and Waterton Lakes National Parks in Alberta. Although we had already completed our goal of visiting all the U.S. national park sites, we were happy to return to three of them on our way home.

We arrived at Waterton Lakes National Park in Alberta, Canada, in the afternoon, and after setting up, we walked into town. We stopped at a small pavilion that described how Waterton Lakes National Park in Canada and Glacier National Park in the United States were officially joined in 1932 as Waterton Glacier International Peace Park. It was the first such designation in the world, but it is now one of 100 such parks. The idea came from a meeting of Rotary International Clubs from Alberta and Montana. It celebrates the peace and goodwill along the world's longest undefended border, as well as cooperation in wildlife and vegetation management. The two parks were established separately and are still managed separately.

Saturday, August 18, 2018

After lunch we headed to the marina to park and wait for our boat trip on Waterton Lake. During the boat ride, the views were very smoky—again. There were more than 600 forest fires burning in British Columbia during our travels there earlier in the month, and skies had been smoky for our entire trip. Even so, we got a good view of the clear-cut Canada/U.S. border.

The border is marked with two stone boundary pillars and a 20-foot-wide "slash" with no trees or shrubs all the way up the mountain. This landscaping was agreed upon as a requirement when the 49-degree latitude was set as the boundary between the two countries.

After about an hour, the boat docked at Goat Haunt in Glacier National Park, Montana, a spot that can be reached only by boat or by hiking. We walked for five minutes along the shore to a pavilion where a national park ranger gave a short talk about the origin and current status of the Waterton-Glacier International Peace Park. Then we had the five-minute walk back to the boat. We were on the island for no more than 25 minutes. I felt really rushed. If we had taken the morning boat, we could have made arrangements to hike for a few hours and get the later boat back to Waterton.[88]

The person narrating the boat trip spoke about local history, animals, and the environment in an informative and interesting way. He pointed out that animals cross the border with no knowledge that they are in a different country. When we crossed the border in the boat, we didn't need passports or any security precautions.

On the way back, someone spotted an eagle, so the captain brought the boat right up to the shore and floated for quite a few minutes so everyone could get a good view. The eagle just sat in the tree the whole time.

Sunday, August 19, 2018

We cooked breakfast and then drove the short distance to Glacier National Park, Montana. Along the way, we stopped at the St. Mary Visitor Center and watched the introductory film. The film matched our memory of Glacier from our previous

---

[88] Passports are needed if you stay at Goat Haunt to hike.

trip—beautiful blue sky and mountains reflected in the lakes. However, this year there were wildfires burning in Montana as they were in Canada. Air quality was poor, and smoke obscured the views. Because of the fires, we could drive only 17 miles on the Going-to-the-Sun Highway, billed as one of the world's most scenic drives. The highway was shut beyond Logan Pass.

I had read that there was a nature trail at Logan Pass, so we decided to do that. However, we missed the sign for the nature trail and ended up on a 1½-mile trail to the Hidden Lake Overlook. If I had realized what this entailed, I never would have attempted it. Much of the trail was a boardwalk with lot of steps with an unusually high rise: 10 to 12 inches high as opposed to the usual 7 inches. Going up and down provided serious leg exercise. There was no railing, and there really should have been bright-colored paint or tape marking the edge of each step. It was very hard to see the edges of the steps as we were coming down.

On the plus side, the trail led through gorgeous fields of wildflowers, especially yellow and pink ones, which were especially vibrant as streams of water flowed through them over colorful rocks. Dick said that the rocks had all formed in different layers of sedimentation and had varied colors depending on the minerals in the original deposits. Some rocks were red, some yellow, some gray, and some brown.

The rocks were also interesting for another reason. Because they were originally deposited in sedimentary layers, they broke apart in layers. Each layer was about one inch thick, and most stuck together to form slabs about one foot thick. The slabs broke across the layers, forming blocks that were then used to make some of the steps in the long stairway up to the overlook.

On our way, there was a lovely waterfall, and at one point we could see two bighorn sheep high up on a cliff. All this was wonderful, but overall the hike was extremely strenuous and the view of the lake mediocre, although it was interesting to see a lake so hidden away. Coming down we were holding hands all the way (mainly because I needed help). A younger couple stopped and asked us how long we had been married. They were impressed with our 50 years and thought it was so cute to see us holding hands. We hiked much of the way with another couple. They were impressed that I was able to do this after having two hip replacements. Me too!

When we returned to the campground for dinner, I went in search of some of the berries I'd spotting people picking earlier. I found lots of bushes of huckleberries. We picked two cups full—good for two batches of pancakes.

The sun that night wasn't quite as red as other nights, but all the time we were in the Canadian Rockies, the sun was a hazy red ball in both the morning and the evening because of the smoke.

Theodore Roosevelt National Park, North Dakota

Tuesday August 21, 2018

Despite rain during the night, the tent was dry in the morning. There must have been wind, but I didn't hear it. We packed up and ate breakfast in the car. It was 46 degrees Fahrenheit when we started.

That day involved straight driving to Theodore Roosevelt National Park, more than 400 miles east. Eventually we drove into better weather—blue sky and 75 degrees. It had been two weeks since we last saw blue sky.

Just before we got to Cottonwood Campground, we saw a bison very close to the road. We had stayed at this campground many years ago with the kids, but I didn't really remember it. There were wild horses at the end of the road across a little river.

Our site was wonderful—quite private, close to the bathrooms, and no fire ban, so we could have a campfire. We had s'mores for dessert for only the second time on this trip.

Another plus for this site was that the evening program was very close. There were a lot of prairie dog towns in the park, and that night's program was on prairie dogs. Their burrows were all over the place. Even though they live in a "town," they don't really cooperate with each other, although they do coexist well with the bison and wild horses. Most burrows have several entrances, so the prairie dogs often escape predators by going down one hole and coming up another. With that in mind, the prairie dogs also have a lot of predators, including snakes, who will go down into the burrows. The bubonic plague, which wiped out whole colonies elsewhere, didn't seem to be as prevalent here, but we were still warned that we shouldn't go near a dead prairie dog.

Wednesday, August 22, 2018

We both slept really well—no loud trains which we had experienced at several of the parks in Canada. At some point we did hear loud howling, which we thought was coyotes, but it didn't last very long. We were awake at 6:30. I was so happy to look out and see bright blue sky. Dick managed to build another fire and cooked huckleberry pancakes for breakfast.

We spent most of our day on the Scenic Loop Road. We hadn't gone very far when we came to a large prairie dog town and lots of bison on both sides of the road. There was at least one mama bison with two young ones beside her. No one who had stopped to take pictures went into the prairie dog town, but we were all very close to the bison, and they seemed oblivious to us. Our next stop was the Ridgeline Nature Trail. In this case, the sign accurately described the trail as moderate with steep stairs. With Dick's help, I managed to do it, although some of the stairs were quite narrow as well as steep. The most striking difference on this trail was the comparison of environments on the sunlit side versus the shaded side of the ridge. The sunlit side was drier with fewer trees and bushes, while the shaded side had more trees and bushes. Many had berries, which the birds like. Back in Montana, it was the bears who ate the berries—100,000 a day per bear!

The whole park is in an area called badlands, so it is dry, and the terrain is rugged. The early settlers used the butte tops as lookouts and the valleys as good places to travel undetected. Much of the area is also grassland. Animals such as bison eat the grass, fertilize the soil with their manure, and pierce the soil with their pointed hooves. This allows rainwater to seep into the ground, thus keeping the grass growing.

I was tired after this hike, but when we got to the Coal Vein Trail, I agreed to try it. Again, it was billed as moderate with some steep trails. The brochure said there was a point where hikers could take a side trail and skip the steep section. I was going to do this, but we never found the side trail, so I plodded on with Dick's help.

The Coal Vein Trail had some ups and downs, but it was less challenging than the Ridgeline Trail. It went over an area where an underground coal vein about 12 feet thick caught fire from a lightning strike in 1951 and burned for 26 years! We saw a flat, sunken area where the coal had burned out and left the dirt and rocks above it unsupported so the whole area dropped about 10 feet.

The layers of rock are different colors. The red, called *clinker*, is what forms when coal is washed down from the Rocky Mountains. The black is coal, and the blue-gray bentonite is clay made of ash from distant volcanoes. The bentonite looks like popcorn when it is dry. It has a lot of different uses and is often part of a formula for cat litter.

Near the end of the trail we saw "chimneys." When the coal fire was burning deep underground, cracks in the rock layers allowed air to be sucked down into the fire. The fire then burned up through the cracks and baked the rocks to form vertical chimneys.

We ate lunch as we drove the rest of the loop road and got back to the South Unit Visitor Center just in time for a tour of the Maltese Cross Cabin. Teddy Roosevelt, who invested in the Maltese Cross Ranch in 1883, had this cabin built. We learned that the Maltese Cross, which looked like two capital letter *I*s put together at right angles, was the brand on the cattle. On the front of the cabin, Roosevelt hammered spent bullet shells to make the shape of the cross. After his wife and mother died on the same day the following year, he came here to grieve.

Roosevelt came from a wealthy family in New York and could afford to have a much fancier cabin than others in the area. His cabin had two rooms, walls that were painted white, and a pitched roof unlike the flat sod roofs of other cabins. Most cabins were built of local cottonwood logs, but Roosevelt's cabin was made of Ponderosa pine, which does not grow in North Dakota. Ponderosa pine logs intended for railway ties had been shipped through the area, and Roosevelt's workers used some that had been left behind. The only reason the cabin has survived is because it was built of Ponderosa pine.

The cabin was important to Roosevelt, and he spent a lot of time there. When he left North Dakota and moved back to New York, he sold the cabin. Ownership may have changed again, because the cabin was shipped to different fairs around the U.S. and put on display several times. Each time it was moved, the cabin was completely dismantled and then reassembled. In 1959 its final movement to its present location in Theodore Roosevelt National Park was done fully assembled on a flatbed towed by a truck.

There is an original rocking chair in the cabin (Roosevelt loved to rock!), a chest with his initials on it, and an exact copy of his writing desk (the original was in very bad shape and could not be preserved). We also learned about Roosevelt's ethics, integrity, and conservation efforts.

After the presentation, we drove into Medora to buy gas and ice and then continued on to the Painted Canyon part of the park. We considered hiking there, but it was a mile-long trail, it was hot, and coming back would be all uphill. We decided just to look at the views from the canyon rim. From the overlook, we saw several hills, all with the same colors and patterns of rock layers from the original sedimentary deposits.

Dick heated our leftovers on a fire and we had s'mores again. Then we went to the evening program on "Vulture Culture," which also covered other corvids, such as magpies and crows. The ranger was young but very enthusiastic about how helpful vultures are. Although they're kind of ugly and have some disgusting habits, they eat dead animals, which removes those dead animals from our environment along with rabies or any other diseases they might be carrying. She also talked about how smart the magpies and crows are.

As we returned to our campsite, we agreed that it had been another good trip. We had taken different hikes from previous trips and learned many new facts. There are so many things to do in every park that each visit is a unique experience—and one that is truly worth repeating.

Indiana Dunes National Lakeshore (now National Park), Indiana

Sunday, August 26, 2018

Indiana Dunes National Lakeshore was on our route home from the Canadian Rockies. Although we could have driven farther, we both liked the idea of one more night in a national park campground.

It was very hot and humid and we could hear thunder in the distance, so after setting up our tent, we decided to drive the lakeshore road rather than hiking. We only had vague recollections of our visit in 1992; after 26 years, nothing looked familiar. We walked down to the shore of Lake Michigan where people were swimming, then stopped to see the "Century of Progress" homes which were built for the 1933 Chicago World's Fair. They featured innovative (for that time period) designs and features such as central air conditioning and dishwashers. One even had a hangar for a plane. All are currently occupied so we could only see the outsides of the houses.

Back at our campsite, we decided that the mosquitoes must have liked our bug spray because it certainly didn't repel them. Nonetheless, we sat by our fire and made s'mores with the last of our chocolate bars and graham crackers.

It was a hot evening but it was very pleasant listening to the sounds of bugs and birds as we fell asleep—a wonderful way to end another trip.

CONCLUDING SECTIONS

Conclusion: What We've Learned

After more than 40 years of camping, we're not ready to stop. We love the natural beauty of the national parks; we love learning about history associated with the parks; we love living outdoors for weeks at a time. Whether you want to tent in your own backyard or in one of the beautiful national parks, here are some recommendations for a successful experience.

In addition to a tent or RV, sleeping bags, pillows, clothes, food, and water,[89] here are some additional suggestions of what to bring:

- **Brown paper grocery bags.** We sit on these when picnic table benches are wet or dirty. The bags take up almost no space and can be dried and reused.
- **Some large manila envelopes for filing.** I label one for receipts; one for reservations; one for addresses, postcards, and stamps; and one for brochures.
- **A small folding table.** This is handy on the rare occasions when there is no picnic table and also useful when it is very sunny and we want to sit in the shade to eat.
- **A clothesline and clothespins.** A clothesline is handy if strung back and forth near the ceiling in the back of a station wagon or minivan. It can also be hung between trees at many campsites.
- **Scrap lumber for firewood.** No fresh-cut wood (with or without bark) can be transported between states and, in some places, between counties.
- **Coleman stove or its equivalent and fuel.** This is especially important during drought conditions or forest fire season when there is sometimes a fire ban. It's also useful when there is rain, because it can be used to cook in a campground shelter or under a car's lift-gate.

---

[89] Meal ideas and recipes appear in the appendix.

- **Reusable sandwich wraps.** These have plastic on the inside and cloth on the outside; they are fastened with Velcro. Many different varieties are available online.

Here are some additional hints that we have found useful.

1. **Don't leave anything outside.** After my sister-in-law's wedding reception, which was held in our yard, we packed all the leftover food into our cooler and took off for a short camping trip to the beach. At the campsite, we left the cooler outside, as we had so often seen others do … and someone stole it. When we woke up in the morning, the cooler and all the extra-special food was gone. We've also seen flocks of birds early in the morning take bags of food off other campers' picnic tables. Keep everything locked in your car. Above all else, follow whatever rules the parks and campgrounds post for food storage to prevent problems with bears or other animals.

2. **Keep a good supply of ice.** We used to try to buy block ice, which lasts much longer than cubes, but it is often hard to find. Now we fill four empty gallon milk jugs with water and freeze them before leaving home. These, along with frozen food, provide ice for a few days. As the ice melts, we heat it for washing dishes. We also cut the tops off four empty milk jugs, which we bring with us. When we need more ice, we buy a bag and pack the cubes into these empty jugs. Because the melting ice is contained, this also means it's not leaking all over the cooler.

3. **Soap the bottom of pans.** When you cook over a wood fire, cleanup can be messy. Before we cook, we rub a bar of soap to coat the outside of the bottom and sides of any pans that will be used over the fire. The layer of soap keeps the smoke and ash off the surface of the pan and makes washing the pans much easier. If you can't wash the dishes right away, put them in a sealed plastic bag.

4. **Protect the environment.** We avoid using paper products, which take up space in garbage dumps, and we use biodegradable soap that can be safely disposed of on the ground. We carry a bag with us to collect recyclable bottles and cans until we find a bin for recycling.

5. **Be active.** Whenever we stopped at rest areas when our children were young, we always encouraged them to run around, kick the soccer ball, play with the hacky sack, etc. Actually, they needed no encouragement at all! Even without children, we stop at least every two hours and walk around for a short while each time.

6. **Buy gifts for future use.** When we come to a gift shop and see something that would be perfect for someone on our gift list, we buy it and put it away. We have learned the hard way that we may not find that special gift anywhere else.

7. **Don't make reservations unless you have specific requirements.** The first year we drove cross-country, which was 1980 (before cell phones and email), my mother wanted to be able to reach us at all times, so we made reservations. Now, however, we rarely make reservations except for really popular national parks or on a holiday weekend. In general, we don't like being tied down. Sometimes the drive is too long, sometimes we want to leave after a shorter time, sometimes we want to stay longer. In recent years we have discovered that many private campgrounds don't offer tent sites. Although we don't usually make reservations, we do try to research a few options before we leave home and have some tentative campgrounds in mind.

8. **Keep a journal.** Initially, only Dick wrote notes about our adventures, but from 1980 on, we all kept journals. I have referred to our journals many times and have shared them with friends who are planning their own trips to places we have visited.

9. **Enjoy the journey.** Put away the electronic devices and look at the scenery. Learn something new at every stop you make. Remember the popular saying that strangers are only friends you haven't met yet and enjoy every moment along the way!

Appendix: Meal Preparation

Planning meals for weekend trips as well as for much longer travels is basically the same except for quantity. Food is more expensive when traveling because it's harder to take advantage of sales, and smaller quantities cost more than bulk items, so I try to bring as many staples as I can. (See list later in this section.)

When we traveled with young children, we learned to eat in the car. We could easily travel 30 miles during lunch, especially when it was prepared and doled out piecemeal: half a sandwich, then some carrot sticks, etc. When we stopped, it was to run around—a quick soccer game, playing with a hacky-sack, a brisk walk—not to sit at a picnic table. Even without children, this makes sense. We all need an opportunity to stretch our legs.

Here are some specific ideas for meals.

BREAKFAST

Our breakfasts include varying combinations of the following:
- juice
- pancakes
- French toast (can be made with leftover hamburg or hot dog rolls, sliced thin, as well as with bread)
- eggs
- bacon
- hot cereal
- cold cereal
- English muffins
- bagels
- coffee cake
- grapefruit
- bananas
- prunes
- yogurt

If we want to make good driving time, we will eat a quick cold breakfast and/or eat in the car while we drive. These eat-in-the-car breakfasts include such things as hard-boiled eggs cooked the night before, yogurt, coffee cake, bagels, fruit, and juice. Cooked breakfasts include bacon and eggs, toasted English muffins, hot cereal, French toast, and pancakes.

LUNCH

Lunches include sandwiches—preferably on Syrian bread, because it doesn't dry out too quickly, or sandwich rounds. We always have peanut butter available and, most of the time, sandwich meat. Then there's cheese and crackers and Logan bread, a recipe our son David got at a winter camp he attended in junior high (see recipe section). It is very nutritious, and it keeps indefinitely without refrigeration, so we can make it ahead. One recipe makes three loaves. We also have carrots, cucumbers, chips, yogurt, melba toast, cookies, and fruit (canned and fresh).

DINNER

Dinner possibilities include the following:
- beef stew (for the second night of the trip; packed frozen, it provides ice for the first two days)
- chicken
- fish
- fruit salad
- ham (canned—the kind that does not require refrigeration)
- hamburgers
- hot dogs
- julienne or chef's salad
- macaroni and cheese
- pork chops
- sausage
- spaghetti
- tuna or salmon (creamed) on chow mein noodles

Accompanying these are
- carrots
- green beans
- peas
- potatoes
- rice
- salad
- squash
- sweet potatoes
- white or wild rice

MENUS AND INGREDIENTS

Menus and ingredients can be varied to suit your family's tastes. When traveling, we shop every three to four days, buying local specialties whenever possible. Last year we camped for 30 days before we repeated a dinner menu. You can eat well and inexpensively while traveling.

Our starting menu is always the same:

DAY 1

- **Breakfast:** Eaten at home
- **Lunch:** Egg salad sandwiches, chips, carrot sticks, fruit, cookies, iced tea
- **Dinner:** Marinated chicken (Italian dressing over chicken in a sealed freezer bag), frozen vegetables, rice, fruit, cookies, iced tea

DAY 2

- **Breakfast:** Orange juice, scrambled eggs, quick bread (banana, zucchini, cranberry, etc.)
- **Lunch:** Sandwiches, cucumbers, fruit, cookies, iced tea
- **Dinner:** Beef stew, biscuits, fruit, cookies, iced tea

DAY 3

- **Breakfast:** Orange juice, pancakes, maple syrup
- **Lunch:** Sandwiches, chips, fruit, cookies, iced tea
- **Dinner:** Hamburgers, tossed salad, fruit, cookies, iced tea

Food to Bring

My list of things to bring includes these food staples.

NONPERISHABLES

- Brown sugar
- Canned French-fried onions
- Canned fruit
- Canned ham (not needing refrigeration)
- Canned juice
- Canned sweet potatoes
- Cereal, cold
- Cereal, hot (measured in baggies in amount needed for the group and stored in a larger plastic food storage bag with directions on the outside)
- Chips
- Chocolate bars (may need to be kept in the cooler)
- Cookies (homemade Monster cookies [see recipe section] and gingersnaps; these don't crumble, and they stay fresh)
- Crackers
- Cranberry sauce
- Dried prunes
- Flour (in plastic food storage bag: enough to make several batches of cream sauce)
- Graham crackers
- Granola bars
- Iced tea mix
- Jam
- Logan bread (see recipe)
- Macaroni and cheese (boxes)
- Marshmallows (may need to be kept in the cooler)
- Packets of catsup and mustard from restaurant leftovers or small containers
- Pancake packets (we mix our own dry ingredients and bring each batch in a baggie, stored in a larger freezer bag with directions on the outside)
- Parmesan cheese, grated
- Peanut butter
- Peanuts
- Pretzels

- Raisins
- Rice
- Salmon (in foil packets with no liquid to dispose of)
- Spaghetti
- Sugar (in a plastic food storage bag)
- Tuna (in foil packets with no liquid to dispose of)

- Water (individual bottles and at least one gallon for use when there is no water at a campground)
- Wild rice

PERISHABLES

- Frozen vegetable (one bag)
- Baking-powder biscuits
- Beef stew
- Bread
- Butter
- Carrots
- Cheese
- Cherry tomatoes (larger tomatoes bruise easily)
- Chicken marinated in Italian dressing in a sealed freezer bag
- Cucumbers
- Egg salad sandwiches (for first lunch)
- Eggs
- Frozen orange juice
- Fruit
- Hamburg
- Hamburg rolls

- Hot dogs
- Hot dog rolls
- Lettuce
- Maple syrup
- Milk
- Onions
- Potatoes (not too many; they spoil quickly)
- Quick bread
- Salad dressing
- Sandwich meat
- Squash
- Yogurt

Recipes

Logan Bread

INGREDIENTS

- 6 eggs
- 6 cups flour
- 1 tablespoon baking powder
- 2½ cups oatmeal
- 2 teaspoons salt
- 1 ½ cups brown sugar
- 1 cup vegetable oil
- ½ cup powdered milk (not reconstituted)
- 1 cup honey
- 1 ¼ cups chopped walnuts
- ½ cup molasses
- 2 cups raisins
- 1 cup chocolate chips
- 1 pound butter

DIRECTIONS

Preheat oven to 350°F. Beat eggs. Add all ingredients except butter, and mix. Melt butter and stir into mixture. Divide mixture into three greased 9x5-inch loaf pans. Bake for 45 minutes or until tester comes out clean.

Monster Cookies

INGREDIENTS

- 6 eggs
- 4 teaspoons baking soda
- 2¼ cups brown sugar, packed
- 1 cup butter or margarine
- 2 cups white sugar
- 3¼ cups peanut butter
- 1½ teaspoons vanilla
- ½ pound chocolate chips (about 1⅓ cups)
- 1½ teaspoons corn syrup
- ½ pound M&M's (about 1 cup)
- 9 cups oatmeal

DIRECTIONS

Preheat oven to 350°F. Mix all ingredients in large bowl. Drop by large spoon or ice cream scoop onto ungreased cookie sheet. Flatten slightly. Bake 12 minutes. Do not overbake. Makes more than 25 large cookies.

Pancake Mix (2 or 3 servings)

INGREDIENTS

- 1 cup flour
- 2 teaspoons baking powder
- 2 tablespoons sugar

DIRECTIONS

Mix flour, baking powder, and sugar. Place in small plastic bag. Label outside with these instructions: Combine ½ cup milk, 2 tablespoons vegetable oil or melted margarine, 1 egg. Add to dry ingredients and stir just enough to dampen. Fry on greased griddle or frying pan.

Potato Bake

INGREDIENTS

- 6 potatoes, peeled and sliced
- ½ pound bacon, crisp-cooked and crumbled
- 1 onion, sliced
- 2 cups cheese, cubed
- ½ cup butter or margarine

DIRECTIONS

Place potatoes onto a large piece of heavy aluminum foil. Sprinkle bacon over top. Add onion and cheese. Slice butter over all. Mix on the foil. Bring up edges of foil and, leaving a little space for expansion of steam, seal well with double fold. Place packet in coals and cover with coals. Cook about 1 hour or until done, turning several times.

Mixture can also be cooked in a large frying pan. Serves 4 to 6.

Bonus: Author Interview

Q. You and Dick have been camping for more than 40 years. How have the vast changes in technology affected your experience?

A. One technological advantage is having a GPS to help us navigate. Cell phones are occasionally helpful when we are in an area where we can get service, but this is often not possible in remote national parks or campgrounds. When Wi-Fi is available, I sometimes send trip updates to friends and family. We have occasionally used FaceTime and What's App to connect with our family. We do not post any stories or pictures on Facebook while we are traveling because we don't want strangers to know that our house is unoccupied.

Q. Dealing with Mother Nature can be a real challenge for campers. What was the worst weather you ever encountered, and how did you deal with it?

A. In North Carolina, we got emergency warnings about a tornado and we checked into a motel. On Prince Edward Island in Canada, the wind was so strong that we had to tie the tent to a nearby fence.

Q. Some of your entries include torrential rains and plagues of mosquitoes. Were you ever tempted to trade in your tent for the nearest hotel? Did you ever give in?

A. We have never gone to a motel because of ordinary rain; we prefer to camp unless there are serious weather warnings such as for tornadoes. If it is raining when we are packing to leave, we work quickly and sometimes spread the wet tent and sleeping bags across our gear in the back of the car. When we reach our next campground, we lay them across the picnic table or hang them up to dry. For cooking in the rain, we can raise the car's lift-gate, put the Coleman stove beneath it on the ground, and sit in the car to eat. If there is thunder and lightning when we are awake, we will sit in the car until the storm passes. At night, we stay in our tent.

Twice on the same trip, we were planning to spend one night with two different sets of college friends. Because of the torrential rain (which lasted over a week, with some highways being closed), we left the campgrounds early and stayed an extra night with each set of friends. We never gave in because of mosquitoes.

Q. Your wildlife encounters included bees, bears, and the occasional snake. Did you ever feel you were in danger?

A. No, we never felt we were in danger. Once, when we discovered bear scat on a path right behind our tent, we stopped taking that path at night and were extra-vigilant.

Q. You've attended some ranger talks on global warming. Did you see a lot of evidence over the years?

A. One glacier we saw on our first trip to Alaska has completely melted. On our second trip to Alaska, we saw glaciers that had retreated considerably from where they were a few years ago. Wildflowers in some parks seem less abundant than in previous years.

Q. If you could go back and do one thing differently, what would it be?

A. I can't think of anything. We've learned from and/or enjoyed practically everything!

Q. If you had to list your 10 favorite parks, which would you choose?

A. That's a really tough question, and one that we have been asked many times. We have liked every park for different reasons, but our top 10 are Acadia, Bryce Canyon, Lake Clark, Big Bend, Great Sand Dunes, Mesa Verde, Capitol Reef, Badlands, Yellowstone, and Glacier Bay.

Q. Where are you and Dick headed next?

A. After finishing visits to all the U.S. national parks, we recently headed to the Canadian Rockies. We drove through that area on our way home from our first trip to Alaska, but during that visit, we only had time for a brief stop. We promised ourselves that someday we would go back, which we did in 2018. We may follow the Lewis and Clark trail next as well as revisiting some of our favorite parks and visiting any new ones.

Quiz

1. How many national park sites are there?

2. What is the largest national park?

3. What does Gateway Arch National Park commemorate?

4. Which national park has Native American cliff dwellings?

5. Name two United States national parks that are not located within the 50 states.

6. Which U.S. president was particularly concerned about conservation and has a national park named after him?

7. What caves, which are now a national park, were discovered because of the evening flight of bats leaving the cave to catch insects?

8. Which park is the most difficult one to visit?

9. At which park can visitors see a sled dog demonstration?

10. Which park was once a Mormon settlement?

ANSWERS:

1. 418

2. Wrangell-St. Elias

3. Westward expansion

4. Mesa Verde

5. Virgin Islands National Park, National Park of American Samoa

6. Theodore Roosevelt

7. Carlsbad Caverns

8. Aniakchak

9. Denali

10. Capitol Reef

Index by State and Territory

Made in the USA
Middletown, DE
02 September 2023

37851448R00203